I0070095

Electricity Auctions: An Overview of Efficient Practices

Luiz T. A. Maurer

Luiz A. Barroso

With support from: Jennifer M. Chang, Philippe Benoit, Daryl Fields, Bruno Flach, Matias Herrera-Dappe, and Mario Pereira

THE WORLD BANK
Washington, D.C.

World Bank Studies are published to communicate the results of the Bank's work to the development community with the least possible delay. The manuscript of this paper therefore has not been prepared in accordance with the procedures appropriate to formally-edited texts. This volume is a product of the staff of the International Bank for Reconstruction and Development/The World Bank. The findings, interpretations, and conclusions expressed in this volume do not necessarily reflect the views of the Executive Directors of The World Bank or the governments they represent.

The World Bank does not guarantee the accuracy of the data included in this work. The boundaries, colors, denominations, and other information shown on any map in this work do not imply any judgement on the part of The World Bank concerning the legal status of any territory or the endorsement or acceptance of such boundaries.

ISBN: 978-0-8213-8822-8
eISBN: 978-0-8213-8824-2
DOI: 10.1596/978-0-8213-8822-8

Library of Congress Cataloging-in-Publication Data
Maurer, Luiz.
   Electricity auctions : an overview of efficient practices / Luiz T. A. Maurer, Luiz A. Barroso; with support from: Jennifer M. Chang . . . [et al.].
      p. cm.
   Includes bibliographical references.
   ISBN 978-0-8213-8822-8—ISBN 978-0-8213-8824-2
 1. Electric utilities. 2. Commodity exchanges. 3. Auctions. I. Barroso, Luiz A. II. Chang, Jennifer M. III. Title.
   HG6047.E43M38 2011
   333.793'23—dc23

                                                                                                    2011019447

Table of Contents

Figures

Tables

Boxes

Foreword

Latin America has been leading the effort to introduce electricity auctions as an instrument to promote competition in electricity procurement. Dozens of auctions have been carried out to date, with noteworthy results particularly in terms of procuring new generating capacity.

The region has conducted a wide range of auctions both "in the market" and "for the market"—from technology-specific, to project-specific and even full competitive procurement, where all technologies compete head to head—encompassing a wide variety of products, from traditional generation forward purchase contracts to more sophisticated electricity call options. Other parts of the world have also implemented auctions, including for capacity payments in electricity markets in the Eastern US, and for trading production rights of power plants in Europe.

Approximately 40 electricity auctions have been conducted over the past 10 years in Latin American countries, mostly in Brazil, Chile, Peru, Colombia, and Panama. Brazil, for example, has successfully conducted about 30 auctions for existing and new electricity generation. As of April 2010, approximately 57,000 MW of new capacity have been contracted for delivery dates ranging from 2008 to 2015, with contract terms ranging from 15 to 30 years and including a wide variety of technologies.

There is increasing interest among World Bank client countries to learn more about electricity auctions as tools for procuring additional electricity generation capacity. In response to client needs, and given the wealth of experience that has recently emerged over the last few years, we felt that the time was ripe to compile the different experiences from electricity auctions and to try to extract lessons learned and best practices. To this end, the report provides a description of several relevant experiences with auctions for electricity, as well as a discussion of the lessons learned regarding policy formulation and program implementation.

One lesson that emerges is that details clearly do matter: every design has to be adapted to the specifics of each power system. Attention should be paid to a variety of factors, including the government's policy objectives, the degree and nature of competition in the electricity market, the interest and prospective role of the private sector, the availability of generation, the variety of different technologies, and the existing regulatory and institutional frameworks in which the suppliers will operate, both for the auction itself and subsequently. Despite the importance of this type of specificity, the report is not meant to be a "how-to" manual on auction implementation. Our goals are more modest for this report and subsequent studies will certainly be useful to help guide policy makers and other actors in the sector.

We hope that this document serves to disseminate knowledge about some of the key issues and options pertaining to electricity auctions. It is also our hope that the information and analyses set out in this report will benefit World Bank client countries, as well as energy specialists in all countries, in gaining an appreciation for the challenges that may lie ahead, and the potential benefits of implementing electricity auctions to enhance power sector competitiveness.

Philippe Benoit
Sector Manager, Energy
Sustainable Development Department
Latin America and the Caribbean Region
World Bank

Acknowledgements

This paper could not have been written without the assistance of many friends and colleagues both inside and outside of the World Bank. These individuals helped us develop an understanding of energy auctions in the power sector worldwide and in their respective countries. They gave freely of their time and insights to make sure that we got the facts right, and understood what they really meant. They include Gabriela Azuela, Suman Babbar, Carlos Batlle, Bernardo Bezerra, Paulo Born, Ashley Brown, Julia Bucknall, Susan Covino, Peter Cramton, Enrique Crousillat, Ahmad Faruqui, Defne Gencer, Christophe de Gouvello, Pankaj Gupta, Mohab Hallouda, Subramanian Iyer, Todd Johnson, Adam Keech, Antonio Fraga Machado, Silvia Messa, Jaime Millan, Sebastian Mocarquer, Lucio Monari, Rodrigo Moreno, Zayra Romo, José Rosenblatt, Dilma Rousseff, Hugh Rudnick, Jordan Schwartz, Dianne Rudo, Mauricio Tolmasquim, Silvana Tordo, Manuel Arturo Uribe, Victor Urrutia, Adriana Valencia, Tjaarda Storm Van-Leeuwen, Juan Diego Vélez, Xiaodong Wang, Peter Wong, and Ariel Yepes.

We are thankful to Judy Wolf for her commitment and the professional manner in which she edited this report, thereby communicating our ideas to a wide audience.

A great deal of appreciation goes to our internal and external peer reviewers, including Pedro Antmann, Beatriz Arizu, Nils-Henrik von der Fehr, Marcelino Madrigal, and Joisa Dutra Saraiva. Frank Wolak provided valuable inputs at the concept stage of this paper.

We also want to express our appreciation to Philippe Benoit, Sector Manager, Energy for the Latin America and Caribbean Region, who had the idea for this report and served not only as its sponsor, but also devoted his personal time and effort to sharpen it.

The report is a product of the Energy Unit with the Sustainable Development Department of the World Bank's Latin America and Caribbean Region.

Needless to say, none of our colleagues and peer reviewers should be held responsible for any errors of fact or interpretation that remain, despite their best efforts to educate us.

Acknowledgments

Executive Summary

The Challenge of Procuring Electricity is Changing.
The Bank's client countries are facing a systematic and sustained increase in the demand for electricity. A key concern for many of these countries is how to efficiently procure new generation resources to ensure that enough capacity is built in a timely manner, and that it is reliable, secure, and acquired at the least possible cost. Historically, this procurement has been very challenging due to factors such as uncertainty in load growth rates, limited access to financing, exposure to construction delays, and deficient legal and regulatory institutional arrangements that fail to provide the necessary incentives. Growing concerns with climate change and the environmental and social impacts of energy projects have added layers of complexity, as the desire for cleaner technologies and energy efficiency solutions are added to the process of selecting the appropriate mix of generation resources.

Many different approaches to electricity procurement have been tried over the past few decades, ranging from direct government investments in the 1950s and 60s, to "power purchase agreements" between government purchasers and producers in the 1970s and early 80s and, with the worldwide power sector reforms starting in the mid 80s, increasing reliance on independent private producers. Although details and circumstances vary widely among countries, all of these approaches have faced major limitations in achieving least cost and reliable electricity procurement. In addition, the liberalization of markets (notably, the movement away from the vertically integrated utility that did it all) and the ensuing appearance of multiple players has changed the dynamic of electricity procurement, presenting both challenges and opportunities. As a consequence, there is great interest in learning about innovative experiences on this topic.

This report assesses the potential of electricity contract auctions as a procurement option for the World Bank's client countries. It focuses on the role of auctions of electricity contracts designed to expand and retain existing generation capacity. It is not meant to be a "how-to" manual. Rather, it highlights some major issues and options that need to be taken into account when a country considers moving towards competitive electricity procurement through the introduction of electricity auctions.

How Can Auctions Help?

Auctions have played an important role in the effort to match supply and demand. Ever since the 1990s, the use of long-term contract auctions to procure new generation capacity, notably from private sector suppliers, has garnered increased attention from investors, governments, and multilateral agencies in general, as a means to achieve a competitive and transparent procurement process while providing certainty of supply for the medium to long term. However, the liberalization of electricity markets and the move from single-buyer procurement models increased the nature of the challenge facing system planners in their efforts to ensure an adequate and secure supply of electricity in the future at the best price.

When competition is feasible and desirable, auctions have proven to be a very effective mechanism for attracting new players, ensuring electricity procurement at the lowest possible price for consumers. An electricity auction increases the competition and transparency of the electricity procurement process, making it less likely to be challenged in the future as the political and institutional scenarios change. Developed power markets with a large number of buyers and sellers in sound financial standing are more conducive to competition. Those markets enable a great variety of electricity-related products to be traded using more sophisticated electricity-related auctions. However, even where competition is modest, and markets are small and still developing, benefits from the use of auction mechanisms can still be derived.

What is an "Auction"?

Simply defined, an auction is a selection process designed to procure (or allocate) goods and services competitively, where the award is made to a pre-qualified bidder and is based on a financial offer. In the most common type of auction with which the public is familiar, such as for artwork or on eBay, potential buyers bid for a product and the highest bid price wins. In most cases involving electricity auctions, the sellers, such as generators, are the ones bidding their products, as they are interested in selling power contracts to large con-sumers or distribution companies, with the bidding process designed in part to select the lowest price. This is the so-called "reverse auction", where the lowest offer is the winner.

There are many types of auctions used to trade electricity-related products. Auc-tions can be organized to trade short, mid and long-term electricity contracts targeted to supply regulated or non-franchised consumers over different time frames.

Within the auctions designed to acquire new generation capacity or to retain exist-ing resources, there is a variety of arrangements: (i) "all-inclusive technologies", in which hydro, natural gas, coal, oil, biomass, etc. compete directly; (ii) renewable-only technol-ogy auctions; (iii) technology-specific auctions (those able to participate, each renewable source has its own, separate auction); (iv) project-specific auctions, such as those used to award concessions to produce energy in a particular hydro site, and (v) auctions for demand resources.

Figure 1 presents a matrix containing the diverse nature of the electricity products and auction schemes utilized in a few select countries.

The most common types of auction designs used in the electricity sector discussed in this paper are: (i) Sealed-bid, (ii) Descending clock (dynamic), (iii) Hybrid, (iv) Com-binatorial, and (v) Two-sided. Details are provided in Chapter 2. The report describes the mechanics of each design, as well as its benefits and/or drawbacks, and why one may be preferable over another, given the specifics of the situation. Some designs have emerged precisely to overcome the shortfalls of others, as in the case of descending clock versus sealed-bid auctions, while others combine designs to get the best feature of each and avoid some of their deficiencies. For the most part, electricity auctions continue to be learning processes, so the extraction of valuable lessons learned from both successful and not-so-successful examples can significantly benefit the implementation of new auctions.

However, there is no "one-size-fits-all" type of auction design. Each has both advan-tages and disadvantages that need to be considered when selecting the option that best matches the specifics of each power sector and products to be traded.

What objectives have countries been seeking to achieve by using auctions?

While auctions as a general proposition are a means to match supply with demand in a cost-effective manner, they can also be and have been used to meet a variety of goals. Recent auctions have met four main objectives:

- Attract new generation capacity—to bridge the supply-demand gap (most frequent);
- Retain and/or replace existing generation capacity;

Figure 1. Auction Organization

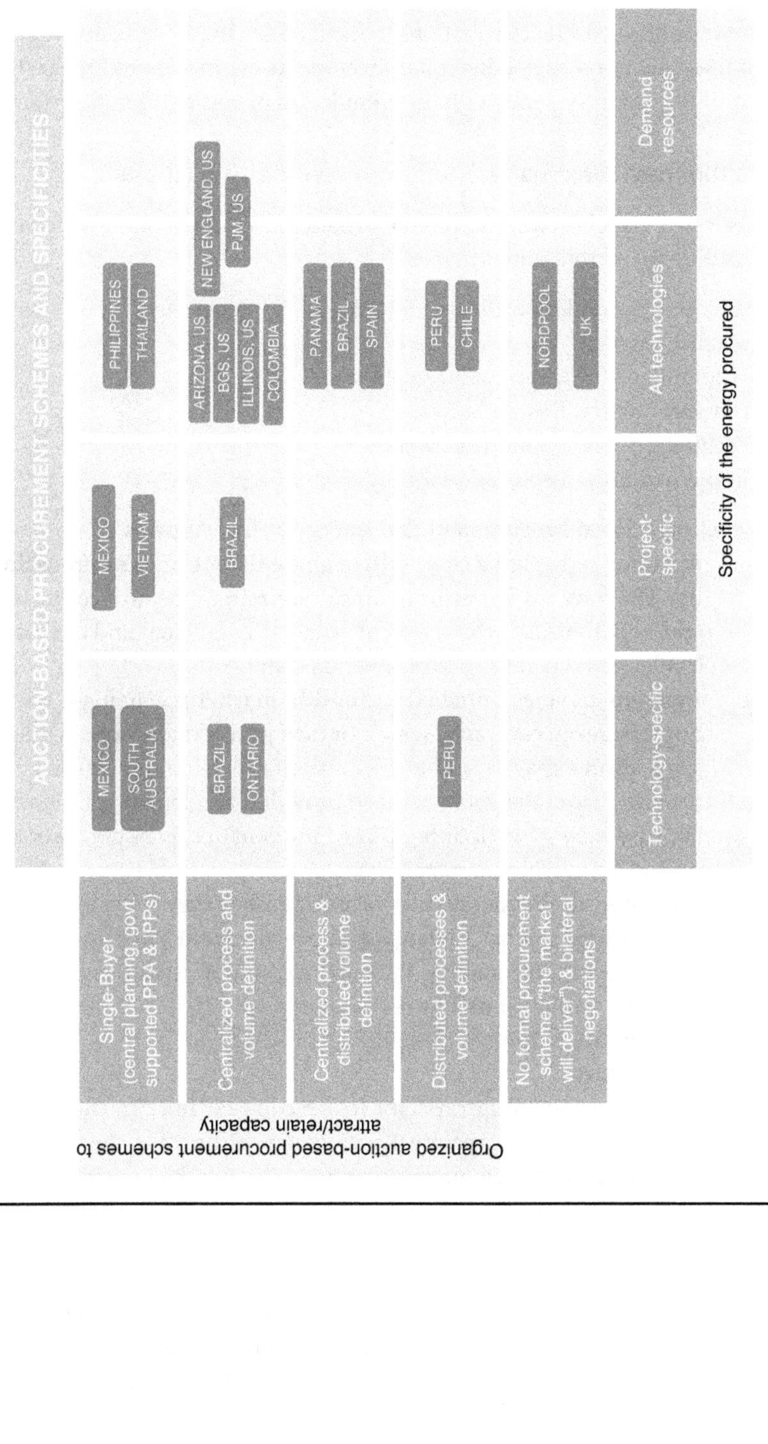

Source: Author's analysis

- Procure electricity for Providers of Last Resort ("default supply auctions") in fully deregulated markets, whereby distribution companies provide energy to those customers who opted not to be served by alternative suppliers;
- Attract newcomers to acquire rights to a portion of the production capacity of existing power plants in order to reduce market concentration, i.e., to carry out a virtual divestiture. These are known as virtual power plant (VPP) auctions.

Many countries have conducted auctions to meet these diverse objectives. What is notable is that these auctions have taken place in contexts characterized by varying levels of demand growth and in systems with different levels of competition (see figure 2).

What are the main lessons learned from electricity auctions?

Numerous lessons can be learned from the experience with auctions, which can be organized according to the following themes:

1. Auction-related Procurement and Energy Policy Aspects
2. Market Context
3. Foundations for a Successful Auction
4. General Auction Design Issues
5. Technology Choice and Renewables
6. Implementation Issues and Participants

1) Auction-related Procurement and Energy Policy Aspects
   a. **Auctions represent a competitive and efficient form of procuring electricity. They are far superior to single sourcing, "beauty-contests," or bilateral negotiations,** which are not necessarily efficient and are more apt to be challenged when the political winds change.
   b. **Auctions have established a credible market mechanism for the allocation of energy contracts, which in turn play a major role in attracting new generation capacity** and also contribute to retaining existing ones. Prices resulting from the auctions have provided an elegant solution to the regulatory challenge of defining what "prudent" costs of generation should be passed on to end-use customers.
   c. **Auctions do not operate in a vacuum; rather they must be an integral part of a country's overall energy and procurement policies** of reforming the power sector, introducing the participation of private generators, harnessing some endogenous sources of energy, and creating competitive pressure to push prices down to benefit the end-user.

2) Market Context
   a. **Auctions of existing capacity foster competition "in the market," while auctions for new capacity foster competition "for the market" and the development of new power plants.** An issue when auctioning contracts to attract new capacity and retain existing resources is whether to have separate auctions for each type of capacity or to carry out just a single auction.
   b. **An effective auction depends on the existence of competition.** Competition or the lack thereof (e.g. market power, collusion) are usually structural issues, which depend, *inter alia*, on the number and nature of players, market concentration, types of products being offered, and specific regulations.

Figure 2. Objectives of Procurement Auctions

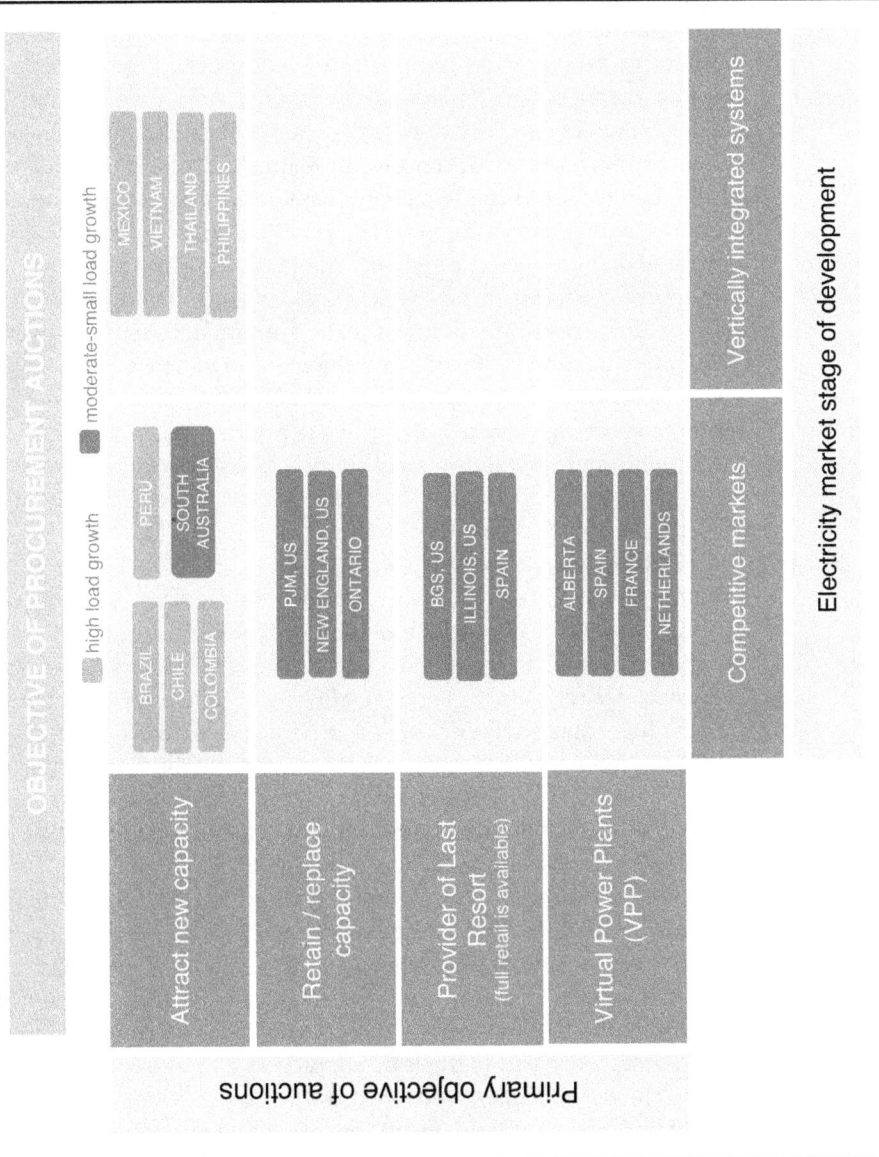

OBJECTIVE OF PROCUREMENT AUCTIONS

high load growth   moderate-small load growth

	high load growth	moderate-small load growth

Primary objective of auctions

Attract new capacity
BRAZIL, CHILE, COLOMBIA, PERU, SOUTH AUSTRALIA
MEXICO, VIETNAM, THAILAND, PHILIPPINES

Retain / replace capacity
P.JM, US, NEW ENGLAND, US, ONTARIO

Provider of Last Resort
(full retail is available)
BGS, US, ILLINOIS, US, SPAIN

Virtual Power Plants (VPP)
ALBERTA, SPAIN, FRANCE, NETHERLANDS

Competitive markets   Vertically integrated systems

Electricity market stage of development

Source: Author's analysis

    c. **Developed power markets with a large number of buyers and sellers in sound financial standing are generally more conducive to competition.** Those markets enable the trading of a great variety of energy-related products using more sophisticated electricity-related auctions.

    d. **Even in places where competition is modest and markets are small, developing countries can still benefit from the use of competitive auction mechanisms.** Less sophisticated, vertically integrated power sectors in low or middle-income countries may also benefit from a fresh look at the competitive procurement options at their disposal. One example is the granting of concessions to build and operate hydropower plants.

    e. **Auctions cannot materially change the structural conditions of the marketplace. However, some auction design features can help mitigate market imperfections.** For example, governments may deal with potentially collusive behaviors or market power by specifying a reserve price that should be high enough to attract a bidder's interest, while and at the same time reflecting particular costs for the power plant being auctioned.

    f. **Many auction practitioners argue that governments should help create a competitive auction by facilitating the entry of as many bidders as possible.** This requires good communication about the auction, elimination of barriers to entry, a clear definition of the product being auctioned, and a good monitoring system to detect abnormal bidding behaviors. It is widely accepted among practitioners that the results of attracting additional bidders are far more effective than limiting the reserve price.

3) **Foundations for a Successful Auction**

    a. **Designing and implementing any type of formal auction system requires a candid assessment of the robustness of the institutions and the regulatory framework.** Independent regulators are of great importance due to the need for regulatory oversight. However, some prior conditions need to be in place—such as rule of law and, in particular, enforcement of contracts. In restructured power sectors, contracts are a proxy for vertical integration. Where cost-reflective tariffs are not the practice, or non-payment is perceived as high risk, auctions for new generation tend to fail or require government support (thus increasing government-contingent liabilities).

    b. **Regulatory stability is a key element to attract investors to participate in competitive auctions.** One of the greatest worries of current and potential investors with regard to auctions is related to regulatory stability and the fact that in some cases the auction rules are constantly changing—sometimes even during the bidding process itself. Occasional changes to improve the auction process are part of the learning process and welcomed by all stakeholders. However, frequent and unexpected changes are a cause for concern.

    c. **Other necessary conditions for the success of an auction process include its transparency as well as investors' perception about the fairness of the process.** Lack of transparency is in part related to the dissemination of information among auction participants before, during, and after the auction. For example, leaving the auctioneer (whose role is often confused with that of the government) with a great deal of flexibility in establishing parameters and formulas in a not-so-transparent way jeopardizes the perception of transparency and fairness.

4) **General Auction Design Issues**

    a. *Nature of the auctions.* **Most of the energy auctions carried out as part of the first generation of power sector reforms have been designed as sealed-bid auctions.** This methodology was the basis for the development of PPAs supporting capacity expansion. It is still used extensively, particularly in places with many sellers and one buyer. **However, alternative designs such as the descending clock auction have revealed many advantages over traditional sealed-bid auctions.** A clock auction enables an efficient price discovery, and is therefore conducive to more aggressive behavior among bidders, thereby resulting in lower prices. Sealed-bid auctions and clock auctions are often combined in hybrid auction designs to achieve "the best of both worlds." Each auction design has advantages and disadvantages that need to be considered when selecting the option that is best suited to the specifics of each power sector and products to be traded.

    b. *Typical Electricity Products.* **Electricity contracts are the most typical products traded in energy auctions.** The electricity product offered in an electricity auction will depend on the nature of the adequacy and reliability constraint of each power system. The product(s) to be procured should be designed according to the adequacy constraint of each individual market. For example, Colombia and Brazil want enough thermal and hydro resources to provide firm energy during a dry period, while in New England the constraint is to have enough capacity to meet the load during peak hours, particularly in the summertime.

    c. *Centralization vs. decentralization.* **In a centralized auction scheme, demand is pooled and procured jointly.** Governments usually play a key role in defining the processes to aggregate demand and in designating an auctioneer to conduct the auction. Centralized auctions seem to be more efficient in fostering competition, compared to carrying out various smaller auctions when demand blocks from different distribution companies are similar.

    d. **Centralized auctions are not tantamount to a formal 'single buyer' scheme (which is also a type of centralized auction).** The government does not have to take the title for the energy, nor does it have to provide guarantees for the contracts.

5) **Technology Choice and Renewables**

    a. **All-encompassing (or technology-neutral) auctions entitle any generation source (and possibly demand-side bidders) to participate in the tender on a level-playing-field basis.** The idea is to foster maximum competition, select the most efficient sources and achieve a least-cost expansion plan. However, it is often difficult for non-conventional renewable sources to compete head to head with baseload coal or large hydro, except under special circumstances. Furthermore, governments may have a preference for particular technologies driven by energy policy concerns or economic policy considerations. For this reason, all-encompassing auctions are seldom used. Governments prefer to establish auctions that target one or more types of technologies. Auctions can still provide the best results for a given set of technologies driven by policy decisions.

    b. *Promoting Renewables.* **Auctions have proven to be an alternative to the traditional, administratively set feed-in-tariffs.** They do not represent a renewable energy policy *per se*, but they have been challenging the well-entrenched feed-in-tariffs that have been responsible for the installation of thousands of MW of renewable forms of energy in the world. Actions foster competition, push prices down in the entire supply chain, and therefore reduce tariffs to end-users, making the whole process more sustainable.

    c. **Renewable sources of energy may call for dedicated auctions.** When conducting auctions for renewable sources, regulators face the choice of establishing dedicated auctions or alternatively blending renewables with conventional sources of energy, therefore fostering "fuel-to-fuel" competition to the maximum extent possible.

6) **Implementation Issues and Participants**

    a. **Moving from auction theory to real-life implementation is not an easy task.** This holds true particularly when auctions are implemented in markets that are not fully functional, or where institutions are not strong enough to support any formal competitive electricity auction procurement schemes. Furthermore, the peculiarities of individual markets may call for very specific auction design and implementation challenges.

    b. **Governments have to specify at the outset who should be allowed to participate in the auctions among all potential buyers and sellers in the market.** This depends, *inter alia,* on the market design, number and nature of participants, the need to foster competition among different energy sources or in some cases, a stated government policy to favor some kinds of technologies such as non-conventional renewables.

    c. **It is of the utmost importance to ensure that new generation projects procured through electricity auctions are built and have adequate operating performance so that long-term system adequacy and reliability is assured.** This depends, *inter alia,* on the proper design of project completion guarantees and penalties for delays and underperformance.

    d. **On the buyer's side, the auctions can be developed exclusively for distribution companies that buy electricity on behalf of regulated users, or extended to free consumers or marketers,** who may be allowed to participate. Moreover, it should be determined whether participation by distribution companies is mandatory or voluntary when serving their captive market. Two-sided auctions also need confirmation regarding who is allowed to bid with demand/energy reduction programs.

    e. **On the seller's side, participants may include existing plants, plants under construction, or green field plants.** An important design and implementation choice regarding policy is to conduct separate or joint processes for existing and new (green field) capacity.

    f. **The "devil is in the details". Well-specified auction rules are critical for the success of the auction, which requires:**
- Comprehensive, complete, unambiguous auction rules with no loopholes, that take into account all possible scenarios, and avoid unintended consequences;
- Specifying what is and what is not allowed, and credible penalties for violating the rules;

- Informing bidders of the rules early on, and providing sufficient time for them to be evaluated. It is not only important to give bidders all the relevant information on the auction process but also to grant them time to process this information;
- Giving bidders the opportunity to comment on, validate, and provide inputs for the rules;
- Explaining auction objectives and operations (seminars and workshops) to all stakeholders and market participants;
- Providing informative training sessions and conducting tests.

CHAPTER 1

Introduction

Objectives of this Report

The objective of this report is to examine the role of auctions for long-term electricity contracts as a mechanism for the efficient procurement of new generation resources, focusing on the lessons learned and experiences that are relevant to most World Bank client countries. It is meant to provide a candid view of successes and failures, areas for improvement, international experiences, and applicability of the different auction mechanisms.

Approach

Several experiences with auctions in both developed and developing countries have been brought together. The lessons learned from these experiences address issues pertaining to the: (i) auction process (including important energy policy decisions or constraints imposed by the stage of development of the power sector), (ii) choice of auction over other selection mechanisms, and (iii) auction design *per se.*

The analysis focuses on the experiences of developing countries, where auctions for long-term contracts have predominated, the objective being to support the expansion of the power sector. Latin America has been the most active region in the world in the implementation of such auctions. Brazil has been leading the effort in the region, having moved from more traditional electricity procurement mechanisms—such as bilateral contracting—to sophisticated procurement schemes, such as simultaneous descending clock auctions involving multiple buyers and sellers. Between 2004 and 2010, Brazil successfully conducted a total of 31 auctions for existing and new energy supply. As of April 2010, approximately 57,000 MW of new capacity have been contracted for delivery dates ranging from 2008 to 2015, with contract terms ranging from 15 to 30 years.[1] Other countries in the region, including Panama, Peru, Chile, and Colombia have also been actively conducting auctions.

Case studies from developed countries supplement the analysis of the experiences of developing nations. Although procurement mechanisms in the developed world typically have different objectives (e.g. capacity replacement or generation divestiture), their experience is valuable for understanding the design of more complex products, auction implementation rules, inclusion of demand resources, and regulatory oversight. In the US, procurement auctions conducted by PJM, ISO-NE, Illinois, and New Jersey concentrate the most relevant experiences for countries interested in centralized procurement processes based on electricity auctions. In Europe, experiences in Spain and France are the most relevant, as they focus on generation divestiture and suppliers of last resort. The UK and Scandinavia provide examples of strong reliance on market forces and existing incentives to buttress the development of new supply on an economic basis.

Who Should Read This Report?

Several audiences should benefit from the analyses and findings presented in this report. Although not exhaustive, the following list is considered to be the primary target audience:

- Countries and professionals interested in learning how to improve the competitiveness of existing electricity procurement mechanisms, taking into account recent academic and empirical evidence;
- World Bank professionals working in countries where current market mechanisms have not achieved satisfactory results in capacity expansion and/or where governments may be considering alternative models to ensure supply adequacy;
- Practitioners and countries operating in emergent power markets that are willing to make their electricity procurement processes more competitive, transparent, and efficient, possibly using auctions as a mechanism to meet market needs;
- Practitioners and countries operating in sophisticated power markets, where auctions have already been held, and are interested in learning from the best practices and other international experiences to improve their current processes;
- Researchers interested in learning more about different types of energy procurement in both developed and developing countries, as well as the different types of energy products being traded competitively.

This document was not designed to provide detailed elements of auction theory, a field that has been extensively debated by academia in recent years and is becoming part of the microeconomic curriculum. A profound knowledge of the power sector is not required, although readers who are familiar with power sector reform and market design are likely to benefit the most. The report tries to avoid entering into technical discussions on the more complex instruments currently auctioned in markets such as the US and European Union. Instead, it focuses on contractual and financing aspects that are most relevant for the procurement of new generation capacity. Details are provided whenever necessary to help the reader understand the nature of the products being auctioned.

Report Organization

The report is organized as follows: Chapter 2 provides some basic concepts of auctions and a historical overview on the emergence of auctions in the power sector: Chapter 3 describes the diverse nature of experiences with electricity auctions in several jurisdictions; Chapter 4 focuses on examples for Latin America, while Chapter 5 examines auctions in other parts of the world, such as Asia, Oceania, Europe, North America, and in multi-country situations, such as power pools; Chapter 6 features experiences with the development of renewable sources of energy and the increasing role played by auctions in expanding non-conventional energies in a competitive way; Chapter 7 provides the main lessons learned in terms of the design, implementation and monitoring of electricity auctions; and Chapter 8 summarizes the principal conclusions. The report is also complemented by a set of Appendixes, which cover such topics as electricity procurement, other uses of auctions in the electricity industry, virtual power plants around the world, some additional experiences with renewables in general (and FiTs and RPS), and lastly, issues relating to descending clock auctions and demand participation in electricity auctions.

Note

1. About 5,800 MW of non-conventional renewables and 17,500 MW of large hydro plants in the Amazon region were also auctioned. Of the total amount of new generation capacity, 49% comes from hydro resources, 44% from thermal resources and the remaining 8% from non-conventional renewables such as biomass and wind power. These figures do not include the amount of energy procured by the non-regulated market or the amount bilaterally negotiated between free customers and generators or marketers.

CHAPTER 2

Auctions — Basic Concepts

This chapter covers some essential concepts about auctions, starting with the definition of an auction. It then moves on to discuss why auctions are used, and finally describes the auction designs most commonly utilized to competitively attract and/or retain adequate generation capacity. This chapter is not meant to be a comprehensive overview on auctions, but it should help readers who are not familiar with the subject.

What is an Auction?

An auction is an allocation procedure based on a precise evaluation criterion specified by the auctioneer, and a pre-defined publicly available set of rules designed to allocate or award objects or products (e.g. contracts) on the basis of a financial bid.[1] It is transparent due to the fact that it is based on a set of rules determined by the auctioneer and known by the bidders before the auction. The award is based on the results of clearly specified financial bids. For the purposes of this study, an auction is an objective mechanism to promote the competitive procurement of electricity-related products.

An auction may be described by its three key rules, namely (i) bidding, (ii) clearing, and (iii) pricing. The bidding rules define how offers should be structured and when they can be submitted. For example, the rules can specify that bidders have to bid just a price, or a set of prices and quantities. The rules may also specify that bids are to be submitted only once (i.e., sealed-bid auction) or successively, in response to the bids made by other auction participants or calls to bid by the auctioneer (i.e., dynamic auction). The clearing rule states how bids will be compared in order to determine the winner(s) and the allocation of the object(s) or product(s). The pricing rule determines the price at which the deal will be closed. For example, in a standard auction where the auctioneer sells several units of the same object or product, the winners can pay their bids (i.e. pay-as-bid or discriminatory auction) or they can pay a price equal to the highest losing bid (i.e. uniform price sealed-bid auction). In a first-price sealed-bid auction, the winner pays the price spelled out on his/her own bid. Or, alternatively the price paid may be that of the second highest (or lowest, in a reverse auction bid).[2]

A typical auction is one where the auctioneer is the seller, who wants to maximize the price of the product sold. This is the situation often described in most of the literature about auctions. When the auctioneer wants to buy or procure objects or products, which is the typical case in this report, the auctions used are called reverse or procurement auctions. In a procurement auction, the auctioneer (e.g. acting on behalf of distribution companies) is interested in the lowest possible prices to be paid for the energy to be sold by generation companies (the bidders). The basic theory on auctions applies equally to either case, as they are mirror images of the same conceptual auction.

Why Auctions?

Auctions have been used extensively outside of the power sector as a procurement mechanism for many years. While the existence of auctions dates back to 500 B.C. in Greece, its use in network industries has been pioneered by telecommunications companies to assign and trade bandwidth, the most notable recent example being the auction of spectrum for 3G mobile services in the UK in February 2000. The gas and oil industries rely on auctions to define prices and allocate exploration rights. In the electricity industry, auctions have been used in different parts of the world as the basis for trading energy and capacity, transmission congestion rights, ancillary services, and other products.[3]

An auction is a transparent mechanism that should achieve a fair, open, and timely procurement process, reducing opportunities for corruption. These are widely sought-after features that minimize the likelihood of future challenges to the selection process and its outcome, avoiding post-auction delays.

By eliciting private information and creating competition, a good auction design finds the real price of the product being auctioned in a competitive way. Hence, an auction is an attractive, less disputable solution to the regulatory issue of establishing the prudent power purchase costs incurred by distribution utilities when serving their captive customers.

Auctions are the ideal selection mechanism when the "product" to be procured can be clearly specified and spelled out in contractual terms on an *ex-ante* basis, and there is sufficient competition. Those conditions, which will be further explored in this report, are not always present. Therefore, auctions are not meant to be a panacea for all kinds of procurement of products in the power sector.

Emergence of Auctions in the Power Sector: Historical Overview

There has been a growing interest in the use of auctions in the electricity industry as a way to promote efficient procurement and foster competition in all sectors: generation, transmission, and distribution. Throughout the world, auctions have been employed in diverse settings ranging from the hourly dispatch of generators in day-ahead markets to long-term contracts for the concession rights to build and operate hydroelectric plants or transmission assets.

With the vertical unbundling of the power sector and subsequent separation of the generation and distribution businesses in the late 80s and early 90s, procurement of electricity started to be carried out by electric utilities or by governments on their behalf. The procurement process typically involved tendering a power purchase agreement to IPPs backed by government guarantees. The product was simply a capacity contract with rights for energy delivery. It was usually tendered through a very simple auction mechanism. In most cases, governments were responsible for the procurement process, for defining the volumes of energy to be procured, and for providing payment guarantees to IPPs.

Auctions were formally introduced in the electric sector as the industry deregulation process was implemented. One of the first uses of electricity auctions was to procure electricity on a short-term basis by independent system operators and thus enable an efficient and least-cost dispatch process. In many formal wholesale markets, generation unit owners and loads submit offers and bids to supply and consume energy at different prices and in anticipation of demand requirements. Using such offers and bids, subsequent market operators set day-ahead prices at every location in the network and day-ahead schedules for generation units and loads.

This kind of auction mechanism has been important to efficiently and jointly coordinate the operation of the generation and transmission network when there are many different owners of generation units and transmission assets. However, no long-term contracts are traded in this market. It was therefore not able to guarantee the expansion of generation capacity, which is an important goal for most WB client countries.

The first auctions for long-term electricity contracts were conducted in the 1990s between state utilities and Independent Power Producers (IPP). In many cases, utilities procured those electricity contracts competitively, floating tenders among pre-qualified IPPs. It basically involved one buyer and multiple sellers. The bidder with the lowest price for the electricity was entitled to sign a Power Purchase Agreement (PPA) with the utility. This mechanism had most of the elements of an auction. When competition was possible and desirable, countries adopted a "First-price sealed-bid" (FPSB) type of auction as part of the first generation of IPP-PPA competitive business models for power trading. The PPA was an essential element to make a new generation project bankable. Thousands of MW of new, green field generation were installed using the IPP-PPA business model. In some cases, procurement took place competitively, while in others PPAs were negotiated directly between utility companies and IPPs.

Distribution companies, or single buyers acting on their behalf, aimed at "outsourcing" the supply of electricity to meet their market requirements. They signed Power Purchase Agreements (PPAs) with Independent Power Producers (IPPs), which were in charge of building a power plant and delivering electricity by a certain date. In many cases, the selection process was based on a competitive procurement. Despite not being referred to as such by industry practitioners, the process had most of the elements of an auction design involving one buyer and multiple sellers, since the selection was based on a financial offer among pre-qualified bidders. Electricity contracts became a proxy for vertical integration.

As electricity markets developed, auctions started to be used as procurement mechanisms for a variety of products in the power sector, including granting concessions, privatizing distribution, generation and transmission assets, and selling several types of financial products. Appendix B outlines different situations in which auctions have been selected as the preferred mechanism for competitive procurement across the entire power sector.

A second generation of competitive business models for power trading has emerged in developing countries over the past few years. In a number of markets, generation expansion has been facilitated by the emergence of dynamic auctions designed to trade a greater variety of long-term contracts that are offered to new generation. These contracts can take different forms, ranging from standard electricity contracts (e.g. PPAs), to reliability options. They usually require physical coverage, which ensures supply reliability, and are auctioned a few years ahead of delivery. Long-term products provide revenue stability to new entrants, helping investors fund new generation, as shown in box 2.1. The pressure to meet an increasing demand growth has made the implementation of auctions of long-term reliability products very active in developing countries.

These new electricity auctions are based on more sophisticated auction mechanisms, offering new products to meet market requirements, as opposed to the tenders of power purchase agreements involving IPPs, which were carried out in the early 1990s. One main feature introduced in this renewed proposal was to centralize the acquisition of the reliability product by means of an auction organized and coordinated by the govern-

Box 2.1. Role of Procurement in Ensuring Security of Supply[4]

A common element in developed and developing countries is the need to ensure supply adequacy (i.e., retain and attract generation capacity) at the least possible cost. For countries with fast-growing electricity consumption, ensuring an adequate volume of new generation is of paramount importance.

For this reason, several countries use electricity auctions as a procurement mechanism, not only to provide a price hedge to consumers, but also to contribute to ensuring supply adequacy and security. These products are thus sometimes referred to as "reliability products" (Battle, Rodilla (2009)). They link the payments received by generators to certain adequacy services provided to the power system. Reliability products can take many different forms, including, for example, requirements of installed capacity, firm capacity, and firm energy (for energy-constrained resources). Despite those products being financial contracts, regulators require them to be backed up by physical assets, therefore contributing to the supply adequacy of the power system.

Determining the product to be acquired from generators may be complex, but is a very important task. The procurement of financial contracts backed by firm energy (or firm capacity), certificates (or tags), and the procurement of energy call options with physical delivery obligations, are examples of some of the products procured in Latin America through auctions under a supply adequacy prospective.

ment. However, the government is not supposed to take title for the energy, but to reallocate contracts among buyers (one or more). The objectives are to increase competition, benefit from economies of scale, and minimize the government's liabilities whenever possible by not being a party in the energy contracts.

Latin America has pioneered the use of auctions to trade long-term products through energy contracts of reliability.[5] Over the past few years, Latin America's use of long-term contract auctions to procure new generation capacity has been getting increased attention from investors, governments, and multilateral agencies. One of the reasons for this interest is the large amount of capacity that has already been contracted. Brazil, for example, has contracted approximately 57,000 MW of new generation from 2005 to 2010, with delivery dates from 2008 to 2015. These contracts are valued at US$ 300 billion. In turn, Colombia has auctioned 3,500 MW of new capacity since 2008. Other countries in the region that have also been actively conducting auctions to procure new capacity include Panama, Peru, and Chile. Two models for energy auctions have been used in Latin America. In some countries, such as Colombia, auctions of reliability products are organized to acquire reliability for the entire demand, including non-franchised customers. In other countries, such as Brazil, Chile, and Peru, auctions are organized solely to provide reliability needs on behalf of the regulated (or franchised) market.

This new business model for competitive electricity procurement and its main features have been garnering increased attention from investors, governments, and multilateral agencies worldwide and will be the focus of this report.

Auction Design

Several different auction designs are used around the world to allocate objects or products. Those most commonly used depend on the products to be allocated. For example, the auctions most frequently used for energy-related products, radio spectrum for wireless telecommunications, art, or wine are not necessarily the same. The aim of this section is not to describe all the possible auction designs, only those used to solve the resource-adequacy problem either directly or indirectly.

Based on experiences in different countries and markets around the world, it is possible to identify the auction designs most commonly used to competitively attract resources to balance the supply and demand of energy. Those auctions are: (i) Sealed-bid, (ii) Descending clock (dynamic), (iii) Hybrid, (iv) Combinatorial, and (v) Two-sided.

Sealed-bid Auctions

Sealed-bid auctions represent a special category whereby each pre-qualified bidder submits a schedule of prices and quantities. *In this type of auction, all bidders simultaneously submit sealed bids so that no bidder knows the bid of any other participant. As bidders cannot see the bids of other participants, they cannot adjust their own bids accordingly. Those auctions may be used when there is a single object or product to be allocated to a single owner, for example, the construction of a power plant* or a transmission line, and the bid consists of a single price. This is the so-called First-price Sealed-bid auction (FPSB), one of the most commonly used in tendering, particularly for government contracts and mining leases. If the auction involves several units of the same product, bids must contain quantities and respective prices (a kind of supply function). The auctioneer has to aggregate those functions and award the lowest-cost bidders. Payment may be based on the clearing price (uniform auction) or on the price offered by each bidder (discriminatory auction). Details of each are presented as follows:

First-price Sealed-bid Auction (FPSB). In this auction, each bidder submits a sealed bid consisting of a single price, for a single object or product. The motivation for the use of the FPSB auction is its simplicity. The auctioneer compares all the bids and selects the one with the lowest price. The bidder who submitted that bid is the winner and receives his/her own bid as payment. This classic auction design has been used extensively in many countries to auction different items with *well-known* values or, alternatively, where the uncertainty surrounding the items' values was reduced and a price discovery process would not bring additional value. FPSB has been used extensively in the World Bank for procuring a great variety of goods and services.

The main disadvantage of FPSB (as well as other sealed-bid auctions) is that it does not allow bidders to acquire information on the price of the product. In a sealed-bid auction, bidders only receive relevant information about the cost of the product being procured once the auction is over. This might give the impression that winning an item in an auction implies bad news for the winner about his/her estimate of the item's cost because no other bidder was willing to bid as little (in a reverse auction) for it. This is known in auction theory as the *"winner's curse."*

Pay-as-bid or Discriminatory Auction. The pay-as-bid auction is used when there are multiple units of the same object or product to be allocated, resulting in different prices. This may be the case when the auctioneer wants to procure five long-term contracts, each one of 100 MW.[6] This design has been the basic procurement of PPAs, particularly when a sole buyer and several bidders are involved. It is also a sealed-bid auction, whereby each bidder submits a schedule of prices and quantities (i.e., a supply function). The auctioneer gathers together all the bids, creating an aggregate supply curve, and matches it with the quantity to be procured. The clearing price is determined when supply equals demand. The winners are all those bidders whose bids, or sections of their bids, offered lower prices than the clearing price. The winners will receive different prices based on their financial offers. The auctions for electricity contracts carried out in Peru and Panama have used a pay-as-bid design. Mexico also uses a pay-as-bid design for its auctions for PPAs.[7]

UNIFORM PRICE SEALED-BID AUCTION. The uniform price sealed-bid auction is also used when there are multiple units of the same object or product to be allocated, resulting in a single price. Bidders are allowed to bid in a similar way as in the pay-as-bid auction, and the process for selecting the winners is the same. The only difference with the pay-as-bid auction is the price each bidder receives. In the uniform price sealed-bid auction, all the winners receive the same price, which is the market clearing price.

Advantages and disadvantages. Sealed-bid auctions, particularly FPSB, are well known among procurement specialists. They have been consolidated through the years among state-owned companies, and are perceived as straightforward. It is clear for bidders how these auctions work, so the cost of participation tends to be lower than in more complex auction designs. The main disadvantage of sealed bids is that all the uncertainty related to the price of a product must be translated into a single bid, which cannot be adjusted when more information is revealed. Hence, if there is significant uncertainty about the price(s) of the product(s) being procured, the potential for an inefficient outcome increases since there is no price discovery. This problem is exacerbated if several products are auctioned simultaneously through sealed-bid auctions. Practical realities such as budget constraints and interdependency in the products' values, in the case of multiple products (e.g., if procuring long-term contracts with different durations), can make bidding in a sealed-bid auction exceedingly difficult unless the auctioneer allows the bidders to express these constraints in their sealed bids, which in turn can make it difficult to determine the winners.

A latent problem in many auctions is the lack of strong competition, with bidders trying to use any available information to coordinate their bidding and increase the final price of the auction. Hence, when competition in an auction is weak, not revealing any information during the auction process becomes an advantage of sealed-bid auctions. There has been some empirical evidence in auctions of frequency spectrum that bidders have colluded by exchanging information in a codified way (via price bids) during a dynamic auction. This strategy reduced the ability of the auctioneer to monitor the behavior of bidders and allowed them to carry on with their pre-agreed collusive practices. The uniform price sealed-bid auction is viewed as a fair auction since all winners receive the same price, which is not the case for the pay-as-bid auction since it discriminates among bidders. However, it may sometimes be difficult to justify having sellers (i.e. bidders) with very different cost structures receiving an identical price for the energy sold. Hence, if the government is the auctioneer, the choice of a uniform price sealed-bid auction may have a high political cost.[8]

One advantage of a uniform price auction is that it attracts the participation of small bidders, which is conducive to stronger competition in the post-auction market. In a non-competitive uniform price sealed-bid auction, bidders bid prices above their marginal cost because they have to "guess" the marginal prices. Hence, large bidders make room for small ones.[9]

Descending Clock Auction[10]

The descending clock auction is one of many types of dynamic auctions. The price is determined throughout the auction process via multi-round bids. Dynamic auctions attempt to overcome some of the disadvantages of the sealed-bid auctions that have been discussed in the previous section. According to this arrangement, the auctioneer starts by calling a high price and asking bidders to state the quantities they wish to

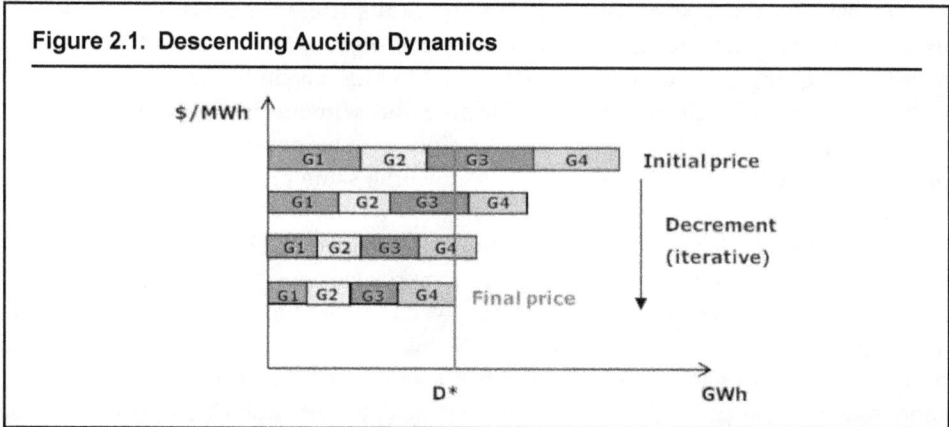

Figure 2.1. Descending Auction Dynamics

Source: Author's elaboration

sell at such a price. If the quantity offered exceeds the target quantity to be procured, the auctioneer names a lower price, and again asks bidders the quantities they want to offer at the new price. This process continues until the quantity offered matches the quantity to be procured or until excess supply is negligible, as illustrated in Figure 2.1. The winners are those bidders who offer a quantity at the clearing price (i.e. the price where supply equals demand). The payment of a winner equals the clearing price times the quantity offered at that price. Figure 2.1 presents the basic concept for this kind of auction. For purposes of simplicity, demand is assumed to be non-responsive to price—or that the response to price has been muted by the auction design, in such a way that buyers are not allowed to express their willingness to pay. This design is often referred to as a one-sided auction.

Through the rounds, the descending clock auction design allows for a strong price discovery, which makes it extremely efficient. Its main advantage over sealed-bid auctions is that a bidder can condition his/her bids based on information from early bidding rounds. By successively lowering prices, bidders get more information on the product's value, allowing participants to revisit their reserve prices (i.e., the lowest prices that bidders would bid), in light of the information revealed by the behavior of other bidders during the auction.

The design of a descending clock auction features several issues that have to be well planned and communicated to the bidders far in advance. Those issues include, *inter alia:* (i) Starting price, (ii) Auction mechanism itself (structure of rounds), (iii) Activity rule, (iv) Information disclosure policy, (v) Clearing rule, and (vi) Information technology. These are described in greater detail in Appendix E.

Simultaneous descending clock auctions can be used when several of the products to be procured are not identical (e.g. baseload and peak-load contracts). This is just a set of descending clock auctions, one for each product, which start at the same time, and do not close until supply matches demand in each of the auctions. In this case, there is one price for each product from one round to another, only the prices of those products with excess supply are decreased. The simultaneity allows bidders to shift supply from one product to another, subject to activity rules that ensure that the supply-quantity curve of each product is monotonically decreasing.

In this case, price discovery plays an important role. By seeing tentative price information, bidders are better informed to make decisions about what to sell, and the quantity of each product to sell, thus helping to resolve the bidder's decision problem. Some products may be complements (e.g., a contract from January to March and another from April to June), while others may be substitutes (e.g., two consecutive three-month contracts and a six-month contract covering the same period of time). The number of possibilities grows exponentially with the number of products. Therefore, bidding in the absence of price information makes the situation much more difficult for bidders. In this case, activity rules may/should not impose any restriction on the bidder's ability to arbitrage across the products, as this restriction can be imposed with respect to the aggregate quantity offered, not the quantities of each product.

The main advantage of dynamic auctions in general (descending clock auctions are one example) is that bidders can adjust their bids based on information revealed throughout the auction, improving the efficiency of the auction and mitigating the winner's curse. However, when competition is not very strong, revealing excessive information can be counterproductive because bidders could use that information to coordinate their bidding, increasing the final price of the auction. There is thus a fine line between enhancing price discovery and facilitating collusion that should not be crossed when selecting the auction design and the information to be revealed.

Even though descending clock auctions might seem more complex than sealed-bid auctions, experience shows that they are not difficult to implement and the implementation cost is not significant. As mentioned earlier, simultaneous descending clock auctions have the advantage of allowing bidders to arbitrage between different products, which cannot be done in sealed-bid auctions.

Practical realities such as budget constraints are alleviated in dynamic auctions since the bidder has the time between rounds to adjust his/her pricing and quantity decisions according to the information revealed during the auction. For example, the bidding team can contact its superiors and request authorization to bid higher prices if he/she thinks that is an optimal strategy given the new information acquired during the auction.

Another advantage of dynamic auctions is that they are less vulnerable to corruption. Since the process used to determine the winners is open, there is no secrecy. In a descending clock auction, the winning bidders do not necessarily disclose the lowest price(s) they are willing to receive in order to supply the product(s), since the auction stops when demand equals supply. This is an advantage of descending clock auctions, particularly when bidders participate in several auctions run by the same auctioneer, because it increases participation.

Hybrid Designs

Most practitioners advocate in favor of descending clock auctions with respect to the sealed envelope approaches. This has been debated for years in academia and industry, and there is still no clear preference. In essence, the uncertainty faced by bidders in the auctions should be considered: the main purpose of a descending clock auction is to grant/allow for "price discovery," i.e., to allow bidders to revise their reserve prices in light of the information revealed by the bidding behavior of other bidders during the auction. However, there are situations where it is claimed that this specific design does not fulfill this objective. For example, Harbord and Pagnozzi (2008) conducted a review of Colombian Auctions for Firm Energy. None of the auction participants they spoke with reported that their reserve prices changed (and would change) during the auction, which may be due to the particular types of uncertainty faced by the bidders for whom the reserve price is a key element to determine their participation in the auction.

This debate has led to the proposal of hybrid auction formats as a way of combining the best characteristics of both approaches in the pursuit of efficiency. Two-phase hybrid auctions that combine different auction designs have been applied, where demand is pooled in a centralized process and there are multiple sellers. They try to combine the most interesting characteristics from each design. There are two common approaches, which will be described next.

DESCENDING CLOCK STAGE FOLLOWED BY PAY-AS-BID AUCTION. The first phase (Phase I—Price Disclosure) encompasses a descending price clock auction. Once it is concluded, a second phase (Phase II—Negotiation), with a final round of bids using a pay-as-bid scheme, is used for the "classified" bidders of the first phase. This auction is generally used to extract value from bidders in auctions of goods with lesser-known values. The objective of the first phase is to provide some price discovery for the players so that those bidders who can sell the product at the lowest cost are selected for the second phase. Since only a small number of bidders might be left in the auction as the price decreases, it is preferable to switch to a sealed-bid stage to minimize the chances of collusion and therefore reduce the final auction price as much as possible.

A simplified version of the design is shown in figure 2.2:

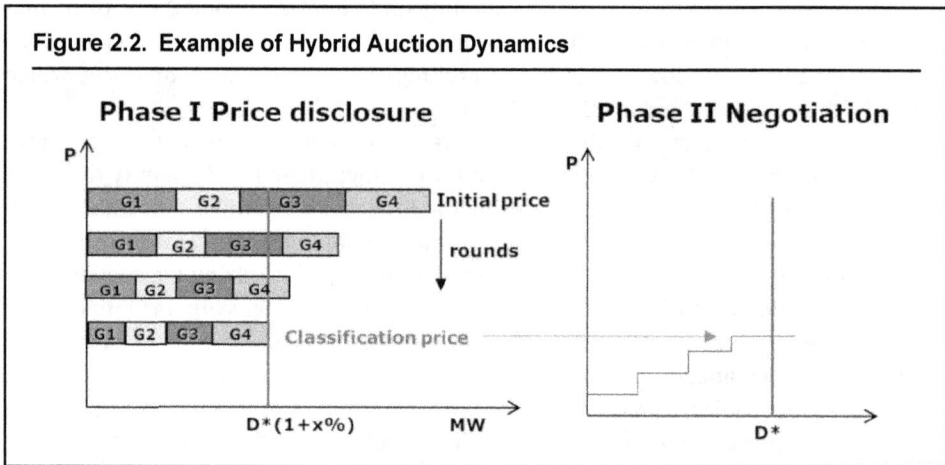

Figure 2.2. Example of Hybrid Auction Dynamics

Source: Author's elaboration

This auction design was selected and has been used since 2004 in Brazilian auctions for existing and new electricity. In each auction, a large block of energy is contracted through a long-term contract in a centralized procurement process. Some auctions have procured multiple items such as long-term contracts with different delivery dates and characteristics but always in a centralized process. Auctions for new electricity have multiple sellers who compete with projects with different technologies and cost structures (hydro plants, coal and gas plants, biomass, etc.). Auctions for existing electricity have multiple sellers with amortized hydro assets, with different opportunity costs and views, who compete for a single (or several) energy block(s). The descending price auction was chosen to be the starting one for these reasons, in order to provide better price information to the bidders and prepare their valuations for the final sealed-bid round, which tries to reduce prices for consumers as much as possible. About 20 electricity auctions were carried out until 2010 in Brazil following this design, contracting about 30,000 MW of new generation capacity. The Brazilian experience is described in box 2.2.

FIRST-PRICE SEALED-BID STAGE FOLLOWED BY AN ITERATIVE DESCENDING AUCTION. In the second hybrid auction approach, there is a first-price sealed-bid round first, followed by an iterative descending auction for the lowest "x" bidders whose offers differ by 5 percent or less. The amount of information released during each round of the iterative auction

Box 2.2. Experience with Hybrid Auctions

The standard design for existing and new energy auctions, which are carried out every year in Brazil, relies on a combination of two mechanisms: descending clock and pay-as-bid (Dutra, J. and Menezes, F. (2005)). The first phase of these auctions follows the design of a classical simultaneous descending clock auction, in which the auctioneer sets a purchasing price and bidders declare the quantity they are willing to sell at that price. As long as total supply is greater than demand by a percentage factor unknown to bidders—an essential point for promoting competition in the second phase of the auction—the price is further reduced. Once total supply reaches this threshold, the first phase ends and the second phase begins. In the second phase, bidders who have remained in the auction up to this point must submit their final offer price following a pay-as-bid design. At this point, the fact that total supply is still greater than demand provides an incentive for bidders to further reduce their bids with respect to the final price of the first phase.

This scheme was first adopted when a procurement auction was held on November 30, 2004 for five types of long-term electricity contracts, referred to as Product 1 to Product 5. Products 1, 2, and 3 were eight-year supply contracts with start dates in 2005, 2006, and 2007. Products 4 and 5 were five-year supply contracts starting in 2008 and 2009. The auction involved the purchase of more than 17,000 average MW.[11] Most of the energy supplied was hydro based.

The same design also applies to auctions in which new generation capacity is procured. In 2007, for example, Brazil held a procurement auction for new electricity, with delivery starting in 2012. The starting price of the first phase was set by the government at US$71/MWh. After eight rounds, the price had decreased to US$69/MWh, marking the end of the first phase. At this point total supply was greater than demand by a percentage factor unknown to bidders—who then had to engage in a second phase that followed a sealed-bid design. Accepted bids in the second phase showed that some bidders gave a further discount of 5 percent over the clearing price of the first phase. This is illustrated in figure 2.3 as follows:

Figure 2.3. Auction Result for Energy Delivery in 2012

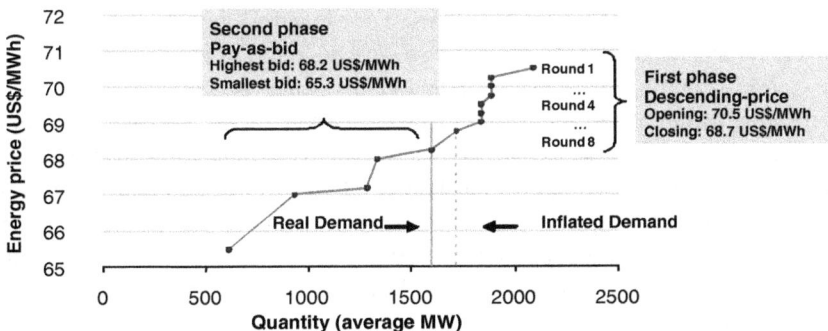

depends on the design: in some cases, the incumbent price is released, while in others only information regarding whether the offer is accepted or not is provided.

This type of auction is generally used for products with better information and knowledge about their values. Hence, since price discovery is not an important issue, the advantage of the first phase is its potential to reduce collusion and increase auction convergence (the auction can finish in the sealed-bid phase if the difference between the lowest bidders is very high). The objective of the iterative phase is to try to achieve a further reduction in prices for consumers after the sealed-envelope phase.

Brazil has been using this auction design to grant concessions and contracts to hydro plants for site-specific, single-product auctions. A concession is needed in order to select the investor who will explore the hydro resources and have rights to the use of water for a specific site—which is a property of the Federal Government—before auctioning an energy contract to the project. Concessions in Brazil were originally granted on a first-come first-served basis, but this has resulted in some investors hoarding several hydro concessions (concessions were acquired but the project was not built). Brazil then shifted to an auction system in 1997 and the current design follows a hybrid auction to select the investor who will explore the concession of a hydro site on the basis of the lowest energy price for the energy to be produced: there is first round (sealed-bid) bidding among all potential investors, followed by a descending iterative auction for the lowest bidders whose bids differed by at most 5 percent. The result of this auction is the granting of a concession to an investor who then participates in a subsequent auction to compete for energy contracts, which then follows a hybrid design.

The same concession's auction design was used in December 2007, March 2008, and April 2010 for specific auctions in Brazil to sell the concession, and an energy contract for large hydro plants in the Amazon. This was the case of Santo Antonio (3,150 MW), Jirau (3,300 MW), and Belo Monte (11,233 MW). All auctions ended in the first round, since the lowest offer was much smaller than the others. Discounts of 36 percent, 22 percent, and 6 percent were obtained for auction starting prices for Santo Antonio, Jirau, and Belo Monte hydro plants, respectively.

A HYBRID INTERNET-BASED ANGLO-DUTCH AUCTION: AN EXAMPLE FOR THE NON-FRANCHISED MARKET. Auctions for energy contracts have also been used when not obliged by regulators or among players in the non-franchised market.[12] A large user, for example, may establish its own auction process to meet his/her load requirements. Even in sophisticated and liquid markets, the number of different forward energy contracts traded is relatively small, including in very active hubs. The energy profiled in those contracts (that is, peak versus non-peak) is pre-determined, and does not necessarily meet the load shape of particular clients. In the US west coast market, for example, standard future contracts are actively traded but only to meet peak load, and are referred to a few major electricity hubs (e.g., Mid-Columbia in Washington and Palo Verde in Arizona).

In developing countries, the non-franchised market is also very active in conducting auctions to procure its electricity needs. In Brazil, Peru, and Chile, energy-intensive consumers, or marketers acting on their behalf, often carry out auctions to buy short, mid and long-term electricity contracts. There are no regulatory requirements imposed on those customers as far as the procurement modality is concerned. The use of auctions reflects a perception that the mechanism has low transaction costs and creates competition among bidders.

When meeting the needs of a particular load curve, buyers may follow a traditional procurement modality, requesting offers among pre-qualified sellers. Alternatively, they can design and conduct their own auctions. Internet-based auctions can yield competitive price offers of capacity options even for products that are not actively traded. The underlying assumption is that bilateral negotiations are unlikely to yield the "best deal" for the buyer because "the value of the negotiation skill is small relative to the value of additional competition." Similarly, competitive price offers may not emerge from an RFO that solicits binding sealed offers from sellers, as the process is a single-round sealed auction with known shortcomings, including conservative bidding by sellers.

An example provided by Lloyd[13] of an internet-based multi-round auction following an Anglo-Dutch design will be described below. The example refers to a voluntary procurement carried out by a municipal utility in Florida with great success. Similar arrangements have been applied by industrial users worldwide. The mechanism was conducted *"in preparation for the utility's winter peaking months, when the highest electricity space heating demand is observed. The utility wanted to acquire a financial option because of its concern over the possibility of an extreme cold spell that can trigger a spot electricity price surge."*

"The auction design entailed an independent auctioneer assisting the buyer in clearly defining the non-price terms of the product to be procured, setting auction rules, inviting & pre-qualifying potential sellers, and contractually binding those sellers to the price offers that they make during the auction. Three rounds were envisioned.

Round 1: Initial offering. All pre-qualified sellers are invited to submit their initial anonymous offers on the auctioneer's auction web site. The lowest prevailing offer is visible to all sellers to aid their assessment of the extent of price competition and inference of the product's market value.

Round 2: Open auction with possible extension time. The auctioneer updates and posts the prevailing best offer in real time as newly submitted valid offers arrive. A valid offer placed in the remaining five minutes of Round 2 automatically extends the round by another five minutes.[14] Round 2 closes at the later of the scheduled time or after five minutes of no bidding activity. The auctioneer then identifies the two or three sellers with the lowest price offers as the finalists for Round 3.

Round 3: Final sealed auction. The auctioneer invites two to three finalists to submit their best and final sealed offers. A seller may choose not to submit a new offer, and its lowest offer from Round 2 becomes its de facto Round 3 offer. As Round 3 creates the risk of losing, it mitigates potential collusion and induces further price-cutting.

Both auctions took less than two hours to complete, and the buying utility and the winning sellers signed the contract immediately thereafter. Hence, the auction process was more time-efficient than an RFO process that typically takes days, or even weeks, to complete because of the time required for bid solicitation and evaluation, and final bilateral negotiation. The Anglo-Dutch auctions yielded competitive price offers to a buyer of capacity options not actively traded in the market."

Results

Figure 2.4 *illustrates the progression of the 2002 auction to procure a capacity option: a three-month, 10-MWh option with a 150/MWh strike price. The option is substantially out of the money because the strike price far exceeds an estimate of marginal generation fuel cost below $60 MWh. The following figure presents the bidding activity for the three rounds.*

The practical usefulness of the auctions is best summarized by an official of the municipal utility who, after the first-time use of the auction to procure an electricity forward contract,

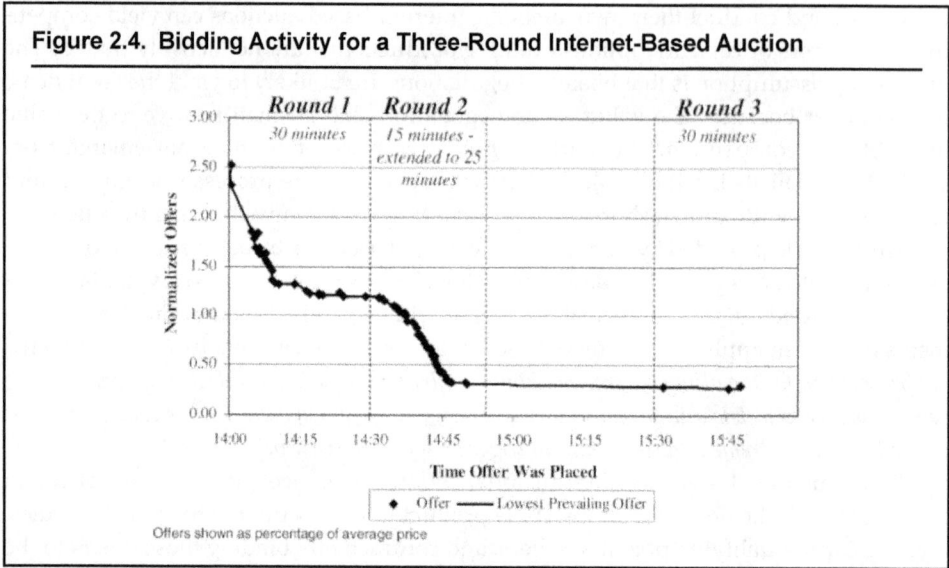

Figure 2.4. Bidding Activity for a Three-Round Internet-Based Auction

Source: Lloyd (2004)

observed that *"the auction resulted in a savings of about 10 percent, compared with what the muni[cipal utility] normally pays . . ."* The same official further remarked *"[t]he process worked tremendously for us. I see this as something that is going to catch on. . . . It's very good for competition. It's unmasking the prices and will save us between $500,000 and $1 million annually."*[15]

SEQUENTIAL AUCTIONS. A fundamental question in the design of energy auctions is whether to have a single auction or to meet the demand over a series of [sequential] auctions. For example, the Colombian regulator will procure forward electricity supply contracts to match the annual forecast demand by means of a sequence of four quarterly auctions (i.e., one fourth of the demand forecast in each auction).

There are reasons for and against spreading the demand over a sequence of auctions, such as:

- *Transaction costs:* When the transaction costs of bidding in an auction are high compared to the profits bidders anticipate making in that auction, participation is expected to be negligible, thereby reducing competition, which tends to increase the cost of procuring the products. The auctioneer may thus prefer a single auction over a sequence of auctions to keep transaction costs low.
- *Price discovery:* If a descending clock auction is not feasible or desirable, a sequence of sealed-bid auctions is somewhere between a single sealed-bid auction and a descending auction in terms of the information revealed through the auctions. Hence, when there is uncertainty about the value of the product being auctioned, a sequence of sealed-bid auctions improves the price discovery relative to a single sealed-bid auction.
- *Risk aversion:* Since the price in an auction might be too high or too low due to some unexpected events, and if bidders are paid the clearing price (e.g., uniform price sealed-bid auction or clock auction), risk-averse price-taker bidders prefer

a sequence of auctions over a single auction. If there is a single auction, bidders might end up receiving too high or too low a price for all their products. However, in a sequence of auctions, this risk is reduced, since the prices bidders receive for their sales are determined at different points in time.

▨   *Weak competition:* If competition in the auction is not very strong, large-scale suppliers can bid to enhance their market power in a sequence of auctions, increasing the cost of procuring the products. Hence, in this case, a single auction might be preferable. For a more in-depth study of this issue, see Herrera-Dappe (2009).

All of these issues should be properly evaluated on a case-by-case basis in order to decide whether or not to spread the demand over a sequence of auctions.

Combinatorial Auctions

A combinatorial auction deals with the simultaneous sale of more than one item, where bidders can place bids on an "all-or-nothing" basis on "packages" rather than just individual items. For the bidder, the question becomes how to combine and price the different products. If there are complementarities on the provision of the products and these are procured through separate auctions, bidders face an exposure problem. For example, suppose the auctioneer wants to procure energy supply contracts and splits the day in four contracts of six hours each, but for a given power plant it is economically optimal to generate for at least 12 consecutive hours. If the four contracts are procured through separate auctions, the power plant is exposed to the possibility of being awarded only one contract for six hours, which is not optimal.[16] Because of the potential risk of exposure to unwanted outcomes, some bidders may refrain from participating in the auction, decreasing competition and in so doing, possibly the efficiency of the auction.

Combinatorial auctions solve the exposure problem by allowing bidders to bid on combinations or packages of the products being procured (usually bidders are still allowed to bid on individual products). Obviously, a product—whether individually or as part of a package bid—can be awarded at most only once, so the auctioneer's objective is to select the set of bids from all bidders that minimizes payments by the auctioneer to bidders, subject to the constraint that each product is awarded no more than one time. Different pricing rules can be applied in combinatorial auctions. One of the simplest is the pay-as-bid rule, where a winning bidder receives the price he or she bids.

There are two different approaches to defining the packages that bidders are allowed to bid on: (i) they can be pre-defined by the auctioneer prior to the auction, or (ii) bidders can be given the flexibility to specify their own packages during the auction. Combinatorial auctions can be designed as single-round sealed-bid auctions or as dynamic auctions with several rounds (i.e., descending proxy auction). For example, Chilean auctions for mid and long-term energy contracts use a sealed-bid combinatorial design with a pay-as-bid pricing rule.[17]

The main advantage of combinatorial auctions is that they solve the exposure problem by allowing bidders to bid on combinations or packages of the products being procured. If the packages are pre-defined by the auctioneer and they happen to be too large, participation in the auction can be low. The main disadvantage of a combinatorial auction is its complexity. Determining the winning bidder can be a complex process where even the bidder with the highest individual bid is not guaranteed to win.

Two-sided Auctions

In two-sided auctions, both bids and asks are allowed. A transaction is created when the bid and ask prices match. One-sided auctions, however, only allow bids and the auction goes to the highest bidder (or lowest, in a reverse auction).

Two-sided auctions enable the active participation of supply and demand resources to compete on a level-playing-field basis, where both are allowed to bid. Although it is one form of demand response, it has seldom been applied, which in part reflects the secondary role assigned to demand response in bridging the supply-demand gap. Appendix F discusses some approaches to entertain demand-side participation in energy auctions.

An efficient two-sided electricity auction mechanism should help control market power and enhance the social welfare of the market. This is particularly important when the supply of electricity is very tight and inefficient generation units have to run and set the clearing price. In the presence of demand response, those units may no longer be dispatched and a significant decrease in the market clearing price may be achieved.

Little activity has been seen in terms of the participation of demand resources in the auction design process to compete with supply resources on a level playing field, and in developing countries, virtually none. Latin American auctions, for example, are one-sided, with multiple buyers and sellers, where only generators are active in the mechanism. The single exception to this is observed in Colombia. Despite not being a full-fledged two-sided auction, an elastic *demand curve* is used as a "proxy" to consumer preferences, as shown in figure 2.5. This price elasticity follows the experience of the US capacity auctions in ISO-NE and PJM.

Two-sided auctions have recently been encouraged by FERC (US) for the competitive procurement of energy-related products. FERC's decision to include demand

---

Figure 2.5. Simulating a Price Elastic Demand Function

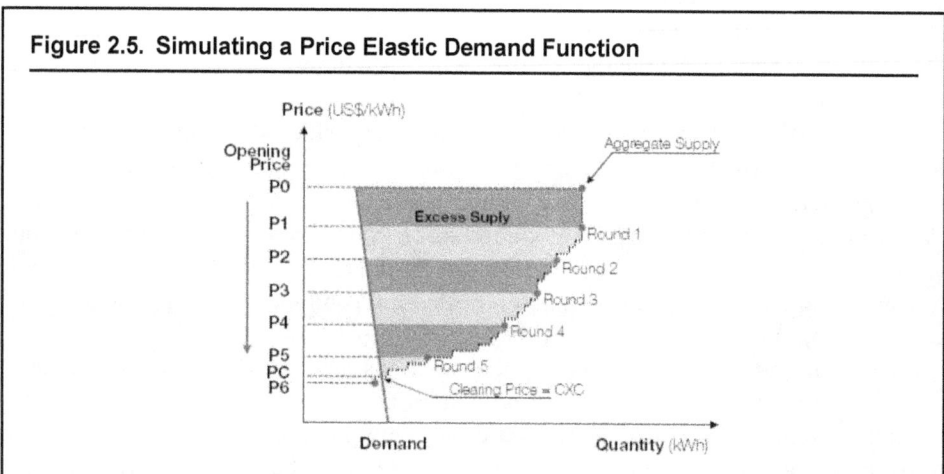

Source: Author's representation

resources in any competitive procurement for electricity resources is a paradigm shift. Developing countries still have a long way to go in this regard, particularly those that do not have a formal electricity market where demand resources could be brought to the table on a level-playing-field basis. Things may change as regulators and stakeholders entertain more demand participation, partly in response to power crises—but it may still take time to overcome obstacles and reduce regulatory uncertainties regarding the monitoring and evaluation of the demand-side gains.

Summary of Auction Designs

A summary of the auction designs described above is presented as follows:

Key Auction Designs

Auction Design	Items	Advantage	Disadvantage	Countries
FPSB (single product)	Concession of power plants and transmission assets	Simplicity, easy to implement Handles weak competition	No price discovery	Vietnam, Peru
Pay-as-bid auction (multiple units of same product)	PPAs, Mid and long-term energy contracts	Simplicity, easy to implement Handles weak competition	No price discovery	Peru, Panama, Mexico
Uniform price auction (multiple units of same product)	CO_2 emission allowances Spot energy Capacity contracts	Simplicity, easy to implement Handles weak competition Viewed as fair Attracts small bidders	No price discovery Possibly high political cost	US
Descending clock auction (single or simultaneous auctions)	Capacity contracts, energy contracts	Easy to implement Good price discovery Suitable for multiple products (simultaneous version) Less vulnerable to corruption (than sealed-bid auctions) Winners do not need to reveal all their information	Possibility of collusion when competition is weak "Seems" more complex	US, Spain, Colombia Ascending clock auction (auctioneer sells): France, Spain, US, Canada
Hybrid auctions (Descending clock phase followed by pay-as-bid phase)	Concessions of power plants, mid and long-term energy contracts	Speeds auction convergence Handles weak competition Good price discovery	(Second phase) Not easy to implement with multiple products Exposure problem (with multiple products)	Brazil
Combinatorial auctions	Mid and long-term energy contracts	No exposure problem Good price discovery if done in rounds	Difficult to implement	Chile
Two-sided auctions	Supply and demand resources	Increases welfare Mitigates anti-competitive behavior	More complex, less familiar Typical difficulties in engaging demand to respond to prices	ISO-NE and PJM

Outcomes of Well-designed Auctions

A good auction design elicits information from bidders regarding their willingness to provide the product being procured. It should also minimize transaction costs and stimulate competition among the potential suppliers of the product being auctioned, with the objective of ensuring a socially more efficient allocation/use of resources.

Well-designed auction systems should achieve the following goals:

- A fair, open, transparent, objective, non-discriminatory, and timely process;
- An efficient price discovery mechanism, minimizing information and transaction costs;
- An outcome in which bidders who can provide a product at the lowest cost will win, ensuring optimal use of resources;
- Minimization of the likelihood of challenges to the selection process and outcome, avoiding post-auction delays; and
- An attractive, less-disputable solution to the regulatory issue of establishing the prudent power purchase costs incurred by distribution utilities when serving their captive customers.

From Theory to Practice

The previous section described the most commonly used auction designs to attract new capacity and/or retain existing capacity. The description focused on the different features of each design such as the timing for submitting bids, how they are structured and compared, and how the price is determined, as well as the advantages and disadvantages of each design. Selecting the best auction design for a particular market and the products to be procured is a prerequisite, but not a guarantee, for the success of the auction. Box 2.3 lists some of the elements that are also needed to ensure a successful auction.

Auctions and World Bank Procurement Guidelines

The World Bank has encouraged its client countries to procure energy competitively. The primary modality recommended by the WB for the procurement of goods and services is equivalent to the FPSB auction. However, when the Bank finances the cost of a project procured under a BOO, BOT, or BOOT concession, the procurement rules are very flexible, provided that the mechanism used for awarding the concession is satisfactory to the Bank and is approved on an ex-ante basis.

The WB Procurement Guidelines specify that *"the concessionaire or entrepreneur under BOO/BOT/BOOT shall be selected under International Competitive Bid procedures acceptable to the Bank, which may include several stages in order to arrive at the optimal combination of evaluation criteria, such as the cost and magnitude of the financing offered, the performance specifications, the cost charged to the user or purchaser, other income generated for the Borrowers or purchaser by the facility. The said entrepreneur selected in this manner shall then be free to procure the goods, works, and services required for the facility from eligible sources, using its own procedures. In this case, the Project Appraisal Document, and the Loan Agreement shall specify the type of expenditures incurred by the said entrepreneur toward which Bank financing will apply."*[18]

The above provisions are remarkable in terms of giving the borrower the necessary flexibility for implementing an energy auction mechanism that makes the most sense for the particular case at hand. For example, if a government is interested in developing a hydro plant in a specific site, it can tender the right to water use in tandem with a PPA, whereby

Box 2.3. What are the Basic Elements for a Successful Auction?

The following elements are necessary for successful auctions, since without them, participation could be negligible, bids may not represent true valuations, and the desired objectives will not be achieved:

- Competition must be ensured.
- Institutions must be solid, independent regulators in order to facilitate successful and sustainable auction implementation.
- A legal or policy framework should ensure that buyers will have cost-reflective tariffs as a means of attracting sufficient and efficient investments.
- Buyers should be creditworthy; if not, then explicit government-backstopped guarantees should be in place.
- Products must be well-defined so that bidders can formulate their valuations for clear, unambiguous products and bid accordingly.
- A complete set of carefully considered rules must be specified for all situations that may arise in the auction, i.e., what the auctioneer and bidders can and cannot do, what information is revealed and when, and penalties for violating the rules.
- There should be no ambiguity about what each bidder is bidding on, the process, who the off-takers are, and the rules of the auction.
- Bidders should be made aware that they are all bidding on the same products and that bids will be compared on an equal (i.e., "apples-to-apples") basis.
- Publication of the auction process through several channels (e.g. road shows), including several target bidder groups, and reasonably timed to attract sufficient interest from participants.
- A regulatory environment that contains basic elements to attract competition and combat collusive behavior.
- A country's reasonable track record on rule of law and contract sanctity.
- A solid and enforceable scheme of guarantees should be in place in order to ensure project completion for new capacity being auctioned.

part or all of the energy produced will be acquired by one or more distribution utilities. The product of the auction should be defined as a future energy contract that is attached to the construction of a hydro plant on that particular site. The winning bidder is the one that offers the lowest price for the energy. The government may propose a FPSB, descending clock or a hybrid auction. If the Bank considers that the product definition and the auction design will be conducive to competition and low cost to customers, it has no objection to the process. The private developer will then be eligible for World Bank financing.

When Not to Use Auctions?

The reasons why buyers in general may not want to use auctions for energy may be grouped into two categories: (i) first, when competition is not possible; and (ii) second, when buyers want to conduct a competitive process, but are not willing to award a bid solely based on a financial offer. Those cases will be discussed as follows:

Competition is Not Possible or Desirable

Guaranteeing the existence of competition is of the utmost importance for successful auctions. Countries where it is not possible to overcome the local incumbents' market, or those whose institutions or regulatory framework are not strong enough to preserve contract sanctity, may create barriers for newcomers and thus jeopardize the procurement process.

Even when competition is desirable, it may not be feasible for structural reasons. This may be the case in highly uncertain scenarios, such as power sectors undergoing a major transformation process. It also may also be the case, for example, when the product is very complex and difficult to specify ex-ante.[19]

Bidders may prefer non-competitive procurement under some circumstances and some of the many arguments are presented in box 2.4. In some cases, they may have some merit, such as the high transaction costs from having multiple bidders analyzing the project and preparing their proposals. Despite their merits, some of the risks and difficulties pointed out by bidders may still be managed to preserve the competitive process and benefits thereof.

Buyers Not Willing to Award a Bid Solely Based on a Financial Offer

There may be some competitive processes for acquiring energy contracts where the buyer wants to take into account non-economic factors, such as maximum plant size, environmental impact, type of fuel, plant efficiency, and others that cannot be factored into a price "handicap" to entitle bidders to participate in the tender on a level-playing-

Box 2.4. Is Competitive Bidding Always Appropriate or Desirable?[20]

Despite the obvious advantages, some private developers argue that competitive bidding may not always be appropriate for infrastructure projects. There are three main cases commonly raised by investors. First, some argue that organizing a competitive bidding procedure takes time and when projects are needed urgently, direct negotiations will be faster. While it is true that competitive bidding processes are relatively complex, the contention that negotiated procedures will always be faster is debatable. Examples abound of negotiations that drag on for very long periods. Besides, hastily negotiated deals may pay insufficient attention to key issues, which may emerge to haunt one or both parties later on.

Second, there may be concern that investors will not take on the often high development costs associated with preparing competitive bids for projects in smaller or more risky markets without assurance or recovering their expenses through the award of the contract. This concern is often said to be particularly true in the case of water supply concessions, where the underground nature of the assets makes due diligence difficult and costly. One response to this concern, as in the case of Buenos Aires, is to undertake a thorough evaluation of the market and underlying assets by an independent consultant before bidding is opened, making this information available to all firms who participate in the bidding process. Limiting the number of prequalified bidders to three or four also increases each candidate's chance of winning and thus their willingness to incur preparatory costs. Finally, an announced policy of reimbursing all or part of the development costs incurred in the preparation of the best non-qualified bid(s) could help attract bidders.

Third, there may also be concern that private sponsors will not take the initiative to develop unsolicited proposals for private infrastructure projects if there is a risk that their labors and intellectual property will not be rewarded through the awarding of the contract. There may be a number of responses to this concern. In the Philippines, for example, a strong framework in support of competitive bidding still allows unsolicited proposals to be accepted through direct negotiation in some circumstances, including a requirement that comparative bids be solicited and, if a comparative bid is received at a lower price, the original proponent has the option of matching the price of the comparative bid and receiving the contract. It may also be possible to provide direct incentives for firms to offer unsolicited project ideas that are later adopted, without necessarily forgoing the benefits of a competitive process; after all, the firm most capable of generating innovative ideas will not always be the one that is best able to implement those ideas at least cost.

A consensus is emerging internationally in favor of competitive bidding. Exceptions should normally be limited (e.g., very small contracts and emergency situations). If it is decided to carry on with negotiated procedures, safeguards can be used to limit the risks inherent in this strategy. Among the most important are the adoption of transparent procedures and the use of external benchmarks, which provide some assurance that the conditions being offered are reasonably advantageous.

field basis. The example illustrated in box 2.5 describes a competitive bidding system used by the state of New Jersey in 1988 for power procurement by utilities from non-utilities sources and identifies the various state policy considerations that the award system tried to incorporate to balance public and private interests. Today, the system would be considered overly cumbersome and intrusive, but it seemed to make sense at that point in time.

High transaction costs are a genuine reason for not using auctions or competitive mechanisms in general. The volume of resources involved in energy contracts and the benefits that may be derived from competition more than offset any transaction cost that the auction may entail. Some more sophisticated auctions, such as dynamic ones, may have higher initial transaction costs to set up the process, to get the systems in place, and to provide training to the stakeholders.[22] However, even in those cases, transaction costs are a fraction of the potential benefits from competition. Furthermore, many of those initial set-up costs will be diluted in subsequent auctions, since most of the processes and systems will already be in place and only some fine-tuning will be necessary.

If Not Auctions—What are the Alternative Procurement Mechanisms?

Auctions represent one of several possible ways to procure products and services. To put them into context, it is useful to provide a range of other procurement possibilities, which is presented below. This list is not meant to be exhaustive; its objective is to show the wide spectrum of possibilities using examples of true cases, while emphasizing that auctions may not necessarily be the best option for allocating scarce resources or procuring services in network industries.

Negotiations

Negotiations are a mechanism whereby buyers freely negotiate the terms and commercial conditions of the product procured. A direct negotiation is the most popular mechanism for energy procurement. Although several electricity-related products are bilaterally negotiated worldwide, this mechanism has several drawbacks. It lacks transparency

---

Box 2.5. Multiple-Criteria Award System for a Competitive Bid[21]

The ranking system included "economic factors" such as the bid price on a linear scale of zero points for a bid at the ceiling price, to a maximum point ranking for projects that submit a bid price equal to 25 percent of the present value of the purchasing utility's ceiling price. Security provisions and dispatchability are also included in "economic factors." The weight assigned to "economic factors" in the point ranking system cannot exceed 55 percent of the total maximum points available.

The second category, "project status and viability factors", has a minimum weight of 25 percent in the overall point ranking and includes, but is not limited to, the following criteria: (1) FERC certification; (2) project schedule and milestones; (3) project permitting plan and schedule; (4) project financing plan and schedule; (5) project development team and experience; (6) project technology; (7) thermal load; (8) engineering design; (9) interconnection and wheeling considerations; (10) site control; (11) stability and security of fuel supply; and (12) the form of liquidated damages funding for failure to achieve commercial operation.

The third and final category, "non-economic factors," had a minimum weight of 20 percent of the overall point ranking and includes, but is not limited to, the following criteria: (1) fuel type; (2) location; (3) environmental benefits; and (3) fuel efficiency.

and its efficiency is largely associated to a definition of a "benchmark" price against which regulators, buyers, and sellers are allowed to compare their negotiated prices. For example, when distribution companies procure energy on behalf of regulated users, it requires the regulator's vigilant eye to define the "prudent" costs of negotiation that should be passed on to final customers. In the absence of a liquid futures market, the definition of "prudent" costs has shown, however, to be very difficult in practice.[23] It is sometimes arbitrary and based on technocratic inputs, and is often disassociated from the market reality. A direct negotiation is also more prone to corruption and nepotism, and therefore more likely to be challenged subsequently as the political winds change.

First-Come First-Served Basis-Feed-in-Tariffs (FiT)

Many countries have used a feed-in-tariff (FiT) process to foster the development of renewable sources of energy. Through this mechanism, the government mandates utilities to procure energy from renewable producers at an administratively set price. Bid selection follows a first-come first-served basis until a desired quota is completed. There is no direct competition among bidders. Chapter 6 provides a detailed description of FiT and other mechanisms for procuring renewables. This mechanism does not necessarily ensure efficiency due to the difficulty in setting a right value for the feed-in-tariff that helps to avoid over or under-investment. On the demand side, Standard Offers are the analogue version of FiT. The regulator specifies a minimum price that utilities have to pay to energy users or load aggregators when submitting projects with the objective of promoting energy savings or demand-side management.

Beauty Contest (or Administrative Allocation)

In this case, a government agency proposes outlines and criteria to be followed in the selection process. "*Typically, a set of guidelines and some measurable criteria are presented, leaving some room for subjective evaluation. Participants present their best case on why they should be awarded the products, covering a variety of aspects (e.g. including business plans). This is typically a subjective, non-transparent selection process that involves a great deal of time, effort, and documentation. Also, it is normally difficult to assess the credibility of the claims made by participants. Due to its lack of transparency, administrative allocation is more prone to corruption and kickbacks*".[24] Appendix A provides an example of the beauty contest used by Sweden to allocate mobile phone frequency spectrum. Borgers and Dustmann (2003) criticize beauty contests due to their lack of transparency, vague selection process, unclear final decision, and bias towards the incumbent.

Output-Based-Aid (OBA)

OBA refers to development aid strategies that link the delivery of public services in developing countries to targeted performance-related subsidies. The service provider will receive subsidies to replace costs associated with providing the service to people, such as user fees. Individual agents will verify that the service is being delivered, and based on the performance of the service provider, a subsidy will be granted, thereby being "performance-based." OBA subsidies are offered in transport construction, education, water and sanitation systems, and health care delivery, among other sectors where positive externalities exceed cost recovery exclusively from the private market.

There are many variations in this kind of performance-based procurement. Some schemes have introduced an element of competition, with the subsidy linked to the number of new connections that a utility company or service provider is able to offer in a certain area. Competition has been based on either the smallest grant to supply a

---

Figure 2.6. Typology of Procurement Processes in the Energy Sector

Non-Competitive	Quasi- Competitive	Competitive		
* Non-solicited Proposals * Direct Negotiation	* Swiss Challenge * Feed-in-Tariff * EE/DSM Standard Offer * Beauty Contest * OBA with Exclusive Concession Rights	* Multi-attribute - e.g. PURPA, weighing of price and non-price factors * Auctions		
		* Sealed Bids	* FBSB * Multi-Product * Descending * Ascending	 * Discriminatory * Uniform Price
		* Dynamic		
		* Hybrid models	* FPSB + Descending * Descending + FPSB	
		* Combinatorial * Sequential		

Source: Author's representation

given number of customers, or the largest number of customers for a given grant. OBA schemes have been criticized for their high administrative costs, which are due to a number of reasons, among which are: the printing and distribution of vouchers can be expensive, and the significant cost involved in effectively monitoring the outcomes of OBA schemes, and in maintaining a process of transparency.

Swiss Challenge[25]

This mechanism is an attempt to introduce some form of competition to unsolicited proposals. "*Swiss challenge is a form of public procurement in some (usually less developed) jurisdictions that requires a public authority (usually a government agency) that has received an unsolicited bid for a public project (such as a port, road, or railway) or services to be provided to the government, to publish the bid and invite third parties to match or exceed it. The original proponent gets the right to match any superior offers given by the third party*".[26] Appendix A provides an example of a Swiss Challenge methodology adopted by the Philippines BOT Law.

Typology of Procurement Processes

Figure 2.6 presents a tentative typology of procurement processes. They are grouped into three major clusters, based on the degree of competition involved. Modalities such as Swiss challenge, beauty contest and others are classified as "quasi-competitive." Those that are competitive are the ones where the award criterion is clearly and unambiguously defined ex-ante, and weights are assigned for each attribute. There is little latitude in the selection and in the negotiation process. Auctions represent one form of competitive selection where the offer is solely based on a price bid. A typology for auctions is also presented for the sake of completeness.

Notes

1. A financial offer *per se* or a bid that can be translated into financial terms (e.g. production share in auctions for oil fields).
2. Called a Vickrey auction, commonly used in eBay-type auctions.

3. A good survey is presented in Klemperer (2000).

4. See Appendix A for details.

5. A reliable system must be both secure and adequate. A secure system should be able to withstand disturbances. An adequate system has the necessary transmission and generation capacity to meet current and future demand growth, even under critical periods. Failures in adequacy result in energy- or capacity-constrained power systems.

6. Another option is that the auctioneer wants to procure long-term contracts for a total of 500 MW, but the size of each contract will depend on the bids submitted by bidders.

7. The mechanism also seems to be applicable to support the acquisition or leasing of containerized emergency generators, which typically come in modules of about 0.8–1 MW. Even a relatively small power system may need 20–30 of those modules during a power crisis.

8. Kahn et al. (2001).

9. Ibid.

10. The ascending clock auction is the equivalent auction when the goal of the auctioneer is to sell products instead of procuring them. The only difference is that the price increases throughout the auction, as its name indicates. It has the same advantages and disadvantages of the descending clock auction.

11. Average MW is an energy unit and reflects the MW that can be continuously delivered by a project. 1 average MW = 8760 MWh over a year.

12. A market in which its customers can freely negotiate the prices of energy to be delivered in bulk. Also called free-market.

13. Adapted from Lloyd, D. et al. (2004).

14. A time extension feature is included to eliminate the strategic value of last-minute bidding by a "sniper" seller in an eBay-style auction.

15. Lloyd, D. et al. (2004).

16. The typical example used in standard auctions (i.e., where the auctioneer is the seller), is the case of the right and left shoe. Buyers value the pair of shoes, not just one shoe. Hence, if both shoes are sold through separate auctions, a buyer is exposed to the risk of only getting one shoe.

17. For a thorough discussion of combinatorial auctions, see Cramton et al. (2006).

18. World Bank Procurement Guidelines. Section 3.13. (a)

19. This may be the case, for example, in the procurement of energy efficiency services, where the definition of the "product" being procured is not always straightforward, and may include goods, works, and services. Services may include project design, operations and maintenance, training, and measurement and verification, while works may involve revamping existing systems, construction of stand-by power and cogeneration facilities and the like. Sometimes the specifics of the work to be executed are known only after a detailed audit is carried out. See Singh et al. (2010).

20. Adapted from Kerf et al. (1996).

21. Adapted from Walker (1988).

22. The total cost of setting up the first large energy auction in Brazil was approximately US$500,000.

23. Arizu et al. (2006).

24. Adapted from Anderson et al. (2005).

25. Based on Kerf et al. (1998).

26. See example of a Swiss challenge scheme on the Philippine Built-Operate-Transfer-Bidding in Kerf (1998).

CHAPTER 3

Electricity Auctions: Experiences in Different Jurisdictions

Introduction

This chapter provides a classification of the experiences related to the implementation of auction cases to be detailed in chapters 4 and 5. Relevant experiences in auctions for different types of reliability-based electricity contracts have been recorded in many developed and developing countries.[1] By comparing and contrasting pertinent issues in auction design, the report should help the reader identify those that are of relevance to their particular area of interest.

Classifying Country Experiences

Experiences from around the world have been classified according to the four main objectives reported by the countries for implementing electricity auctions. These include:

(i)   Bridging the supply-demand gap by (in most cases) attracting new generation capacity;

(ii) Retaining and/or replacing existing generation capacity (e.g., replacing older plants with low-carbon alternatives);

(iii) Procuring energy for Providers of Last Resort ("default supply auctions"), where full retail competition is available, and;

(iv) Attracting newcomers to acquire rights to a portion of the production capacity of existing power plants in order to reduce market concentration, i.e., to carry out a virtual divestiture.

The four primary objectives for holding auctions and each country's stage of development of electricity markets are illustrated in figure 3.1. A wide range of auctions can be implemented in competitive markets, from VPP-type auctions to auctions for long-term contracts to support capacity expansion. The latter is the primary objective in vertically integrated power sectors.

Examples from the developing world can be divided into two main groups, both having the objective of increasing generation capacity. In the first group, the procurement process is characterized by a single buyer and potentially multiple sellers, as in the cases of Mexico and Vietnam, where auctions have been used by state-owned companies to procure electricity from Independent Power Producers. The second group includes multiple buyers, either through a centralized or distributed process, and multiple sellers, as in the cases of Brazil, Colombia, Peru, Panama, and Chile, where auctions for long-term contracts among multiple buyers and sellers are used to attract investments in new capacity. These auctions can be used to bridge the country's projected total future capacity gap, focusing in some cases on the captive market, or on the total market, if the auction is carried out for the specific purpose of bridging the supply-demand gap.

Figure 3.1. Auctions: Objectives and Electricity Market Stage of Development

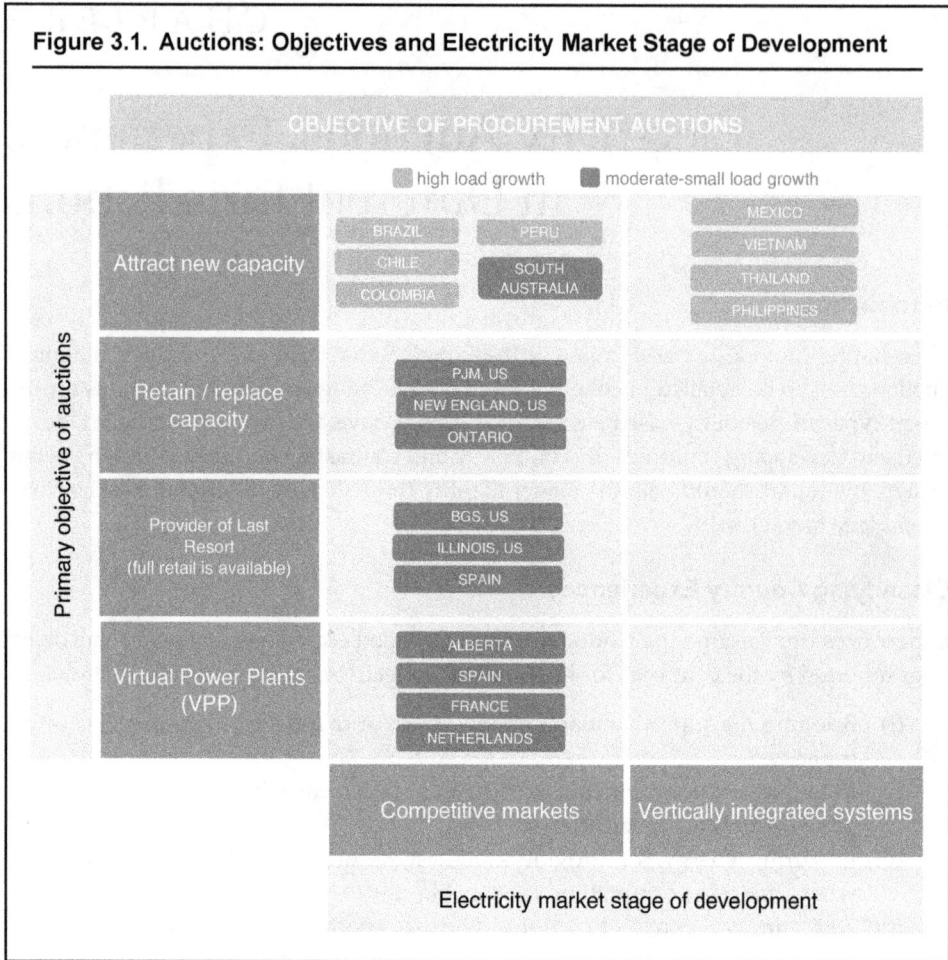

Auctions have also been used by distribution utilities in fully deregulated markets to procure energy to their customers, acting in their capacity of providers of last resort ("POLR"). Even in the case of full competition, some customers have not opted out, and want to be served by the incumbent utility. Auctions are a mechanism used to ascertain that energy is procured in the most efficient way; they have not been designed with the aim of solving resource adequacy problems (i.e., to attract new capacity). However, they can be helpful in retaining existing capacity by providing medium-term supply contracts to generators through auctions that are carried out on a recurrent basis. For this reason, such experiences are included in this chapter, together with cases where the auctions' main goals are to either attract new capacity or retain/replace existing capacity.

The virtual power plant (VPP) auctions that have been implemented throughout Europe and in Canada are also auctions for electricity supply contracts. Their goal is not to solve the resource adequacy problem, but to increase competition in the wholesale energy market by reducing the incumbents' market share and facilitating new entry. Interested readers can find examples of VPP auction implementation in developed countries in Appendix C.

For a more extensive comparison of experiences around the world, it is important to keep in mind countries where investments are driven solely by market forces and/or bilateral negotiations (such as the case of the highly developed and mature markets of the UK and NordPool). In places where auctions are the preferred procurement scheme, there is a variety of ways to actually implement them, ranging from the Single-Buyer framework—through a centrally planned process where the government provides contract guarantees—to a distributed environment whereby distribution companies are free to organize auctions whenever they feel necessary and can purchase whatever volumes they deem appropriate. Within this range, there are centralized processes where the volume to be procured is either centrally defined or defined by the distribution companies on a distributed basis. However, in both the centrally planned or distributed process, contracts are made between the distribution companies and the gencos, without the government taking contractual positions in the market or providing guarantees.

Country experiences may also be classified based on the scope of the auction process. Some auction arrangements may be technology-specific (e.g., renewable sources), while others may be open to all technologies, including demand resources. Moreover, some schemes may be project and location-specific when the government's objective is to auction the rights of a particular hydro site. The other aspect is the institutional organization of the auction-based procurement scheme, which ranges from the typical single buyer concept, based on central planning and government-backstopped PPAs, to institutional arrangements such as the Nordpool, where auctions for the procurement of long-term contracts are non-existent. In this case, auctions are only used as a mechanism to dispatch the power system efficiently by selecting and committing the least-cost power plants according to their merit order. Figure 3.2 presents several country experiences classified according to those two aspects.

Figure 3.2. Auction-based Procurement Schemes and Specificities

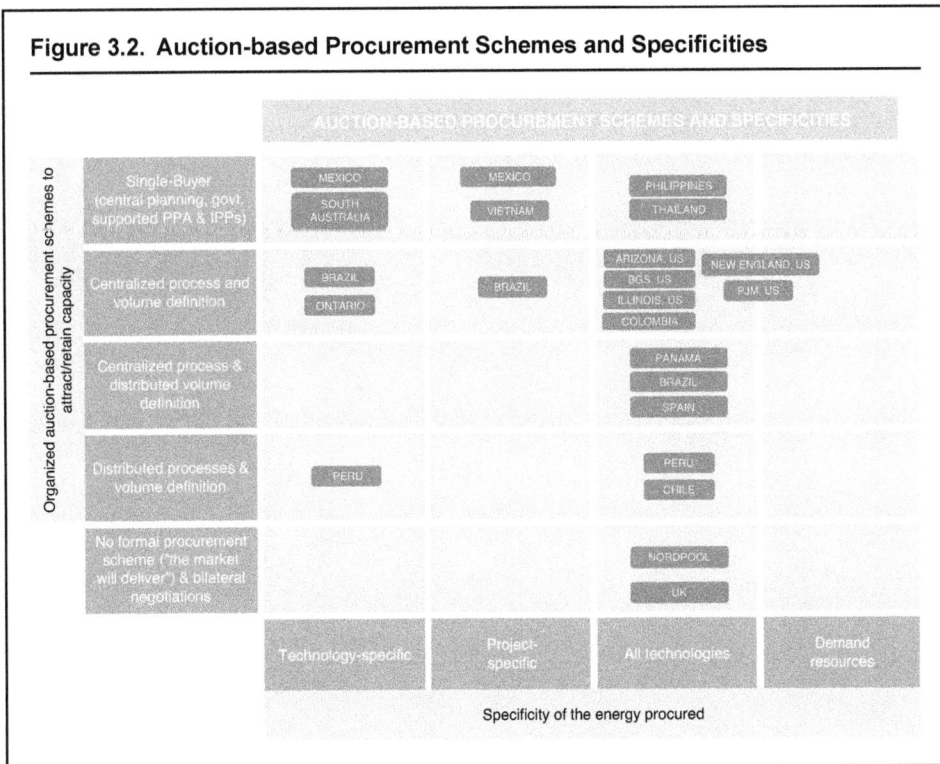

Selected experiences from Latin America (Brazil, Peru, Chile, Colombia,[2] Panama, and Central America), Asia and Oceania (Vietnam, The Philippines, Thailand, and South Australia), Europe (Spain, UK, and Nordpool) and North America (PJM, NEPOOL, California, New Jersey, Illinois, and Ontario) will be discussed next.

These regions have been selected because of the diversity of settings where auctions are applied. Latin America is the region where the experience with contract auctions to foster the entrance of new capacity—which is the main focus of this report—has developed most. Europe and Canada have a concentration of the most useful experiences with auctions for virtual supply procurement (further discussed in Appendix C), while Europe still has countries without specific supplementary mechanisms to foster capacity expansion (UK and the Nordic countries). The US experience is also of relevance in presenting auctions for default supply procurement and in capacity auctions to attract and retain resources. Demand resources have recently been included in the US auctions, which are a pioneer in this field. Finally, some experiences with cross-border auctions for energy procurement are also provided.

Three layers of information are provided for each case study presented in Chapter 4: (i) classification of the country (or market) with respect to its general market characteristics, (ii) classification with respect to the procurement schemes used, and (iii) classification with respect to the attributes of the auction mechanism employed.

Notes

1. Appendix B discusses more situations where auctions are used in the electricity industry, such as for day-ahead dispatch and the allocation of financial transmission rights.
2. Colombia was classified in "All-technologies". However, regulations enabling several technologies to participate are still missing (e.g. wind). See Botero et al (2010).

CHAPTER 4

Auctions in Latin America

Auctions for long-term contracts are extremely relevant for developing countries, where the expansion of generation to meet demand requirements is of paramount importance, and demand often presents high and erratic growth rates. Spot markets alone are too volatile and risky to support the building of new capacity by the private sector, particularly for hydro-based systems. Developers have good reason not to invest solely based on the price signals conveyed by the spot market, whose rules may also be altered by government, particularly during times of energy or capacity scarcity. Hence, long-term contracts become tantamount to sustainable generation expansion (see Appendix A for details).

Although the use of long-term financial contracts cannot fully mitigate spot price volatility, they give investors the chance to better control risks by fixing the contracted volume and price. This hedging reduces barriers to entry, making the market more contestable, and facilitates generation financing and adequacy. Granting contracts through well-designed auctions benefits consumers by ensuring that bid prices reflect competitive levels according to real-market cost expectations and risks. Overall, auctions are intended to make the contract market more transparent and competitive.

Latin America has had the most experience with auctions with multiple buyers and sellers. Different auction mechanisms that have been adopted in this region over the past few years are presented below.

Brazil

Power System Characteristics

The Brazilian power system is the largest in Latin America, with an installed capacity of about 116,000 MW, peak demand of 70,000 MW, and annual consumption close to 470 TWh/year.[1] Hydropower accounts for 75 percent of the installed capacity but usually for almost 90 percent of the energy produced. Hydro plants have large reservoirs that are capable of multi-year storage capacity and are spread out over a complex cascaded system along 12 main river basins. The remaining generation mix includes natural gas-, coal-, nuclear- and oil-fired plants. Three new non-conventional renewable sources have recently emerged as options for generation expansion: small hydro plants (SHPs—less than 50 MW capacity and reservoir area smaller than 3 km^2), wind power, and bio-electricity (co-generation from sugarcane bagasse).

Captive (regulated) consumers constitute 70 percent of the country's load and are supplied by the local distribution companies, which are responsible for procuring energy on their behalf. Free consumers (i.e., those who may individually procure an electricity supplier) account for the remaining roughly 30 percent of total consumption.

Reform Process and Market Structure

The regulatory framework for electric energy in Brazil is the result of the interaction between different factors. The country's electricity industry sector has undergone considerable reforms and has advanced significantly over the past 15 years, evolving from a government-run, tariff-subsidized unsustainable business, comprised of several state-owned inefficient utilities, to a partially competitive environment with both private and government-owned companies, and a relatively independent regulatory agency. The current power sector model relies on a combination of competition and planning to guarantee supply adequacy and provide a relatively predictable environment for attracting new investors. The principal driving force is the hydro predominance in the country, with huge reservoirs that control multiple river systems distributed over a vast area. Historically, this has inspired a strong tendency towards centralized hydrothermal coordination for the system's operations and dispatch. Another influential factor is the system's recent history, starting with the financial difficulties that plagued the former government-owned and controlled model, which practically brought expansion to a halt. The need for expansion to ensure supply adequacy was one of the basic reasons for power sector reform in Brazil. This paralysis led to a first round of reforms starting in 1996, which were partially successful. However, it was stalled by political opposition and successive court challenges, and was to some extent responsible for the serious supply crisis that resulted in the energy rationing of 2001–2002. The current government, elected in 2003, put the reform back on track, which led to the present regulatory framework.

Sector reform has also led to the creation of a number of institutions. ANEEL is the federal electricity regulator, while ONS plays the role of the national independent transmission and system operator, dispatching the system according to a least cost, centralized tight pool. The wholesale energy market operator (CCEE) is responsible for spot price setting, contract settlement, and, more recently, conducting energy auctions. The planning functions are carried out by EPE, a company recently created to fill a 15-year gap, when the centralized, indicative planning had virtually stopped. There are several other government institutions that have direct influence on the power sector, such as regulatory agencies (e.g. ANP for oil, gas, and biofuels), environmental agencies, and state governments.

One of the fundamental elements of any power market is the process through which plants are dispatched and the energy spot price is established in the wholesale market. In order to preserve hydrothermal coordination, the system scheduling is centrally carried out by the Independent System Operator (ONS), which uses a multi-stage stochastic optimization model that takes into account the plants' operating characteristics and inflow uncertainties. The least-cost dispatch does *not* take into account any bilateral contracts or other commercial arrangements and, as a result, determines the dispatch of every plant in the system and also the short-run marginal cost, which is used as the clearing price in the short-term energy spot "market."

Energy spot prices are very volatile, being influenced by hydrology and by the assumption used to run the dispatch model. Therefore, as is the case in many other power systems, it is very risky for a generator to enter the system with a merchant plant. In hydro systems with many years of storage, low spot prices are more likely and may last for long periods of time. During times of scarcity, the government temptation to interfere in spot prices is very high, limiting the upside that merchant plants could have and jeopardizing their economics. In order to hedge against this high price volatility in Brazil, generators must sign bilateral contracts, which are purely financial instruments, but are essential for the commercial feasibility of new projects. Long-term contracts form the backbone of the regulatory model in the country. Competition for those long-term contracts is thus perceived as the most important mechanism for ensuring least-cost expansion. This is an essential ingredient when demand grows at about 5 percent per year, representing an annual additional capacity of 4,000 MW.

A system based on mandatory reliability contracts was introduced in 2004[2] as an incentive to the entrance of new generation. Its three main rules are:

1.   First, all loads (captive consumers from distribution companies and free consumers) must prove to be 100 percent covered by energy contracts. Energy load coverage is verified monthly by the CCEE, certifying that the accumulated MWh consumed over the past 12 months does not exceed the accumulated MWh contracted in the same period. Any shortfall is penalized at a price that mirrors the cost of new energy.

2.   All contracts, which are financial instruments, should be covered by 'firm energy certificates' (FEC). FEC are defined in GWh/year, and are issued by the Ministry of Energy. The methodology for their calculation is fairly complex. It basically reflects the sustained energy production of each generator when interconnected to the grid. The FEC of a plant is the maximum volume of energy that can be sold through contracts and establishes the reliability assured by the generator backing up the contract. It is therefore a critical parameter for the feasibility of a power plant. This rule is verified by comparing[3] the volume of energy sold in a contract with the amount of FEC held by the seller. Again, any shortfall is penalized at a price that mirrors the cost of new energy.

3.   In order to promote the most efficient procurement mechanism for regulated (captive) consumers, the contract obligation scheme for distribution companies operates in tandem with the use of energy auctions of long-term contracts as the main mechanism for energy procurement. On the other hand, free consumers can procure their energy needs as they please (as long as they remain 100 percent contracted).

Use of Auctions

Auctions thus act as the backbone to incentivize efficient purchases by distribution companies when acting on behalf of captive consumers. Auction prices are then passed on to energy tariffs, thus avoiding the need to define benchmark prices as a cap for the energy cost. This was the system used in Brazil before and proved to be very arbitrary and controversial.[4] Since 100 percent of the load needs to be contracted, the spot market serves to settle (positive or negative) differences between a plant's physical production, scheduled by ONS, and its energy contracted.

It is important to emphasize that the regular electricity auctions carried out in Brazil are designed to meet the needs of the franchised (regulated) market only. Free consumers are expected to procure their own needs independently and will select their own preferred procurement mechanism, which may or may not include energy auctions. However, given the success of the auctions conducted for the franchised market, large customers and marketers have often used some of the very same auction arrangements when trading to meet the needs of the non-franchised market.

Separate auctions are carried out to procure new energy (green field generation) or to renew existing contracts (from existing power plants) in the regulated market. The reason for this separation was a matter of risk allocation between generators and distribution companies: a new plant needs long-term contracts to ensure project financing. In contrast, if long-term contracts are given to existing plants as well, the contract portfolios of the distribution companies would become inflexible and difficult to adjust to an uncertain load growth. Hence, existing plants are offered shorter contracts, typically from a few months to eight years.

Procurement of new generation projects is carried out regularly at known intervals, through two public auctions every year, for electricity to be delivered three and five years later (usually referred to as A-3 and A-5 auctions).[5] Each auction offers long-term energy contracts (15-year duration contracts for thermal plants and 30-year duration contracts for hydro plants). These can be standard financial forward contracts, where generators bid an energy price of $/MWh for their FEC or energy call options, an option premium ($/MW), and an energy strike price ($/MWh). In the call option proposal, the consumer notionally "leases" the plant from the investor, paying a monthly fixed amount of $/MW for its availability (to allow recovery of investment and fixed costs), reimbursing the plant's owner on its declared variable operating costs ($/MWh) whenever the plant runs. Figure 4.1 shows the general energy contract auction scheme. Auctions for existing energy follow the same design mechanics as new energy auctions.

The contract auction market is organized by the government as a centralized scheme, carried out jointly to satisfy the total load increase. The objective of the joint auction is to allow smaller distribution companies to benefit from economies of scale in the new energy-contracting environment. However, the government does not interfere with the demand forecasts, which are directly declared by distribution companies, nor does it take ownership for the energy contracts. Each winning Genco signs separate (private) bilateral contracts with each of the distribution companies in proportion to their forecasted loads. In other words, this is *not* a typical single buyer model: the government *does not* interfere with the contracts, nor does it provide payment guarantees. It is a fundamentally different scheme of centralized procurement.

This auction mechanism follows a hybrid design, combining an iterative descending clock auction with a final pay-as-bid round (see Dutra, J. (2005) for details). By means of a specific committee, the government is in charge of proposing all the relevant documents, including auction and energy contract design, and price caps for each auction.

Finally, all technologies compete jointly in the regular new energy auctions. Contending generators require either a concession (in the case of medium and large hydro) or an authorization to operate (all other plants).

Figure 4.1. Energy Auctions in Brazil

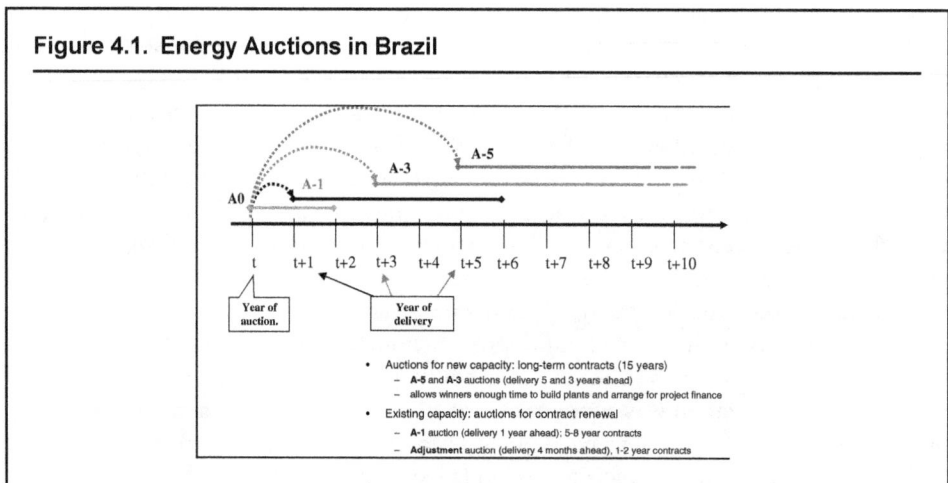

- Auctions for new capacity: long-term contracts (15 years)
  - **A-5** and **A-3** auctions (delivery 5 and 3 years ahead)
  - allows winners enough time to build plants and arrange for project finance
- Existing capacity: auctions for contract renewal
  - **A-1** auction (delivery 1 year ahead); 5-8 year contracts
  - **Adjustment** auction (delivery 4 months ahead), 1-2 year contracts

Source: PSR

The government (MME) is responsible for providing an initial "menu" of new generation capacity options (new hydro projects with pre-granted environmental licenses), which are based on technical studies conducted by the planning agency. Investors are encouraged to add other projects, i.e., thermal plants, international interconnections, etc., if they were not completed in the least-cost plan. Any projects should have prior environmental licenses before a plant participates in an auction.

The Brazilian regulation also allows the use of auctions as a backstop mechanism for the development of specific technologies, if they are to be driven by energy policy decisions. Project-specific auctions for particular projects are also allowed by the regulations in order to increase competition among investors.

Technology and project-specific auctions can be carried out within the framework of the regular new energy auctions described earlier, i.e., to supply the regulated market. In this case, the selected projects or technologies have priority in contracting their FEC and do not compete with other candidate technologies. Project-specific auctions for supplying the regulated market have been carried out to develop large hydro plants in the Amazon region. Three hydro plants—Santo Antonio (3,150 MW), Jirau (3,300 MW), and Belo Monte (11,233 MW)—were auctioned in specific procurement processes carried out in 2007, 2008, and 2010, respectively. The government understands that these hydro plants are strategic projects for the country, which were already accounted for during the power sector's reform.

The government has the prerogative to call an auction to contract a given quantity of energy even if it was not contemplated in the demand forecasts prepared by the distribution companies. These auctions, named "reserve energy auctions", are organized in order to increase the reserve margin, or to foster the development of particular sources of energy, such as renewables. Their details are fully stipulated by the government, including the definition of the technology (or project) and the demand to be contracted. The cost of the energy acquired in the reserve energy auctions is shared among all consumers (regulated and free) through tariff uplift. Technology-specific auctions following this modality have been used to contract renewable generation and were utilized by the government in 2008 to contract energy from sugarcane biomass, and in 2009 for an auction to contract wind power.

Results

Auction schemes have helped create competition "for the market", where investors compete to enter the market through long-term contracts. These have been the basis for the emergence of new capacity. Overall, new capacity auctions in Brazil have attracted the interest of both national and foreign investors. Potential suppliers have included a wide range of technologies such as new hydro projects, gas, coal and oil-fired plants, sugarcane biomass, and imports from neighboring countries using international interconnections. Brazil has successfully conducted a total of 31 auctions for existing and new energy thus far, including those for renewable sources and large hydroelectric projects. From 2005, when the mandatory mechanism was put into practice, until April 2010, approximately 57,000 MW of new capacity were contracted for delivery, starting as early as 2008 and as late as 2015, with contracts ranging from 15 to 30 years. This includes some 5,800 MW of non-conventional renewable and 17,500 MW of large hydro plants in the Amazon. Out of the total contracted new generation capacity, 49 percent comes from hydro resources, 44 percent from thermal resources and the remaining 8 percent from non-conventional renewable sources such as biomass and wind power. Despite Brazil's untapped hydroelectric potential, difficulties in the processes for obtaining environmental licenses have led to fewer-than-expected hydro projects participating in the auctions. These figures do not include the volume of energy procured by the non-regulated market, or the volume negotiated bilaterally between free customers and generators or marketers.

The evolution of prices in the new energy auctions, along with the total amount of average MW contracted at each one is shown in figure 4.2. It also presents the split between thermal and hydro resources.

A summary of the outcomes of the technology- and project-specific auctions is presented in figure 4.3.

Despite the positive aspects related to the introduction of auctions in Brazil, there are still some areas of concern. Lack of transparency has been an issue: some intrinsic parameters of the auction mechanism (demand allocation between hydro and thermal candidates is an example) are defined by the auctioneer with little transparency, potentially having a direct impact on the auction outcome. When comparing different thermoelectric technologies in the auctions, a scoring rule based on the expected electricity cost for the consumer is used (see Bezerra (2010) for details). This is calculated based on dispatch scenarios set by the government, which are perceived to be excessively optimistic and have made oil- and diesel-fired thermal plants artificially more competitive. The competition between private and public participants has also been hotly debated. The behavior of state-owned companies with respect to economic rationale has been a source of concern ever since the auctions were designed in Brazil, and it remains a general concern worldwide. Investors worry about the low rates of return (hurdle rates) that are ultimately expected by the public sector. This concern is further aggravated by the fact that in some cases the auctioneer is both the buyer of energy and owner of these companies, which creates an obvious conflict of interest.

An additional point of concern was raised recently when the government determined that the second "A-5" auction held in December 2010 would be specifically for hydroelectric projects (including small hydropower plants), thus ruling out the participation of any other technologies—including conventional thermal, biomass and wind plants. Given that "A-5" auctions are the only ones capable of inducing competition among all projects and technologies—since the five-year period is sufficient to allow for any project to start producing energy—the decision to allow only hydro projects to participate was heavily criticized due to the fact that the exclusive right given to hydroelectric plants to supply energy would discourage competition among technologies. The criticism gained even greater support after the final results of the auction were made public: the total volume of energy offered by the participating hydro projects fell short of the auction's demand by 1,190 GWh/year. Interestingly, however, the auction resulted in the lowest average energy price in the history of all new energy auctions in Brazil: US$ 37.39/MWh.[6] In this regard, the government had previously announced that the A-3 auction to be conducted in 2011 would be exclusively for wind, small hydro and biomass technologies. Nevertheless, given the perspective of having abundant natural gas from the new offshore oil fields, the government has now declared that natural gas plants will be allowed to participate in A-3 tenders.

Colombia

Power System Characteristics

Colombia has a hydro-dominated power system, with 67 percent of the 13.5 GW of total installed capacity represented by hydroelectric plants. Thermal plants fueled by

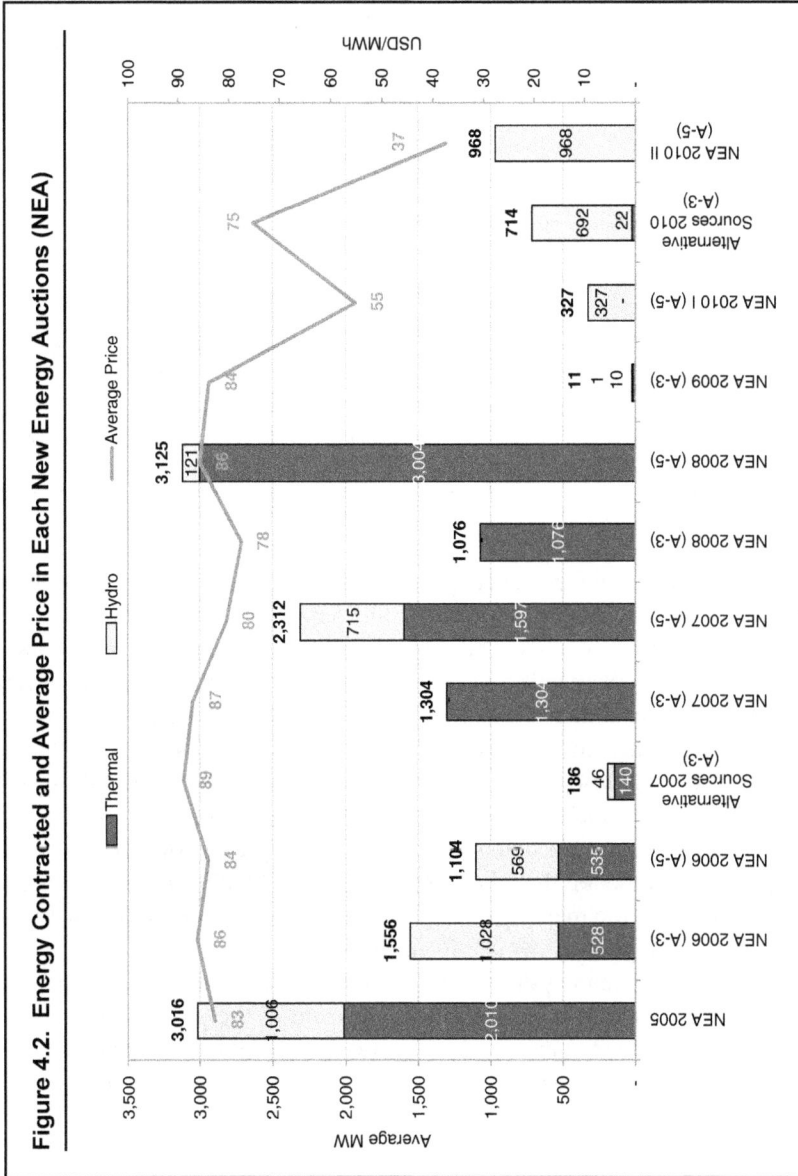

Figure 4.2. Energy Contracted and Average Price in Each New Energy Auctions (NEA)

Source: Data from CCEE (2010), compiled by the authors

Figure 4.3. Results of Technology- and Site (project)-specific Auctions

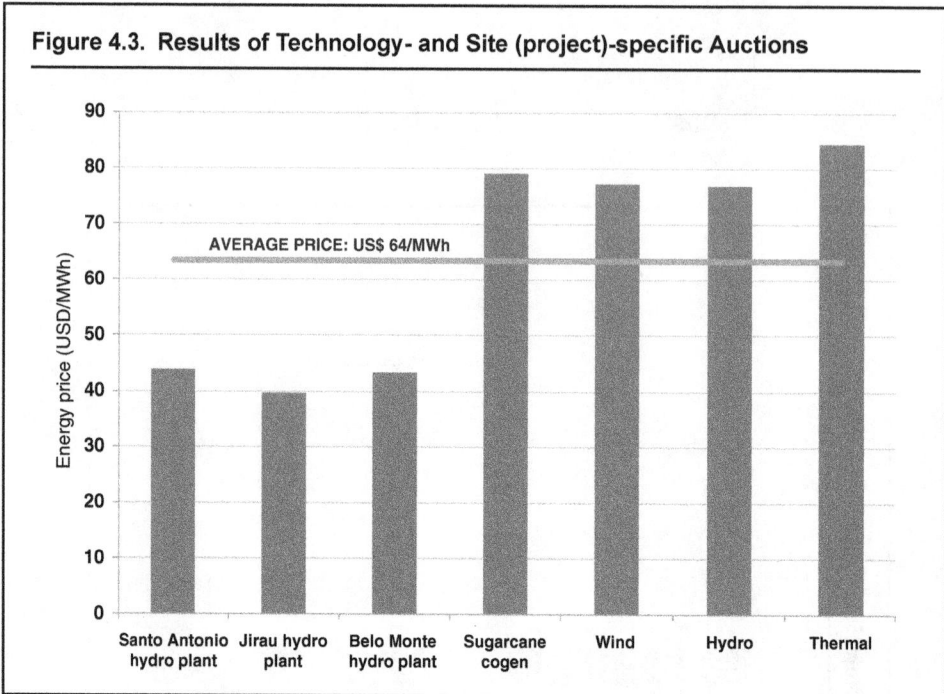

natural gas, coal, and fuel oil represent approximately 20 percent, 7 percent, and 3 percent, respectively.[7] Only a very small fraction currently comes from small wind and cogeneration projects. Colombia is estimated to have roughly 100 GW of potential hydropower, but most new hydro projects face significant environmental constraints, as is the case in Brazil. In addition, coal-fired generation is expected to increase over the next few years due to the existence of large reserves in the country. Annual demand is about 54 TWh and the average growth rate has been close to 4 percent over the past few years. Generators encompass both public and private players, including international investors. While there are 44 generation companies registered as being active in the market, six represent over 80 percent of the installed capacity, with the top three holding 55 percent: EMGESA (private subsidiary of ENDESA, 21 percent of the market), Empresas Públicas de Medellín (publicly owned, 20 percent), and Isagen (publicly owned, 16 percent).

Contrary to the Brazilian system, only 6 percent of Colombia's hydro plants have reservoirs with multi-year storage capacity: 15 percent of the plants have run-of-river reservoirs that can be depleted in a single day, and 55 percent have reservoirs that allow monthly regulation. This modest storage capacity mix makes the system vulnerable to hydrological risks, thus affecting supply security.

Reform Process and Market Structure

With the enactment of the Public Utilities Law (Law 142) and the Electricity Law (Law 143) in 1994, the following elements were implemented: (i) the desire to introduce competition, (ii) the implementation of electricity markets at wholesale and retail levels, and (iii) an enabling environment for private sector participation by defining a mechanism and procedures for regulating activities in the electricity industry. Activities that are natural monopolies (distribution and transmission) were separated from those conducive to competition (generation and retailing). A wholesale power market has also been implemented.

Colombia relied on regulated capacity payments to stimulate the installation of new megawatts. According to this scheme, which was implemented in 1996, regulated payments were given to generators in proportion to their available capacity. Determining a value for the capacity payment and the design of a mechanism to ensure the availability of the generators receiving it turned out to be a challenge. The capacity payment scheme produced mixed results. To overcome these obstacles, in 2006 the Colombian Comisión de Regulación de Energía y Gas (CREG) introduced a new regulatory scheme to ensure the long-term reliability of the electricity supply in Colombia: the Firm Energy Market. Implemented in 2008, it was inspired by the forward capacity market of New England ISO in the United States.

The electricity market has the following four components:

Day-ahead spot market: Based on day-ahead bids, the system sets the hourly spot energy price and determines the generation schedule. There is a single spot energy price for each hour and bids of generators include prices and available capacity for the next day.

1. Bilateral financial contracts (OTC) market: Generators and electricity suppliers freely agree on contract prices and quantities. This market is mainly used by market participants to hedge against volatile spot prices.
2. Ancillary services market: This market includes Automatic Generation Control (AGC) and generator imbalances.
3. Firm energy market: Designed to ensure sufficient energy reserves for the system, particularly during exceptionally dry periods, when energy generated by hydro-power plants is limited. The firm energy market provides an additional payment for security of supply, which is disconnected from the energy generated.

The existence of the firm energy market is closely linked to Colombia's electricity market's strong reliance on hydroelectric generation. The reliability adequacy requirement for supply security in the Colombian power sector aims at ensuring that there are sufficient thermal and hydro reservoirs to provide energy during dry periods. Hence, firm energy here refers to the ability to provide energy during dry periods.

Use of Auctions

The firm energy market pays generators a reliability charge based on the results of auctions for Firm Energy Obligations (OEF—in Spanish—"Obligaciones de Energía Firme") in exchange for a commitment to provide energy at a fixed price whenever spot prices exceed a pre-defined "Scarcity Price." An auction to contract OEF is carried out at the CREG's discretion, i.e. whenever it estimates that demand for electricity in future years cannot be covered by existing and new planned generation capacity. This means that the total demand—not only the regulated consumers' demand—is bought in the reliability auction market. In order to participate in an auction for Firm Energy Obligations, bidders have to be backed by physical resources certified as capable of producing energy during a dry period. The "scarcity price" is established by the CREG and updated monthly based on the variation of the Fuel Price Index. It essentially indicates the time when the different generation units or plants will be required to fulfill their OEFs, which occurs when the spot price exceeds the scarcity price and is the price at which this energy will be paid. The firm energy market thus provides price hedging for all spot prices above this value. Those features distinguish the Colombian auction from others in Latin America.

The firm energy market and its associated payment have been designed to guarantee long-term economic signals to provide incentives for investors to build and operate efficient generation resources so as to meet the country's development needs. The auctions to contract OEFs are mainly characterized by the following elements.[8]

▨ *Product:* The firm energy product is a financial call option backed by a physical resource (generation units) certified as being able to generate energy (i.e. provide firm energy) when the scarcity conditions are present. This call option is essentially composed of:

  ○ Underlying asset: firm energy, which is the energy that the generator is able to generate even under scarcity conditions;

  ○ Strike price: it is considered that scarcity conditions have arisen when the pool price exceeds the scarcity price;

  ○ Premium: in exchange for this commitment, the generators receive a premium (reliability charge), provided that they honor their obligations. This premium is fixed, certain, and defined through the auctions.

  This energy product has important risk-hedging features. On one hand, the financial call option hedges demand from high energy spot prices during periods of scarcity. On the other hand, the supplier's generation units and fuel availability provide a physical hedge to limit the risk of selling the call option. Also, the investor risk is lower than in an energy-only market, since the reliability charge payments represent a more predictable and stable cash flow than the highly variable rents from the spot market. When spot prices are above scarcity price, generators with OEFs are called to deliver their firm energy obligation. The daily obligation is equal to its share of firm energy, distributed through the day based on the hourly dispatch. Thus, a baseload-generation firm energy obligation is equally spread throughout all hours of the day, while a peaking hydro plant with high opportunity costs will have its firm energy obligation distributed mainly during the peak hours of the day. This definition—tying a unit's obligation to its hourly dispatch during scarcity—is expected to mitigate market power and improve the spot market's performance.

▨ *Planning period:* The planning period refers to the time between the primary auction and the beginning of the supplier's commitment. For the first auction, the planning period was 4.5 years. Projects with longer lead times could sell firm energy for up to seven years ahead of the start of the commitment. From the seventh to the fourth year ahead, the supplier sells the firm energy as a price taker.

▨ *Commitment period:* The commitment period for existing generation is one year, and for new generation resources it is between one and 20 years. New generation resources select their preferred commitment length during the auction qualification. The firm energy price is indexed with US inflation during the commitment period.

▨ *Cost of new entry* (CE): A parameter in the auction is the cost of new generation entry. The CE was initially estimated by CREG, and will be set based on competitive auction results later on.

▨ *Demand curve:* The demand curve specifies how the quantity of firm energy purchased depends upon price. At CE, load purchases are equal to 100 percent of estimated firm energy required to supply projected demand. As illustrated in

Figure 4.4. Demand Curve for the Auction of Firm Energy Obligations

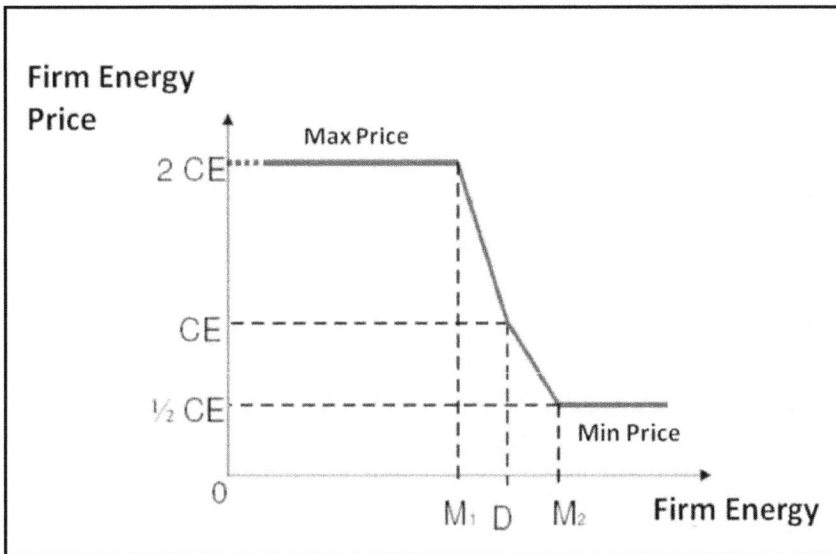

Source: XM, Colombia

figure 4.4, at higher prices, load purchases are reduced to slightly less than the target firm energy quantity, while at lower prices load purchases are slightly more than the target quantity. The firm energy price has a ceiling of two times CE and a floor of 50 percent of CE.

- *Auction mechanism:* A descending clock auction design was selected with the purpose of promoting efficient price discovery. At the beginning of each round, the auctioneer determines the opening and closing prices of that round, as well as the volume of excess supply in the previous round. Each bidder then submits a supply curve for the currently valid price range, respecting a simple activity rule: as the price declines, participants may only maintain or reduce quantities. Thus, a participant's offers must be consistent with an upward sloping supply curve. This process continues until supply and demand are balanced, which determines the quantity awarded to each supplier and the price to be paid to all suppliers during the commitment period, as illustrated in figure 4.5.

- *Fail-safe mechanism:* The auction design recognizes the possibility that there may be either adequate supply or insufficient competition. The fail-safe mechanism specifies the rules to apply in these unlikely events.

- *Transition:* The new reliability charge market scheme started in December 2006, including a transition period until December 2012, during which payments will be settled at the administratively determined price of US$13.05/MWh, to be periodically adjusted. Once the transition period is over, the reliability charge for all generation will be set by the clearing price of firm energy competitive auctions. The main goal of the new scheme is to ensure that sufficient and efficient new generation capacity is available to ensure energy reliability from 2012 onward.

Figure 4.5. Descending Price Clock Auction with Intra-round Bids in Colombia

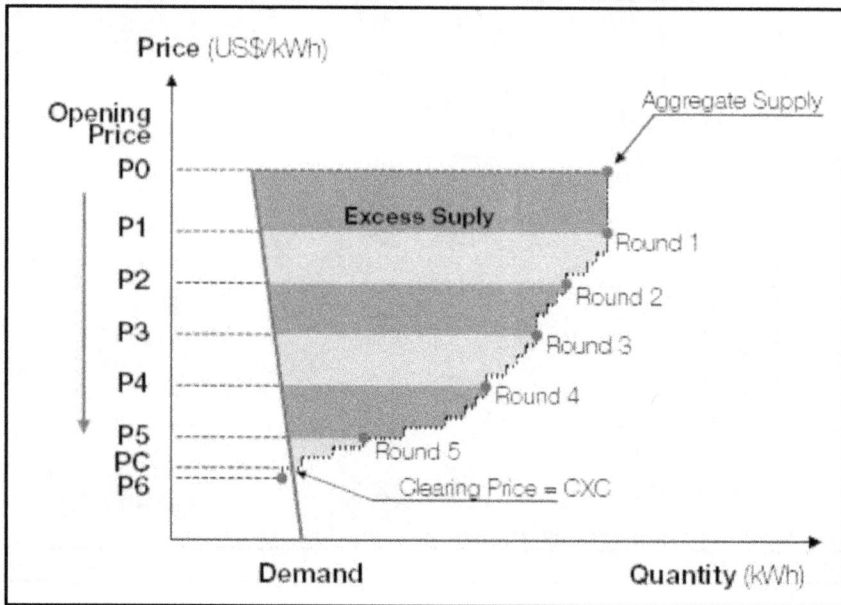

Source: CREG

To facilitate supplying the demand in critical conditions as well as the fulfillment of the OEFs of the generators, the market design has a built-in set of instruments known as "Safety Rings".

The first safety instrument is the Firm Energy Secondary Market, a market of bilateral contracts, in which only generators participate. The sellers are those with firm energy that was not sold in an auction, or has not been committed in the secondary market, while the buyers are the generators that temporarily need firm energy to honor their OEFs. When a generator anticipates that it cannot generate sufficient energy to honor his OEFs, or when he/she is planning the maintenance of one of his/her generation plants or units, he/she can come to this market to negotiate with another generator the total or partial backup of his Obligation. The agreement that formalizes this negotiation is called a Backup Contract. Backups between generation plants or units belonging to the same owner or commercial representative are also registered in this market. These agreements are called Declarations.

The second instrument is the Voluntarily Interruptible Demand. This safety ring allows the generator who foresees that he/she does not have enough energy to honor his/her OEFs to contact, through the retailers, the users of the SIN that are able to reduce their energy consumption either because they own backup generation equipment, or because they can modify their productive processes. In this case, the users' reduction of demand will be deducted from the Obligation of the generator, who will remunerate the retailer that represents the users at a previously agreed-upon price.

The third instrument is known as the Last Instance Generation Assets. This mechanism uses generation assets that do not take part in the auction or in the MEM. In other words, these assets are used purely and exclusively to fulfill OEFs already assigned to an agent in the auction.

The initiative to make use of these safety rings is that of a generation agent, who also assumes the cost that it entails, with no possibility of passing it through to the demand side. The second and third instruments have not yet been implemented in the MEM.

Finally, there are the Reconfiguration Auctions. After the Auction for the Allocation of OEFs has taken place, it is the CREG, on behalf of the users of the SIN, who determines the need to use Reconfiguration Auctions in the case that an excess or default of firm energy is foreseen for a particular year.

Results

Two auctions were held in May and June 2008. The first (main) auction was conducted 4.5 years in advance (the "planning period") of the commitment period in the form of a descending clock auction for new resources, and the second was effectively a sealed-bid auction for existing power plants (since bids from existing plants had to be submitted before the beginning of the auction, and could not be modified afterwards). In this auction, new resources were able to lock in a firm energy price for up to 20 years, beginning in December 2012, while prices for existing resources were set for only one year.

In the first auction there were seventeen participants. Most of the capacity offered came from existing plants (62,860 GWh per year). Ten new power plants also participated, with a combined yearly capacity of 9,185 GWh—only three, however, were successful in the auction: (a) coal-fired Gecelca 3 of 150 MW, (b) hydroelectric Amoya of 78 MW and (c) fuel oil-fired Termocol of 201.6 MW bid by Poliobras, a new entrant in the Colombian market. Table 4.1 below summarizes the breakdown of new capacity offered by existing players and new entrants.

Table 4.1. Composition of New Capacity Offered in the First Primary OEF Auction

Generating Companies	Power Plant	Technology	OEF Offered (GWh)	Market Share	Share of new capacity
Isagen	Amoyá	Hydro	214	12%	2%
Gecelca	Gecelca 2,3 & 7	Coal	2,979	16%	34%
Poliobras	Termocol	Fuel Oil	1,678	0%	18%
Cosenit	Termodial 1	Petroleum	208	0%	2%
Meriléctrica	Merilectrica-cc	CC-Gas	602	2%	7%
Proeléctrica	Termoandina	Gas	766	1%	8%
Termocandelaria	Termocandelaria	CC-Gas	1,449	2%	16%
Termotasajero	Tasajero2	Coal	1,290	2%	14%

Source: Author's representation

The second auction ("the GPPS auction") was designed for new generation projects with longer construction periods, and allocated OEFs for periods of up to twenty years, beginning in December 2014. The reserve price in this auction was the "market clearing" price established in the first auction. If insufficient supply was offered to cover demand, as turned out to be the case, then the reserve price was to be paid; if supply exceeded demand, a sealed-bid auction was to be held. Six new hydropower projects participated in the auction. The reserve price in this auction was the "market clearing" price established in the "descending clock" auction. Since the incremental supply offered by bidders was less than the incremental demand every year, the reserve price was paid to the six bidders for power plant projects commencing from December 2014 to December 2018. Therefore, a sealed-bid auction phase was not necessary for any delivery year.

As a result, some 9,000 GWh per year of OEFs were allocated to new resources, along with 62,860 GWh per year allocated to existing generating plants at an auction-determined "option" price of approximately US$14/MWh. In total, OEFs were assigned to 350 MW of new coal and gas-fired installed capacities, along with 3,100 MW of new hydro capacity. Subsequent auctions will be held whenever the CREG estimates that electricity demand in future years cannot be covered by the existing and/or any planned new generation resources that will enter into operation.

The Colombian experience was very successful. Sector specialists indicate that a critical assumption of the reliability energy market is that it has to be competitive for new entrants. Thus, as part of the market implementation, it is important for regulators to take steps to reduce barriers to entry. A second critical assumption is that suppliers have faith that the market, once implemented, will be functional for the lifetime of new plants. Hence, it is important for the government to make a commitment to the approach and to honor the commitments. Entry barriers and political risks can undermine even the best market designs. Regulators and the government must recognize and address these challenges; otherwise the market could provide high-cost, not least-cost, investments.

There are, however, some specific areas for concern. As pointed out by Harbord and Pagnozzi (2008), it was felt that the first (main) auction's planning period was not long enough to attract large hydro projects. Consequently, it attracted primarily thermal generation, while the GPPS auction attracted only hydro projects. This might have reduced competition and efficiency in both auctions. Ideally, auctions should have longer planning periods and cover a sufficient number of years, so that all types of plants can compete in the same auction. An important aspect to note is whether generators will be able to deliver their firm energy obligations when the call option is exercised. This might be a special concern for hydro plants, whose production capability has a negative correlation with spot prices (when spot prices are higher, hydro availability is lower).

Chile

Power System Characteristics

Chile has an electric infrastructure that is divided into two main independent power systems, the Northern and Central Interconnected Systems, and various isolated grids that serve remote locations, especially in the far south of the country. Recent data[9] indicate a net installed generation capacity of 12.8 GW, split between 62 percent thermal and 38 percent hydro resources—with the Northern System's 3.6 GW being 99 percent thermal, and the Central System's 9.1 GW being 52 percent hydro. Strong, but volatile, annual demand growth rates of about 6 percent have been observed. Record peak demand is currently approximately 8 GW for the two main interconnected systems and energy consumption of 57 TWh was observed in 2009.

Reform process and market structure

Chile became the first country in the world to deregulate its power sector in the early 1980s. At that time, strong regulatory oversight was established with regard to tariff issues from the very beginning and, according to the 1982 regulatory model, electricity prices between regulated consumers and generation were calculated by the regulator on a six-month basis. These prices reflected the expected marginal cost of supply on each of the main nodes of the network over the next six months. Like Colombia, Chile also relied on regulated capacity payments to stimulate the entrance of new capacity. Payments were made in proportion to the generator's firm capacity certificates calculated by the system operator.

In the late 1990s, the country was faced with some major difficulties with respect to the adequacy of supply, resulting in a power crisis and energy curtailment during a severe drought in 1998–99. The main reason for these supply problems was the lack of incentives to foster a well-diversified generation mix. Fundamentally, the economic signal provided by the energy spot market was too volatile and did not adequately stimulate the entrance of new capacity.

In 2004, the power sector in Chile was once again faced with several supply problems. The tariff system was highly regulated and inflexible, prices in the spot market were very volatile; capacity payments only represented a small part of the overall generator income, whose role was limited by the uncertainty of the energy spot market; and curtailment of natural gas exports by Argentina constrained thermal generation. New generation capacity was needed, but the risky investment environment inhibited the closing of financing for new projects, increased the end-user generation price, and made development of new capacity more difficult. These factors ultimately prompted various changes to the regulatory model, particularly with regard to tariff policies. The government therefore sought solutions by exploring long-term contracts at a price to be determined by a free bidding process in order to ensure profitable cash flows for investors, thereby stimulating the entrance of new generation.[10]

A new regulatory model was implemented in the country by incorporating a real market signal in consumer prices through auction mechanisms. The old energy price calculation would be phased out, as contracts procured through auctions were to replace existing contracts. The aim was to reflect the cost expectations of generators and investors and the existence of an attractive market with high but competitive yields. The fundamentals of the new regulatory model are:

- Distributors must be 100 percent contracted all the time, at least for the next three years;
- Distributors must contract their needs through auctions, which must be public, open, transparent, and without discrimination;
- Each distributor auctions its consumption requirements according to its own criteria (i.e. auction design is freely decided by each distributor);
- A coordinated group of distributors is permitted to organize a process in order to simultaneously auction their net demand;
- Distributors can auction contracts for up to 15 years at a fixed price (indexed according to changes in the main variables);
- The government sets a price cap for the auction. The capacity price is also fixed by the government (indexed according to CPI);
- Each generator offers a price and a volume of energy (the amount of capacity is computed by means of a load factor) and the auction is cleared at an optimum point that balances cost minimization and demand coverage maximization. Contract prices are passed directly to consumers by means of a pass-through mechanism. Distributors thus have a constant yield for their assets, regardless of auction results.

The Chilean auctions focus on ensuring the security of supply for the regulated market. Free consumers are expected to procure their own supply requirements independently and select their preferred procurement mechanism, which includes energy auctions.

Use of Auctions

Because the auction trades different contracts, these are allocated to every generator simultaneously by means of a combinatorial sealed-bid mechanism. This allows different contracts to be auctioned in a single process, in which every generator bids for a specific set of contracts. In addition, to increase the level of competition, generators are allowed to bid for a net amount of demand higher than their capacities. After bidding, generation capacities are re-incorporated into the process for delivering a feasible allocation. All contracts are allocated by means of a multi-objective combinatorial sealed-bid mechanism that seeks to minimize costs and maximize demand coverage. The sealed-bid combinatorial auction scheme used is shown in figure 4.6 below.

One of the most unique aspects of the Chilean auction framework is that distributors design and manage their own auctions to then supply electricity to their regulated markets. Given the fact that distributors auction their demand at any time depending on their needs, and design their mechanisms and contracts depending on their own criteria, the current regulation dictates that all proposed mechanisms and contracts must be revised and ultimately approved by the regulator before the auction takes place.

To ensure system adequacy, generators must give a yearly justification to the National Energy Commission (CNE, for the Spanish equivalent *Comisión Nacional de Energía*) of their firm energy necessary to supply all the regulated contracted demand. Generators can use a combination of existing and new plants to justify their capacities. Thus, the general auction process is not divided between existing and new generation auctions, as is the case in Brazilian auctions. Generation capacities need to be justified by bidders, providing sufficient and credible supports with regard to existing and future projects. The aforementioned supports, and decisions about their credibility, are evaluated at the distributors' discretion.

Figure 4.6. Chilean Auction Mechanism

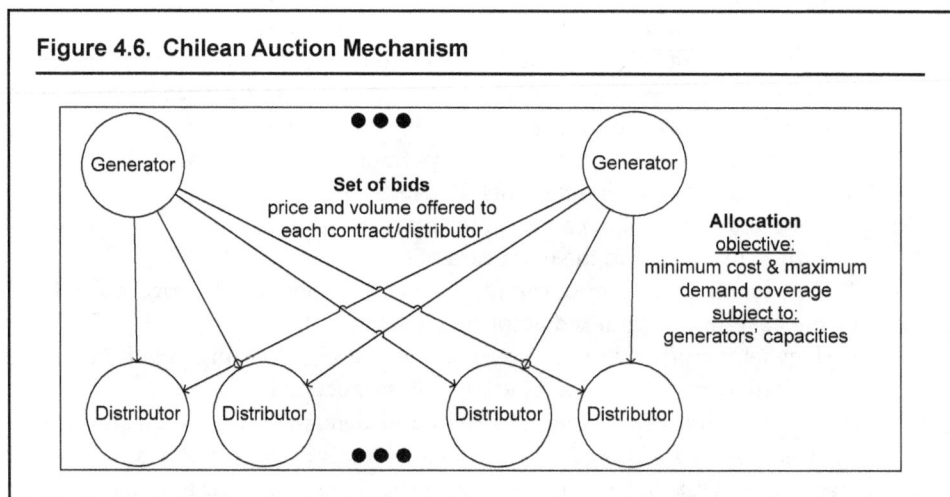

Source: Systep, 2008

Although generators trade two products in the market, energy and capacity (or peak demand supply), competition is only set in terms of energy, so generators compete by offering a volume and price of energy. Nevertheless, the final contract includes volumes and prices of both energy and capacity. The latter is calculated according to pre-established load factors.

Furthermore, each distributor separates its demand into two groups: base energy blocks and variable energy blocks. The base energy blocks represent the fixed energy that will be consumed, while the variable energy blocks represent the energy increase that will be consumed due to demand growth. Both base and variable energy have different natures and conditions. Distributors can auction base and variable blocks separately in different contracts or combine base and variable energy in a single contract since they are free to design their own contracts, as established by regulation.

As this is a long-term contract allocation process, indexation formulas are used so as to hedge mid and long-term risks, which then force the auctioneer to take a risk position when allocating contracts. With regard to design, the formulas are determined and published by the regulator in the form of a multivariable linear function of fuel and inflation indexes in which each multiplying factor is ultimately adjusted by each bidder according to its power source and fuel supply agreements.

In the case of Chile, there is no formal requirement to cover the generation offered by firm capacity certificates: each distributor accepts (or not) the adequacy guarantees given by generators at their own discretion. This market-driven scheme implicitly forces distributors to assess their own adequacy risks and may also force them to assume consequences if the wrong decisions are made, e.g. a distributor may be obliged to shed its demand if there is a lack of system capacity caused by its supplier. Indeed, if lack of capacity is assumed by those with failed contracts, market-driven policies should deliver the efficient level of adequacy. However, in most cases, a lack of supply adequacy during load shedding is allocated according to social welfare-based criteria.

Results

Three auctions have been carried out from October 2006 (first auction) to 2010, offering an average demand of 28 TWh/year to be served between 2010 and 2025. A summary of these results appears in Table 4.2.

Chile has not carried out technology-specific auctions. Monte Redondo was the first wind plant to obtain two contracts from auctions by directly competing with conventional power plants.

The decentralized organization of the Chilean auctions has raised some concern as to their overall efficiency. As discussed in Moreno (2010), an immediate consequence of this high degree of decentralization is that contracts cannot be standardized (i.e. they are not similar). This, in turn, allows generators to have many possibilities for which they can bid, i.e. they

Table 4.2. Contracted Energy and Prices per Generator and Distributor

Summary from 2005 to 2009 Prices at Quillota 220kV busbar and indexed November 2010

Generation Company	Average price US$/MWh	Contracted Energy GWh/year
AES Gener	89.9	5,419
Campanario	139.3	1,750
Colbun	85.3	6,782
Endesa	75.6	12,825
Guacolda	74.4	900
Emelda	141.2	200
EPSA	141.2	75
Monte Redondo	141.2	275
Chilectra	62.0	12,000
Chilquinta	110.7	2,567
EMEL	80.3	2,007
CGE	121.4	7,220
SAESA	80.9	4,432

Source: CNE and Systep

can present different bids simultaneously (volume and price) for various types of contracts according to their preferences (risk, supply period, etc.). The mechanism has led to a substantial price differential among the diverse contracts and geographical areas, as generators can choose different price-volume strategies for each contract auctioned. It has also led to a discussion about the (correct or perverse) incentives of distributors to design a mechanism that yields low prices to the end-users. Indexation formulas are not taken into account by the auctioneer during the allocation process, thus avoiding any type of risk assessment from the auctioneer's side. This aspect has triggered a debate in the Chilean electricity market because the set of winners can dramatically change if price forecasts are incorporated into the mechanism. Finally, with regard to the auction mechanism itself, it appears to be very difficult for the auctioneer to define the criterion or set of rules to tune and balance two different objective functions (cost minimization and demand coverage maximization) in the combinatorial auction design adopted. As explained in Moreno (2010), a controversial heuristic procedure has been used to achieve this multi-objective clearing mechanism in the auction. However, its final outcome has proven to be greatly influenced by the auctioneer's (distributor's) discretion.

Peru

Power System Characteristics

The Peruvian power sector has an installed capacity of approximately 6,000 MW (2009), split in almost equal parts between hydro (49 percent) and thermal plants (51 percent). It is essentially comprised of the National Interconnected Electric System and some isolated grids scattered around rural areas of the country. However, according to data provided by COES[11], total hydro plants account for about 60 percent of actual energy production. The participation of natural gas plants has been increasing steadily, using gas from the Camisea basin. Energy consumption in 2009 was 29.8 TWh and industrial users account for about 57 percent of it. Peak demand that year was 4,300 MW.

Peru has experienced an annual demand growth rate of approximately 8 percent over the last decade, while total installed capacity has increased only 4 percent per year during the same period. Increases in consumption in 2006–2007 and 2007–2008 have been 11 and 9 percent, respectively, in line with overall economic growth. Investments in generation capacity have been growing over the past five years at close to 30 percent per year to meet demand requirements. Private investments have been the major driving force behind the expansion of the country's generation capacity.

Reform Process and Market Structure

The reform of the Peruvian power sector dates back to the early 1990s, when the electricity industry deteriorated significantly due to negligible investments in infrastructure caused in part by the absence of cost-reflective tariffs to support new investments. Limited investments in maintenance and the destruction of infrastructure by terrorist groups led to a power crisis in the 1990s. Existing supply covered only 74 percent of the demand requirements and distribution losses were over 20 percent. Less than half of the population had access to electricity. The structural reform process that started in 1992 led to the privatization of the electricity sector. The restructuring process, articulated in the Electricity Concessions Law (LCE, for the Spanish equivalent *Ley de Concesiones Eléctricas*) of 1992,[12] unbundled the vertically integrated state monopoly into generation, transmission, and distribution, and paved the way for the introduction of private operators and competition in generation and commercialization. Open access to the transmission grid was also established. The process of granting concessions and transfer of generation assets to private companies began in 1994 and was bolstered in 2002.

Regulated consumers served by distribution companies represent only 54 percent of the total load, while free consumers—who can contract their electricity supply directly with generators or distribution companies through bilateral, freely-negotiated contracts—account for 46 percent of the market. This is a sizeable share compared to other countries in the region where free users represent no more than 30–40 percent of total energy consumption. It also has a tremendous effect on the electricity market, since electricity suppliers can negotiate contracts without the restrictions of a regulated price for a large portion of the demand.

On the generation side, the power sector reform introduced five key elements in the Peruvian power system:

a)   Centralized generation scheduling (on a least-cost basis) by a system operator ("COES"). Energy spot prices are defined as the marginal costs of the scheduling model, which is based on stochastic hydrothermal scheduling tools. Hydro plants are dispatched based on their water values, meaning that they cannot make price bids in a "market". Price bids of thermal plants are cost-based and audited.

b)   There is competition at the wholesale level (generation) and for financial contracts. The wholesale market is managed by COES, which serves as a market to settle differences between quantities contracted and physically scheduled by COES.

c)   A capacity payment scheme was introduced in the 1990s. A regulated capacity payment is defined based on the annualized investment and O&M costs of a peak-load generation unit of "adequate capacity in relation to the size of the system and the reserve requirements". The regulator determines the main characteristics of this unit each year to be applied in the periodic review of generation tariffs.

d)   Energy transactions are carried out in a spot market whose prices are set hourly by the computational model defined above. Contracts are negotiated bilaterally, but the pass-through limit of the distributor's purchases to regulated users is capped to a "busbar"[13] energy tariff. This is exogenously calculated by the regulator every year based on a three-year economic operation simulation and assumptions on the expected evolution of demand and generation supply capacity, fuel prices, etc.

e)   Payments to/from final users and between wholesale market participants are then based on a two-part tariff system—very similar to the classical scheme of peak-load pricing—composed of the capacity and energy charges of (c) and (d).

Use of Auctions

The power sector market design used in Peru was very similar to the one implemented in Chile at that time. As in the Chilean model, the remuneration of generators in Peru relied on a combination of a capacity payment and a calculated busbar energy price as defined in the contracts signed with distribution companies. The calculation of such a price has always been very controversial and a decoupling from actual market conditions was sometimes observed. In 2004, marginal operating costs increased significantly while the price paid to generators remained low. It was then observed that those prices were insufficient to foster the development of new generating capacity. As a consequence, generators decided not to renew existing contracts with distribution companies. The same occurred in 2004–2005 in Chile, which had the same busbar concept implemented: in this case, gas supply constraints from Argentina increased the energy spot prices, but this change was not conveyed in the busbar price, thus reducing the incentives to contract.

In 2006, the Ministry of Mines and Energy in conjunction with the government planning agency proposed to substitute the exogenously defined busbar price with new ones to be defined as a result of a competitive process (auctions) for energy contracts in order to properly remunerate investors and improve financing conditions. In July 2006, Congress passed Law N°28832 to "Ensure the Efficient Development of Electricity Generation." This new law introduced important changes to the LCE, mainly regarding generation and transmission regulation, the administration and functioning of the electricity market, and the determination of electricity prices. The LCE and Law N°28832 constitute the legal framework of the electricity sector in Peru. Once again, the new market model is very similar to the one implemented in Chile a year before.

A key change in the generation sector brought about by the revised electricity law was the adoption of an auction-based system by distribution companies to ensure service to regulated users. The mechanism was intended to foster contracting in the forward market. In addition, a new procedure to determine the generation energy tariff for regulated users was defined, whereby prices resulting from the contract auctions became the main driver of the generation cost component.[14] Capacity payments remained unaltered.

The basic principles of the Peruvian electricity auction system are:

a) The expected demand of regulated users should be fully contracted by distributors, at least for the next few years. This is monitored and enforced by the regulatory agency.

b) Distributors should call for supply auctions at least three years before their demand requirement, and with a contractual duration of no less than five years, which would be insufficient for developing medium to large-scale hydro plants.

c) Distributors design and manage their own auctions (including the selection of the demand to be contracted and the auction mechanism), but the process is subject to general approval and supervision by the regulator (Osinergmin) and should follow the specific guidelines set forth in the regulations.

d) Distributors can combine their demands to participate jointly in a supply auction. Free users can request that their demand be incorporated into a supply auction organized by a distributor.

e) The regulator establishes a price cap for each auction, above which no offer would be accepted. The maximum price is only revealed if a given auction "round" does not cover all the demands put out to tender and at least one bid received is rejected because it is higher than the maximum price.

f) In case the situation described in (e) occurs, a new tender is called (i.e., a new auction round). There is no restriction for participating in a new invitation to bid for the same process: if a company participates in the first invitation to bid, it is not obliged to continue participating. Participation in the first invitation to bid does not oblige companies to participate in the second invitation to bid.

The product auctioned in an energy contract includes a demand and its "associated" peak and off-peak energy. Prices offered are only for energy (peak and off-peak) and the peak value is remunerated by means of the regulated capacity payments. The energy requirements are then split into two parts: a minimum fixed portion, which will be provided/taken (and paid) by generators/distributors, and a variable additional optional quantity (up to 20 percent of the fixed quantity) requested by distributors. The fixed part is considered a take-or-pay portion, and the additional volume is paid as taken with no obligation for a minimum take. Energy contracts awarded are indexed to local fuel prices, inflation, and exchange rate.

Adoption of energy auctions has not eliminated the administrative calculation of busbar prices. Generators can therefore contract with distributors in two ways: bilateral and direct contracting at a price no higher than the administratively determined busbar price, or through the energy contracts awarded in the auctions.

The Peruvian regulatory system also allows the procurement of particular technologies through specific auctions. The guidelines and principles for these auctions follow the same ones as those described previously. The key difference between technology-specific auctions and a typical auction is the fact that the government defines the demand to be put for bid, and the energy cost is shared among all users (regulated and free) by means of a specific levy.

Auction implementation in Peru has been envisioned in two basic phases. During the initial three-year transitory period (2006–2009), the auctions traded products with durations of less than five years, to be delivered over a three-year interval. This first phase also adopted the first-price sealed-bid auction as the main mechanism. Generators were allowed to supply monthly quantity offers (non-decreasing) and the clearing mechanism was applied on a monthly basis. The main purpose of this transitory period was to stimulate generation contracting in order to cover the portions of the distributor's portfolio that were not contracted due to the "refusal" of generators to contract supply at the regulated tariff. An important part of the regulated demand was not covered by supply contracts, so the distributors involved were "taking" their required supply from the wholesale energy market, being exposed to the spot prices but receiving their payments based on the regulated generation tariffs.

Some revisions of auction principles were put forward in 2008, and a new phase for Peruvian auctions was launched. Different rules have been applied for tenders called from 2009 onward, which are summarized as follows:

- A descending clock mechanism has become an alternative to the pay-as-bid auction implemented during the transition period. Now distributors are free to select their preferred auction mechanism. However, pay-as-bid auctions have been the preferred alternative.
- Each bidder may submit up to three "regular" offers (i.e., offers that span the entire duration of the contract) and three "optional" offers (referring to new generation projects that may begin operations up to 24 months after the contract's starting date). The latter are only considered in case the "regular" offers of all bidders are not enough to cover demand.
- In the case of new hydroelectric projects, a discount factor is applied to the energy price offered by other bidders for comparison purposes. As of 2010, the discount has been set at 15 percent. This serves as an incentive for the development of hydro generation, but investors receive payments based on the price they actually submitted in case they become the winning bidder.
- The selection mechanism accepts the offers until they match the total of the Fixed Power Required or until there are no further bids.

Results

Peru conducted several electricity contract auctions during the transition period, with mixed results. Numerous processes were annulled, several resulted in low demand coverage, and a significant number of invitations to bid for the same tender occurred, with the subsequent revelation of the maximum adjudication price—possibly indicating a strategic behavior on the part of the bidders.

As previously mentioned, the new rules were approved in 2008 and became effective in 2009. The first auction process following the new rules took place on April 14, 2010. On the same day, four different auctions were carried out successively for a total demand of 3,015 average MW.[15] Long-term contracts with a total duration of eight, 10, and 12 years were auctioned. A summary of the auction results—in which a total of 575 MW of new generation capacity was contracted—is presented in table 4.3.

On August 18th, 2010 another tender process, organized by the distribution company Luz del Sur and supervised by the electricity regulator OSINERGMIN was carried out. It attracted the participation of four other distributors and 14 power generators. Long-term contracts for the purchase of electricity between 2014 and 2023 were auctioned at an average price of US$39/MWh.

Technology-specific auctions have been conducted a number of times in Peru, the last of which took place in February 2010 and was aimed at renewable energy sources. It resulted in contracts being awarded to wind, small hydro and solar plants for a total of 400 MW. Further details on these auctions are presented in Section 6.3.

One major challenge of the auctions previously described has been to attract the participation of new hydroelectric plants. The major constraint has been the three-year interval between the actual auction and the delivery of electricity. This is felt to be too short a period to allow the participation of new hydro plants even with the application of an economic "handicap" (the discount factor) in their offers to be compared with those from other technologies. In response to that, ProInversión, a specialized government agency whose main role is to promote private investments in infrastructure, has organized specific electricity contract auctions exclusively for hydroelectric plants. In 2009, ProInversión organized an auction that awarded a 10-year contract to a 168 MW hydroelectric project. The agency has scheduled a second auction for 2011. ProInversión auctions can have their own design, which includes longer lag times for the electricity delivery. On the other hand, ProInversión can decide the demand to be contracted and it is not clear how this is reconciled with the declaration of demand by distributors

Table 4.3. Peruvian Energy Auction Results After 2009

Year	Tender	Rounds	Date	Covered	Average Adjudication Price (US$/MWh)	Maximum Adjudication Price (US$/MWh)
2010	Edelnor	1	04.14.10	100%	38.92	Not disclosed
		2	04.14.10	100%	40.88	Not disclosed
		3	04.14.10	100%	42.63	Not disclosed
	Total			**100%**		
	Distriluz	1	04.14.10	95%	40.29	Not disclosed

Source: Osinergmin

to the regular auctions supervised by Osinergmin. The fact that ProInversión auctions "compete" directly with the regular auctions supervised by Osinergmin fragments the electricity procurement process and can potentially affect its overall efficiency.

Unlike the auction system in Chile, auctions in Peru are carried out separately, thereby mitigating the complexity of combinatorial auctions. However, both share the same conceptual design issues and present the same challenges, as they are decentralized auction processes.

Panama

Power System Characteristics

Panama's total installed capacity is currently over 1,600 MW, almost evenly divided between hydro and thermal resources (53 percent and 47 percent, respectively). The country still has great hydroelectric potential and some geothermal potential, but fossil fuel reserves are virtually non-existent, thus creating a dependency on international markets. Total electricity generation is about 6.3 TWh per year, with peak consumption of 1,222 MW. Current forecasts indicate a growth rate of 5.7 percent over the next few years. Panama is a member of the Central American Regional Market, and the SIEPAC project will provide a 300 MW interconnection between all countries by the time it is finalized in 2011. There are also studies being conducted for a high voltage DC interconnection line with Colombia, which is scheduled to be in service in 2012.

Reform Process and Market Structure

The electricity sector in Panama was restructured in 1997, following the main guidelines of similar reforms implemented throughout the world: privatization, vertical and horizontal unbundling, open access to the transmission grid and distribution networks, and creation of a wholesale electricity market. Regulation above all determines the existence of two short-term markets: the hourly energy spot market (in which differences between contracted energy and actual generation/consumption are cleared) and the daily generation capacity spot market (where the clearing between contracted generation capacity and the participation of each demand in the daily peak and actual availability of each generator occurs). The other market environment established by the reform process was the Contract Market, in which bilateral power supply agreements are arranged. These contracts function as risk-management tools that help stabilize prices for the final customer and the cash flow to generation companies.

Use of Auctions

After a five-year transition period during which the state-owned transmission company (ETESA) acted as the manager of the procurement process, distribution companies became responsible for organizing tenders for energy contracts, following rules and regulations set forth by the government. In a nutshell, distribution companies could organize and manage their contract auctions, i.e., with bid documents and contracts being prepared by those companies. All information had to be reviewed and approved by the regulator. This scheme was conceptually very similar to the current Chilean approach and resulted in a number of implementation problems, such as the development of documents and contracts with various schemes and conditions. The procurement auctions were very different from each other, and investors ended up being confused by the successive changes of rules. Auction approval by the regulator was also very time-consuming because tender documents were not standardized, sometimes presenting conflicting clauses that assigned excessive market risk to the generator or even to the distributor. Furthermore, the obligation to contract was not enforced among the buyers during some periods, which discouraged the implementation of auctions for offering long-term products and attracting new capacity to be built. Requests for bids were eventually made but the contracts offered had a very short duration (up to four years) with no sufficient lead time to allow new investments to compete in the process. No new generation was attracted. Between 2006 and 2008, the lack of new capacity led to inadequate reserve margins, high spot prices, and a dearth of interest from existing generators for contracts, as they preferred to sell in the spot market. Customer tariffs ("pass through" of spot prices) became very volatile and the risk of load shedding was imminent.

The lack of enforcement of the 100 percent contracting requirement rule led to the offer of short-term contracts in auctions, which did not support the emergence of new capacity. Hence, in 2008, two key modifications that tried to overcome the aforementioned challenges were introduced:

- Minimum levels of contracting into the future (100 percent for the next two years, 90 percent for the following two years, 80 percent for years five and six and thereafter, until 40 percent in years 13 and 14) were established in order to foster the auctioning of long-term contracts and attract new capacity.
- The regulator convinced distribution companies to centrally procure all new energy, adopting uniform standard rules for the power-purchasing processes. This change reduces the risk for the investor through clear, stable, standardized rules.

The contracts cover up to 14 years from the bidding date, but with a lead time for the contract to start 24 to 72 months after contracts are awarded. The procurement auction is open to all technologies, with indexation allowed. Indexed bids are evaluated using a standardized fuel inflation forecast and compared at present values. A first-price sealed-bid auction design is used.

A new regulatory change was again implemented in 2009, and the centralized procurement process started to be managed by ETESA. The volume to be procured is defined jointly by ETESA and the distribution companies (which are consulted by ETESA to verify their needs) but ETESA offers no guarantees on contracts, which are signed directly between generators and distributors. ETESA also forces generators to bid their available firm capacity in the auction.

Results

The country has finally been witnessing the construction of new generation capacity since these adjustments were made. The first auction under the new procurement rules was carried out in 2008, involving 10-year contracts for 350 MW starting in 2012 or 2013.

Central America

Power System Characteristics

The Central American region is a land bridge connecting North and South America. Its six countries (Guatemala, El Salvador, Honduras, Nicaragua, Costa Rica, and Panama) have an installed capacity of 10,000 MW. Hydroelectricity accounts for about 40 percent of this capacity, but in some countries (i.e. Costa Rica, Panama, and Guatemala), hydro generation supplies more than 50 percent of energy demand. Load growth in the region hovers around 6 percent annually. Energy consumption per capita in 2008 shows that Costa Rica and Panama have much higher demands than the other countries, mainly due to economic activity, type of consumption, and level of electrification. Guatemala and Panama have a structural advantage in terms of integration with other electrical systems due to their location: Guatemala with the Mexican system and Panama with the Colombian one.

Market Structure

All countries in the region enacted Energy Laws in the mid-1990s. Competitive wholesale markets were introduced in Panama, Guatemala, Nicaragua, and El Salvador. Honduras and Costa Rica are still vertically integrated systems. Private participation, however, is considerable in the region, mainly in the distribution segment. Investors have been participating in generation expansion through IPPs in all of the countries in the region. These are either tendered by the vertically integrated utility (Honduras and Costa Rica) or procured in a market-based framework.

There are several organization models for CA's energy procurement:

- Guatemala, Nicaragua, and Panama have organized competitive markets with a high level of regulatory intervention to ensure security of supply. Regulated capacity payments are offered and there are mandatory requirements for distribution companies and large users (i.e. final users authorized to find their own source of supply in the market) for contracting forward their expected peak demand plus some defined security reserve margin. However, this procurement mechanism has not been fully tested in Guatemala and Nicaragua. Only Panama has been carrying out and mastering procurement auctions of long-term contracts.
- El Salvador initially organized an energy-only market, with little regulatory intervention to ensure adequacy. As a result of decreasing reserve margins over a period of several years, the country introduced amendments to the law to incorporate some level of intervention on this and other topics in 2002. In essence, capacity payments are being reintroduced and mandatory requirements for distribution companies and large users for contracting forward their expected peak demand will be implemented.
- Costa Rica and Honduras created single buyer competitive markets, maintaining a centrally planned system, and allowing private participation in generation through Power Purchase Agreements (PPA) with Independent Power Producers (IPPs). Contracts are signed between IPPs and with the integrated utility (Empresa Nacional de Energía Eléctrica (ENEE), as in the case of Honduras, or with Instituto Costarricense de Electricidad, in the case of Costa Rica (ICE)), where private participation is limited to 30 percent of the country's total installed capacity.
- Central America (CA) is implementing a Regional Electricity Market (MER), whose main objective is to enable the construction of regional generation projects that will take advantage of economies of scale and provide cheaper electricity to consumers in the region. To support this type of project, the MER market design includes firm regional supply contracts that will need to be acquired in tandem with firm transmission rights in order to be accepted by local regulators as a source of supply comparable to generation, located within the country's

Figure 4.7. Central America Regional Power Market

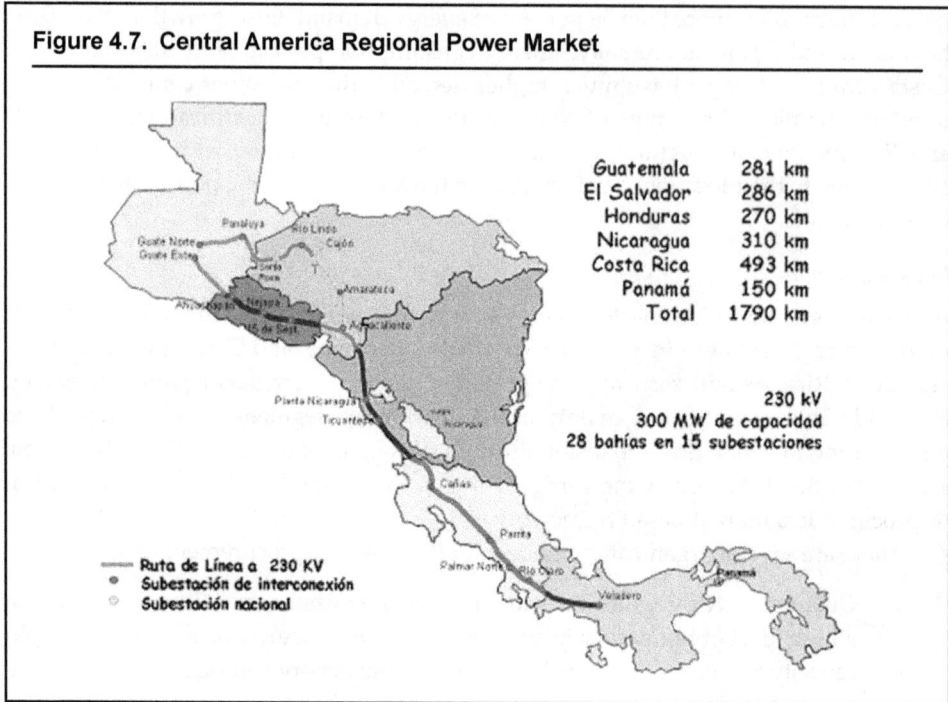

Guatemala	281 km
El Salvador	286 km
Honduras	270 km
Nicaragua	310 km
Costa Rica	493 km
Panamá	150 km
Total	1790 km

230 kV
300 MW de capacidad
28 bahías en 15 subestaciones

—— Ruta de Línea a 230 KV
  • Subestación de interconexión
  ◦ Subestación nacional

Source: CIER

borders. The MER will effectively allow an integrated approach to adequacy through the concept of regional firm contracts. A second objective of the MER is to increase effective competition. The possibility of CA distributors procuring energy in the MER to fulfill their obligations, rather than in their national markets, substantially increases the level of competition. The MER is just a "seventh market," in addition to the six existing domestic markets, and is illustrated in figure 4.7 below.

Use of Auctions

The power system in Central America is poised to be the first market in the developing world to adopt electricity auctions across borders. The transmission infrastructure is being built connecting the countries to each other, and extending it to Mexico and Colombia. The transmission network may potentially enable the construction of large hydro plants with economies of scale, as long as they can be shared (and even owned, if a "Felou" or "VPP" kind of scheme is envisioned) among multiple off-takers, including national utilities or large customers. Auctions seem to be an elegant solution to share those resources on a competitive basis.[16]

Mexico

Power System Characteristics

Mexico has approximately 52 GW of installed generation capacity with about 76 percent of this capacity being fossil fuel fired. Major fuels include fuel oil, natural gas, coal, and small amounts of diesel. The remaining capacity consists of hydropower (22 percent), nuclear (2.7 percent), geothermal (2.2 percent), and a small fraction of wind. The most notable change in the generation mix over the last decade has been the large increase in natural gas-fired capacity, which has replaced fuel oil plants. The demand for electric power in Mexico has been growing faster than GDP over the past few decades, a trend that is likely to continue for the foreseeable future as electricity use continues to increase in all sectors. Specifically, electricity consumption has grown at a continuous pace of 4.1 percent over the last 10 years, reaching 209.7 TWh in 2007.

Market Structure

The Comisión Federal de Electricidad (CFE), a major state-owned enterprise, has a monopoly on the electricity sector, controlling its generation, transmission, distribution, and trading. Serving more than 97 percent of the population, CFE has consolidated its position with the recent acquisition of the utility company serving the metropolitan area of Mexico City. Since the late 1990s, the private sector has participated in the generation side as independent power producers (IPPs), mostly with gas-fired combined cycles. The IPPs generate and sell power exclusively to CFE under long-term contracts. In 2010, IPPs represented about 23 percent of total installed capacity in Mexico, and generated 33 percent of total electricity.

Use of Auctions

Mexico runs a classic Single Buyer procurement scheme backed by central planning and carried out by the CFE, which determines energy volumes. It then calls a first-price sealed-bid auction to contract IPPs to build, own, and operate (i.e. BOT scheme) the projects it has identified according to the long-run plan and provision. Independent producers are awarded a long-run power purchase agreement (PPA). Pricing of these agreements follows a two-part structure: one proportional to firm capacity actually made available to the CFE, and another that covers the variable costs incurred for producing energy whenever the plant is dispatched by CFE. In 1997, the government of Mexico created a financial mechanism—Proyectos de Impacto Diferido en el Registro de Gasto (Projects with Deferred Expenditure Impact) (PIDIREGAS)—to finance long-term oil, gas, and power projects, and also provides a government guarantee to private investments.

Global generation companies also got involved in the Mexican energy-generation business by constructing combined-cycle plants all over the country according to the CFE's demands. The Spain-based Iberdrola and Union Fenosa, as well as EDF, InterGen, Transalta, AES, and Mitsubishi, among others, have developed projects since 1999.

Results

The Mexican experience of IPP participation has generally been very successful. None of the projects launched has failed and all payments have been executed according to the terms and provisions, to the overall satisfaction of all parties. Approximately 11,000 MW of CCGT have been installed since 1998. The current total installed capacity by IPPs is 11,500 MW. However, the program's overall efficiency has been challenged, with some question as to whether the risks of implicit guarantees are growing significantly, and if there are alternative schemes to develop the program more efficiently.

Notes

1. Source: ANEEL, EPE, and ONS, 2010.
2. Law 10.848/04 and Decree 5.163/04.

3. Again, a moving average of 12 months is used.

4. As discussed in Arizu et al. (2004).

5. The two-auction scheme is a mechanism to hedge against load growth uncertainty, in the absence of which it would be risky for a utility to procure all load growth requirements in a single auction.

6. The low observed price should be interpreted carefully. It is probably due to the low price of 32.42/MWh offered by the 1,800 MW Teles Pires hydro plant. Its consortium members were primarily state-owned utilities or state pension funds.

7. 2009 data as provided by the Colombian market operator XM at http://www.xm.com.co/Pages/DescripciondelSistemaElectricoColombiano.aspx.

8. See Cramton and Stoft (2007) for details and Rodilla et al. (2011) for a simulation model of the dynamics of the Colombian auctions.

9. Data provided by CNE (National Energy Commission) at http://anuario.cne.cl/anuario/electricidad/php_electricidad-01.php.

10. Rudnick, H. (2006).

11. COES is the Committee for the Economic Operation of the National Interconnected System. The data is available at http://www.coes.org.pe/Dataweb2/2009/STR/estadistica/anual/anual.htm.

12. The Electricity Concessions Law (ECL) and its regulations; Law N°25844 and Supreme Decree (DS) N°009-93-EM.

13. The term "busbar" is commonly used in the power systems field to refer to the network nodes of the transmission grid (usually the main substations of the system). Generation prices are calculated for each of the main nodes (the difference in prices between nodes are the result of transmission losses).

14. Camac, D. (2006).

15. Representing the average production in MWh divided by 8,760 (hours in a year)

16. The same rationale applies to Central and South Asia, where resources are available but unevenly distributed among countries.

CHAPTER 5

Auctions in Asia, Oceania, Europe, North America, and Multi-Country

Asia and Oceania

Energy procurement experiences in Asia and Oceania have generally revolved around tenders for specific BOT or BOO contracts for hydro and/or thermal projects organized by government-linked institutions and tendered to IPPs. The numerous experiences using this scheme have relied basically on simple first-price sealed-bid auctions. Four country experiences have been selected: Vietnam, Philippines, Thailand, and South Australia.

Vietnam

Power System Characteristics

Vietnam's installed capacity is about 11,000 MW with a diversified generation mix involving hydro (45 percent), coal (25 percent), and gas-fired plants (30 percent). Electricity demand has increased steadily over the last decade, but the country's per capita energy consumption remains one of the lowest in Asia.

Market Structure

State-owned Vietnam Electricity (EVN) is responsible for electricity generation, transmission, distribution, and sales throughout the country. Foreign and private sector participation has been permitted on a more permanent basis since 2002, but the lack of a regulatory regime has hindered investments.

Use of Auctions

In order to meet load growth, the government decided to promote private sector participation of foreign-owned IPPs through specific BOTs. The World Bank assisted the government in preparing and conducting the bidding for the Phu My 2-2 (715 MW) gas-fired power project under a BOT scheme. The procurement process was carried out using a first-price sealed-bid auction design. Six solid international consortia submitted bids, and the EDF-led consortium was awarded the project in 1999, being one of the first private groups to participate in the Vietnamese power sector. Key project documents including the BOT contract were signed and the Investment License was issued in 2001. Financing documents were signed in 2002 and the plant was commissioned in early 2005. The private generator is selling power to the state-owned integrated utility EVN under a 20-year PPA. The project became the first infrastructure project in the country where the sponsor was selected through competitive bidding, as well as the largest foreign investment outside of the oil and gas sectors.

Results

Although the general experience seems to be positive, the finalization of the process, including financial closure, took a long time, which made the Government of Vietnam ("GoV") reluctant to repeat it a few years ago. The main cause for the delays was an incomplete legal and regulatory framework, leaving several issues to be negotiated and agreed upon after the award. A simple lesson learned is that any tender process requires a suitable framework in place that covers the main issues for financial closure, licensing, and implementation.

During the years following this tender, Vietnam developed and improved the legal framework for foreign and private investments. The country issued the Electricity Law in 2004, as well as related implementation decrees. The GoV also established the electricity regulator and is developing the full regulatory framework for the electricity industry. A competitive procurement carried out today would be simpler and faster than at the time of Phu My 2.2. Moreover, a BOT tender for a coal-fired power plant is currently in progress.

Philippines

Power System Characteristics

With 7,000 islands to cover, the Philippines faces unique electricity market challenges in providing services throughout the country. Of the three largest islands—Luzon, Visayas, and Mindanao—Luzon (which includes Manila) accounts for 75 percent of the energy demand and 87 percent of installed capacity. Geothermal power accounts for the country's largest share of indigenous energy production, followed by hydropower, natural gas, coal, and oil. With the exception of a downturn from 1991 to 1993, and again during the Asian crisis in 1998–99, growth in the GDP has ranged from 4 to 7 percent.

Reform Process, Market Structure and Use of Auctions

The financial and political crises of the 1980s dried up government resources and eliminated the support from the government's presence in the power industry. The massive power shortages that followed in the late 1980s and 90s prompted the passage of the BOT law in 1990. This regulatory move created the mechanism through which the government contracted over 40 Independent Power Producers over the next years, following a first-price sealed-bid auction design for power purchase agreements (PPAs).

The IPP sector in the Philippines developed in three main waves. First, the plants contracted in the early 1990s to address the power crisis were largely oil-fired plants with 5–12 year PPAs. These tended to be expensive because of short-term PPAs (which led investors to aim for a rapid capital recovery) and the high costs from oil plants that were dispatched as baseload during the crisis. Second, a wave of large baseload coal plants—for a total of over 2,500 MW of installed capacity—became operational between 1996 and 2000 and had longer PPAs (up to 25 years). Third, a number of large hydro/irrigation projects and natural gas plants became operational from 1998 to 2002, with approximately 4,000 MW of installed capacity.

In 2001, electric industry reform was implemented by the Electric Power Industry Reform Act (usually referred to as "EPIRA"). The EPIRA law essentially seeks to further liberalize the electricity sector, including a fully private generation market, in which power producers compete in a private bilateral contract market for sales to distribution companies and large-scale users, as well as the establishment of a spot market for system balancing.

Auctions have proved useful and are now being used for the privatization of generation assets, and PPAs—the Power Sector Assets and Liabilities Management Corporation—created during the 2001 reform process, have so far sold a total of 4,300 MW in generation capacity from 20 plants that were previously owned by the government.

Thailand

Power System Characteristics

Approximately 70 percent of Thailand's electricity supply is sourced from natural gas-fired power plants, being supplemented by other resources such as fuel oil, coal, and hydro. The development of energy-intensive industries and high rates of GDP growth spurred a consistent and rapid increase in the electricity demand since the 1990s, though this trend was seriously affected by the Asian financial crisis. Thailand's electricity industry is linked to that of Laos and Malaysia.

Market Structure and Use of Auctions

State-owned EGAT (Electricity Generating Authority of Thailand)—which is responsible for over 60 percent of the electricity generated in Thailand and also controls the entire transmission system and distribution to a few large customers—has been implementing several programs of Independent Power Producers (IPP), Small Power Producers (SPP), and Very Small Power Producers (VSPP). The IPP program launched in December 1994 was a significant departure from the previously centrally coordinated and planned Thai electric power sector.

In the case of IPPs, EGAT-procured power from private power producers on a Build-Operate-Own (BOO) basis, whereby private power producers construct the facilities, becomes the sole owner of the assets without having to transfer them to the government at the end of the contract. The payment structure is output-based and is made under the Power Purchasing Agreements (PPAs) that are assigned to investors following a competitive tendering process according to a first-price sealed-bid design. Payments resulting from these PPAs are divided into two components: (i) availability payment (intended to cover fixed costs) and (ii) energy payment (for the reimbursement of the costs of energy actually produced).

The IPP projects implemented by EGAT have been deemed successful and have included the tendering of import hydro IPPs located in Laos, and of PPAs for new local thermal (gas and coal-fired) IPPs.

The SPP program focused on smaller developments and defined requirements as to the type of power plants that may be eligible. More specifically, they are required to be non-conventional renewable sources—such as wind, solar, small hydro, and biomass.

South Australia

Power System Characteristics

Total generation capacity in South Australia is about 4,000 MW, the majority of which comes from gas-fired plants. Coal generation exists, while hydro participation is very modest. A significant expansion of wind power has been observed over the last few years. There are currently 11 wind farms operating in the region with an installed capacity of around 900 MW. South Australia is interconnected to the Victoria region.

Reform Process and Use of Auctions

Back in October 1998, at the time of market reform and the privatization of electricity assets, the Electricity Reform and Sales Unit (ERSU) issued a Request for Proposals for the development of a natural gas project named Pelican Power Station, to be located in South Australia. Following demand forecasts and with the aim of ensuring supply reliability—particularly during peak periods—the RFP defined a schedule that determined that a minimum generation capacity of 150 MW should be available by November 2000, increasing to 250 MW by November 2001.

The procurement process had four major objectives: (i) to meet specific time frames for both the first 150 MW and the total 250 MW, (ii) to maximize financial benefits for the government, (iii) to minimize (ideally eliminate) subsidies or government underwriting, and (iv) to increase competition in the state electricity market.

Given the relative urgency to make the generating capacity available, the government provided the necessary approvals and offered a 20-month fixed-price contract for 200 MW of electricity output and a three-year gas supply offer. Bidders bid for the right to explore the site with related approvals, plus the off-take and gas agreements, also recognizing that penalties would apply if deadlines were missed.

Results

A total of 24 companies initially expressed an interest in the process and 16 were eventually shortlisted to attend a bidders' conference. Prospective bidders were requested to submit an indicative bid, which was used as a further shortlisting process from which four companies were chosen to submit final bids. The bids essentially consisted of determining how much money the company would be willing to pay the government for the right to build the power station.

In February 1999, the contract for the construction of a 500 MW combined-cycle project was awarded to National Power, which completed the project ahead of schedule and provided a net benefit of $40 million to the government. Although the auction demand was 250 MW, the winning project offered a capacity of 500 MW.

This success was the result of a well-structured and credible process, a good communication strategy to encourage participation, and having bids on an executable agreement, thus avoiding the delays and vagaries of post-bid negotiations.

Europe

Spain—Default Supply Auctions

Power System Characteristics

The Spanish power system has an installed capacity close to 94,000 MW. The capacity mix includes hydropower (18 percent), natural gas (30 percent), coal (12 percent), nuclear (8 percent), fuel oil (5 percent), and so-called Special Regime—wind, small hydro, biomass, and other renewable sources (34 percent). Load has experienced a solid growth until 2007, when it started to decrease.

Use of Auctions and Results

Ministerial Order ITC/400/2007 implemented a quarterly auction procedure, the so-called CESUR auctions[1], to support the calculation of the energy price to be passed through to regulated consumers. The National Energy Commission (CNE, *Comisión Nacional de Energía*) was appointed as trustee of the auctions. The Commission contracted an independent consulting firm to conduct the first five auctions, which started in June 2007. The outcomes of these auctions, both in terms of prices and bilateral contract volumes, are allowed to be passed on to end-users under regulated tariffs since they are recognized as part of the allowed costs of distribution companies. However, the quantities auctioned have always been much smaller than the amount needed to fulfill regulated consumers' needs. In the first auction, only three-month baseload contracts were auctioned (6,500 MW, or less than 40 percent of the expected needs). In the fourth auction, six-month duration baseload contracts were introduced, but the quantity was still 7,000 MW. In the fifth auction, 1,800 MW quarterly baseload contracts and 900 MW for the six-month contract were tendered. From the sixth auction onward until today, the managing body responsible for organizing and managing the auctions has been OMEL, the market operator. In the seventh auction, peak-load contracts were introduced.

The first auction began with 25 domestic and international sellers participating in the bidding. Contracts were awarded to 21 winning suppliers, including retailers, generators, and marketers. In the last one, the 11th, held in June 2010, 33 market players bid in the auction. All CESUR auctions were designed as simultaneous descending clock auctions. The first auction closed after 25 rounds and the last one after 14.

Currently, the new suppliers of last resort are responsible for meeting the needs of customers whose contracted capacity is below 10 kVA, i.e. small businesses and domestic consumers. The ministry still sets a maximum price that these suppliers are allowed to charge. In order to fill the gap between the quantities auctioned and the actual needs, suppliers of last resort are allowed to pass through a risk premium (4 percent shopping credit).

United Kingdom: The "Do-nothing" Approach and Ongoing "Visible-hand" Proposals—The Central Buyer

Power System Characteristics

The UK (England and Wales Pool) had an installed generation capacity of 78,000 MW in 2009. Most electricity generation comes from coal, oil, and gas-fired generation (77 percent), followed by nuclear (13 percent), international links (3 percent), and renewable sources (7 percent).

Reform Process and Market Structure

The electricity supply industry in England and Wales was under public ownership until 1990 when its chief utility—the Central Electricity Generating Board (CEGB)—was restructured and privatized along with a full restructuring of the power sector. It was touted as one of the most comprehensive and successful reforms of the 1990s. A full market-based scheme anchored in spot pricing theory was introduced, aiming at providing market signals for system operation and expansion. In this power pool, which operated between 1990 and 2001,[2] the underlying assumption was that if investors would forecast an increase in short-term market prices, due to load increase for example, they would react accordingly by building new capacity. This new capacity could enter the system as merchant plants or by hedging part of their price and market risks with financial instruments, particularly forward contracts (the so-called contracts for differences). Consistency would be assured because long-term contracts could be priced relative to the futures market, where the prices are in turn projected from short-term market prices and expectations of future changes in supply/demand conditions. The power generation sector added

9.5 GW of capacity in combined cycle gas turbines during the period 1990–96 (nearly 20 percent of peak demand), while demand rose less than 6 percent. Half of the new capacity was installed by new entrants.

The England and Wales Pool had a capacity adder (tariff uplift) that was calculated taking into account the expected loss of load probability (LOLP) of the power system. The capacity adder increased sharply as the system approached full capacity utilization and the reserve became tight, and it was paid to all generators selling into the Pool. There was also an availability payment for generators who had not sold energy into the Pool but remained available during the day.

Some generators allegedly abused their market power to manipulate the capacity payment, which was one of the reasons why England changed the market model from a gross pool to a balancing market in 2001. The previous generator-type capacity adder methodology was explicitly removed in favor of assumed security delivery through energy market prices. A major driver for the New Electricity Trading Arrangements (NETA) project was the perception that the previous market mechanism (including its capacity adder) delivered an average price that was too high, leading to excess capacity development. Indeed, soon after the NETA market introduction, the obvious excess capacity from the "dash-for-gas" period led to a price collapse and older plants were quickly closed or mothballed.

Much of the new UK capacity was not built to meet load increases, but to replace older plants with the introduction of gas-fired combined cycle plants. Natural gas has been historically abundant in the UK, which relied on large reserves in the North Sea. Security of supply was assured by keeping older plants as cold reserves through explicit standing reserve option contracts offered by the transmission system operator.

A great deal of existing capacity in the UK is, however, at risk of closing over the next few years. This is the case for the existing coal capacity—which is facing carbon constraints—and for the current stock of nuclear capacity, also scheduled for closure with no clear sign that new nuclear capacity will be developed, despite the government's encouragement. There is an explicit government policy to "de-carbonize" the energy matrix and avoid building new coal plants, which may constitute a long-term liability for the power sector if payment for CO_2 emission ever comes to fruition.

Supply Adequacy Threats and Possible Use of Auctions

In early February 2010, OFGEM, the national gas and electricity regulator, launched a public consultation for "Options for delivering secure and sustainable energy supplies."[3] OFGEM recognized that large parts of the UK's ageing energy infrastructure will need replacement, and some rapid progress towards its substantial de-carbonization will have to be embraced by the power sector at the same time. Five key issues[4] were identified as concerns for attracting the unprecedented levels of investment to be sustained over many years under difficult financial conditions and against a backdrop of increased risk and uncertainty.

The OFGEM document stated that short-term price signals at times of system stress do not fully reflect the value that customers place on security of supply.[5] As a result, price incentives to increase peaking capacity may not be strong enough. Several different policy measures have been merged into five possible policy 'packages'. In some packages, OFGEM includes the concept of long-term capacity tenders covering renewable sources and low-carbon generation to facilitate their financing. In one case, long and short-term capacity tenders are combined for all generation and demand-side response.

A Central Energy Buyer option package envisages a single entity responsible for coordinating the procurement of new energy supplies, or at least certain forms of energy supplies. According to one of the proposals, the Central Energy Buyer would underwrite long-term contracts to lower the financial cost, giving increased confidence with regard to specific outcomes on power expansion.

The proposals being floated are still the subject of much debate and many contributions, and approval may take a while. However, they seem to point towards a centralized scheme for energy procurement through long-term contractual commitments.

North America

ISO New England—Forward Capacity Market to Retain/Attract Generation

Power System Characteristics

Created by the FERC in 1997, ISO New England is a regional transmission operator whose system consists of 13 interconnections to three neighboring systems in the US and Canada: Maritimes, New York, and Quebec. Covering an area of 6.5 million customers with a population of 14 million inhabitants, the power system has 32,000 MW of installed capacity, distributed over 350 generators. The peak load reaches 28,000 MW in the summer. The capacity mix includes gas (38 percent), oil (24 percent), nuclear (14 percent), coal (9 percent), and hydro (6 percent). Natural gas and nuclear meet most of the energy demand (70 percent). In 1999, ISO New England began managing the restructured regional wholesale power markets.

Market Structure

The New England ISO operates a locational forward capacity market (FCM) intended to send competitive price signals to procure new investment in capacity and retain existing resources required to ensure resource adequacy. The locational aspect is to ascertain that capacity additions (or auctions for load reduction) are executed in critical areas of the grid. The FCM was implemented in 2006 to ensure that adequate resources are available to meet customers' needs for reliable electric energy through the most efficient combination of existing generation, new investments in generating capacity, and demand resources. It provides a market structure to attract investments in new generating capacity and to price capacity resources.

Use of Auctions

The Forward Capacity Market is a mechanism set up to procure enough installed capacity to meet the region's reliability criterion, or the Installed Capacity Requirement (ICR).[6] In practice, for each one-year capacity commitment period, a Forward Capacity Auction is conducted to procure the Net Installed Capacity Requirement (NICR) of the New England Balancing Authority Area. The FCM design incorporates several key features:

- The primary capacity auction is held three years before the delivery year. The three-year planning period facilitates the participation of new capacity resources and fosters competition among new proposals.
- The new capacity projects proposed compete in the market, set capacity clearing prices, and have a choice of an extended commitment period ranging from one to five years. That is, new capacity can have an N-year commitment, where the supplier chooses an N between one and five years at the time of qualification. Both new and existing capacity resources are paid the same market clearing

price the first year, provided there is sufficient competition and an adequate supply. The price paid to new capacity after the first year is indexed for inflation. Existing capacity participates in the auction each year and has a one-year commitment.

- Demand and intermittent resources compete equally with traditional generation resources to provide capacity. This limits the potential for market power in the capacity and electric energy markets while enhancing economic efficiency.
- Resource adequacy is addressed at both regional and capacity zone levels.[7] In the FCM, import-constrained zones, sometimes referred to as "load pockets", can have higher prices if needed, in order to attract a sufficient amount of new resources. Export-constrained zones can have lower prices if they have too much capacity. Locational price signals provide incentives for new resources to be located where and when new capacity is needed.
- Before the auction, the ISO determines the minimum capacity required in each zone and in the system for the first year of the commitment period.
- A simultaneous descending clock auction is used to determine the capacity clearing prices and capacity suppliers for each zone. A starting price for the auction, which is twice the cost of new entry (CONE), is specified before the auction begins. The auction clearing price is used to update the CONE in subsequent auctions.

The product procured is a call option backed by a physical resource.[8] The call option represents a financial contract that entitles the buyer of the option to receive from the seller any positive difference between the spot market price and a predetermined reference price, known as the strike price, for each MW purchased under the option contract. This holds true for every hour within the time horizon for which the option is defined as being active. In exchange, the seller receives a premium. In other words, every time the spot price surpasses a defined strike price, all the units committed in the FCM will have to sell their energy at the strike price instead of the spot market price. This strike price is calculated to serve as a threshold for determining scarcity situations. All units thus have the incentive to produce during periods when the system needs them most, because otherwise they would be forced to purchase the energy at a very high spot price. Hence, the risk of not having enough resources to supply the demand shifts from the consumer to the generation producers' side.

Each type of resource, including intermittent generation, has a resource-specific set of rules for qualification that enables it to participate in the forward capacity market. Qualification occurs between five and 13 months before the auction. All existing resources are automatically entered into the capacity auction and assume a capacity supply obligation for the relevant commitment period at the lower end of their summer- or winter-qualified capacity, unless they submit a "de-list bid" that subsequently clears in the auction. A de-list bid indicates that a resource does not want to assume a capacity supply obligation below the price of the bid.

Results

ISO-NE has conducted two forward capacity auctions (FCAs) to date for the commitment periods of 2010/2011 and 2011/2012, achieving its objective of attracting and retaining the capacity needed to meet the region's ICR for the first two commitment periods. The first FCA (FCA #1) was conducted in February 2008 for the capacity commitment period of June 1, 2010 through May 31, 2011. The second FCA (FCA #2) was conducted in December 2008 for the capacity commitment period of June 1, 2011 through May 31,

2012. Table 5.1 shows that both auctions cleared at the floor price with surplus capacity above the Net Installed Capacity Requirement.

The most interesting aspect of the FCM in NE is that it treats supply and demand resources on a level-playing-field basis, thus participating in the same auction processes. Energy efficiency and other demand resources were able to compete with generation to meet system reliability. Demand resources are expected to represent possibly 15 percent of market needs in the future. This is an area that will likely experience significant growth, as metering technology and two-way communication enable the participation of a larger number of players in the wholesale market. Box 5.1 describes this experience.

Table 5.1. Forward Capacity Market Results—ISO-NE

Cleared Resources (MW)	FCA #1	FCA #2
Generation	30,865	32,207
Demand resources	2,279	2,778
Imports	934	2,298
Total cleared	**34,077**	**37,283**
NICR	32,305	32,528
Excess cleared	1,772	4,755
Price (US$/kW-month)	**4.5**	**3.6**

Source: ISO-NE (2009)

Box 5.1. Demand Resources Participation in New England

A noteworthy provision in New England's FCM is the fact that energy efficiency and other demand resources could compete with generation to meet reliability needs for the first time. Instead of meeting capacity and reliability needs by simply paying generators additional money, there is an **auction** for all new capacity, and demand resources are eligible to participate and compete in the auction. Resources that can meet power needs are allowed to bid in the auction and the bids determine the price for capacity in the region. One of the most interesting results of the first two auctions was the large volume of demand-resource capacity that cleared in each auction. Capacity from these resources represents about 7 and 9 percent of the total requirements in the first and second auctions, respectively. Results for the first auction are shown below (ISO New England (2009)).

New Demand Resources
(1,188 MW)

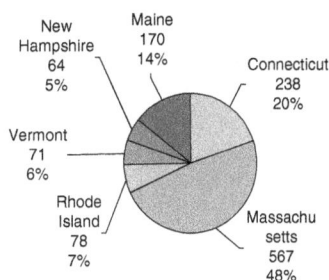

New Hampshire 64 5%
Maine 170 14%
Connecticut 238 20%
Vermont 71 6%
Rhode Island 78 7%
Massachusetts 567 48%

New Supply Resources
(626 MW)

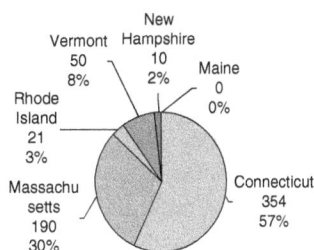

Vermont 50 8%
New Hampshire 10 2%
Maine 0 0%
Rhode Island 21 3%
Massachusetts 190 30%
Connecticut 354 57%

Values represent MW and percent

Demand resources improve the efficiency with which the region uses capacity. The region's low load factor means that there is considerable opportunity for demand-side management to improve the efficiency with which the region uses existing capacity.

PJM—Reliability Pricing Model to Retain/Attract Generation

Power System Characteristics

PJM Interconnection is a regional transmission organization (RTO) that coordinates the movement of wholesale electricity in all or parts of 14 states in the US, namely Delaware, Illinois, Indiana, Kentucky, Maryland, Michigan, New Jersey, North Carolina, Ohio, Pennsylvania, Tennessee, Virginia, West Virginia, and the District of Columbia. PJM, whose initials represent Pennsylvania, New Jersey, and Maryland, was designated an RTO by the FERC in 2001, following FERC's Order 880 that began the deregulation of traditional utility companies. It expanded to a much larger region and currently manages about 163,500 MW of generating capacity over 56,350 miles of transmission lines. The marginal fuel types are coal and natural gas. More than 51 million people live in the PJM region. The all-time peak load of 144,644 MW was set in August 2006.

Market Structure

PJM operates a capacity-market model named the Reliability Pricing Model (RPM) that is designed to create price signals to procure needed investments and retain existing plants, thus maintaining reliability in the PJM region. Implemented in 2007, the RPM is based on making capacity commitments three years ahead and shares several similarities with New England's FCM. The long-term RPM approach, in contrast to PJM's previous short-term capacity market, includes incentives that are designed to stimulate investment both in maintaining existing generation and in encouraging the development of new sources of capacity—resources that include not just generating plants, but demand response and transmission facilities.

The RPM model works in conjunction with PJM's Regional Transmission Expansion Planning (RTEP) process to ensure the reliability of the PJM region for future years. The RPM includes the continued use of self-supply and bilateral contracts by load-serving entities (LSEs) to meet their capacity obligations that result from the reliability criterion defined by planning studies. The capacity auctions under the RPM obtain the *remaining* capacity that is needed after market participants have committed the resources they will supply themselves or provide through contracts.

Use of Auctions

The RPM provides:

- Procurement of capacity (residual capacity after specification of self-supply and bilateral contracts) three years before it is needed through a sealed-bid auction;
- Locational pricing for capacity that reflects limitations on the transmission system's ability to deliver electricity in an area and to account for the different needs for capacity in various areas of PJM. This way, some zones have been defined where the capacity requirements are calculated independently. The fact that Cost of New Entry (a relevant parameter used to define the demand curve) may differ from one location to another is also taken into account;
- A variable resource requirement to help set the price for capacity, i.e., the demand is represented by means of a downward-sloping curve. The downward-sloping demand curve reduces market power concerns. Figure 5.1 illustrates the use of a downward-sloping demand curve by showing the supply and demand in the 20011/2012 Base Year Auction:

Figure 5.1. Downward-Sloping Demand Curve

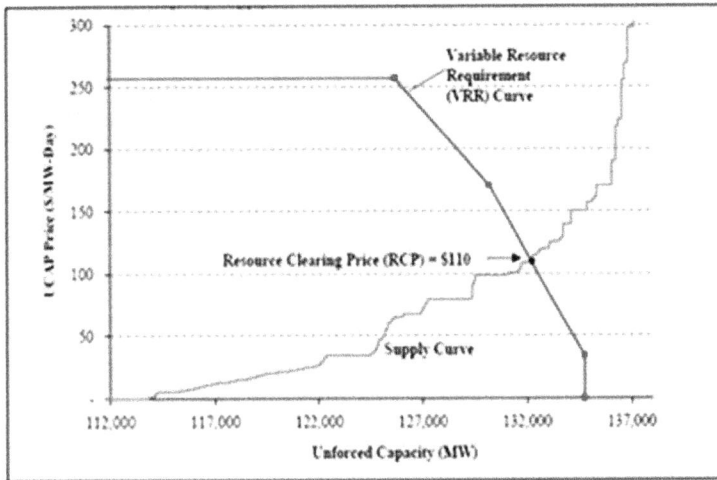

Source: PJM

- The opportunity for Transmission and Demand Resources to participate, which allows direct competition between various options, including new generation resources and demand response, to address reliability requirements;
- A backstop mechanism to ensure that sufficient resources will be available to preserve system reliability.

Results

Four auctions have been conducted thus far and the role of demand response is growing in PJM's capacity market. One of the key features of the Reliability Pricing Model (RPM) is the ability of demand response to compete with and be paid the same as generation. More than 2,000 MW of demand resources cleared in the May 2008 auction; these resources must be in service for the 2011/2012 delivery year. The trend of Demand Response Participation before and after RPM Implementation is illustrated in figure 5.2 as follows:

New Jersey—Default Supply Procurement (BGS)

Market Structure

The state of New Jersey is part of the large, mature, liquid PJM market described above. It has embraced full retail competition, whereby every customer has the legal right to buy from an alternate supplier. But even though all customers have the "right to choose", very few retail customers have actually exercised this right (opted in). As a consequence, some entity needs to be the "default supplier" for the energy requirements of those customers.

Every year since 2002, the four New Jersey Electric Distribution Companies (EDCs) have procured electric supply to serve their Basic Generation Service (BGS) customers through a statewide auction process. Those companies include Public Service Gas &

Figure 5.2. Demand Response Participation in RPM

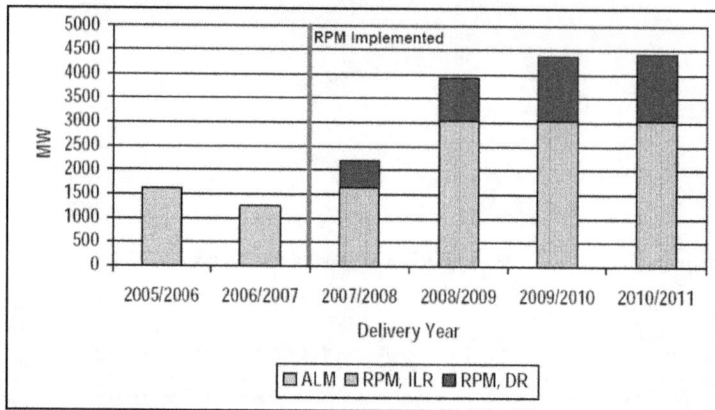

Source: PJM

Electric Company (PSE&G), Atlantic City Electric Company (ACE), Jersey Central Power & Light Company (JCP&L), and Rockland Electric Company (RECO). BGS refers to the service of customers who are not served by a third party supplier or competitive retailer (because they have not opted out to leave the incumbent utility). This service provided by the utility is sometimes known as Standard Offer, Default Service, or Provider of Last Resort. The auction process consists of two simultaneous auctions, one for larger customers on an hourly price plan (BGS-CIEP) and one for smaller and mid-size commercial and residential customers on a fixed-price plan (BGS-FP).

Use of Auctions and Results

This auction mechanism has been successful ever since it first started. As discussed in Loxley and Salan (2004), the first BGS auction was completed in February 2002, when New Jersey utilities purchased 17,000 MW for 12-month contracts starting in August of the same year. That was the first time that a simultaneous descending clock auction was used for the procurement of power. The auction finished after 73 rounds, from February 4 to February 13, 2002, where 21 bidders offering 29,600 MW of supply competed for the opportunity to serve 17,000 MW of load. Fifteen winners were selected and the total value of the auction was US$4 billion. The design of the simultaneous descending clock auction pioneered by BGS was inspired by simultaneous multiple-round auctions used earlier for spectrum in the US, and for selling electricity in the form of PPAs in Canada.

Bids are made for the right to serve full requirement tranches of load, equal to roughly 100 MW of peak load for the smaller and mid-size customers, and 75 MW of peak load for the larger customers. In the case of the smaller and mid-size customers, each year the EDCs procure one-third of the load for a three-year period. In the case of larger customers, the supply term is only one year. Tranches were designed in order to minimize the risk for the suppliers, but winners are responsible for the risk of the demand profile, i.e., variations in demand associated with normal fluctuations in business activities and weather. It was felt that this risk was fairly well known and manageable for the prospective bidders.

The distribution companies do not actually conduct the procurement. The Regulatory Commission hires its own consulting firm to review the design and implementation of the auction.[9]

Contrary to a pure Single Buyer model, distribution companies in New Jersey do not take title to the power. They act as agents for those retail customers taking the default service, as opposed to the more traditional role of distribution companies as buyers and resellers of power. Self-dealing is allowed, and at least three of the winning bidders were affiliates of the buyer. But there have been no allegations of unfair favoritism towards these bidders. This presumably reflects the fact that the actual auction was conducted by a third party and the winners were selected solely on the basis of their willingness to supply at specific prices rather than the more subjective combination of price and non-price criteria, as is the case for auctions conducted in other parts of the US (e.g. Florida).

This kind of competitive auction used to serve default customers could also be employed in situations where there is no mandatory retail competition. Even in the absence of retail competition, a Regulatory Commission could require that a distribution company conduct an auction process to serve some or all of the electricity needs of their retail captive customers. Alternatively, the Regulatory Commission could set the rules itself and organize the auction in a centralized fashion. This might be the case for most World Bank client countries with some level of vertical de-integration of their power sectors.

Among the many attempts to have distribution companies procure electricity in their capacity as providers of last resort in the US, the New Jersey central purchasing arrangement has been considered very successful, and other states have adopted or are about to adopt it.

Illinois—Default Supply Procurement

Market Structure and Use of Auctions

In 2007, the electric power generated in Illinois came primarily from coal (47 percent), nuclear (46 percent), and gas (5 percent). The Illinois electricity market is under the jurisdiction of two regional transmission organizations. Commonwealth Edison (ComEd) is a member of the PJM Interconnection, and Ameren is part of the Midwest Independent Transmission System Operator (MISO).

The power market in the state of Illinois has also implemented electricity auctions. In 1997, the result of the restructuring of the Illinois electric industry was that the two utilities, namely ComEd and Ameren sold their generating assets to affiliates or third parties. A transition period of 10 years was set, in which the residential and small commercial tariffs were artificially frozen and the Illinois utilities met demand using long-term contracts. In 2004, the Illinois Commerce Commission started a series of workshops and studies to figure out what to do after the end of the transition period. One of the recommendations was to use auctions as a procurement method for short and mid-term contracts, following the example of other states in the United States such as New Jersey. In 2006, the Illinois Commerce Commission approved the use of the auction proposed by ComEd and Ameren. The auction was held in September 2006 and the impact on tariffs started in January 2007.

Results

Eight different products were procured at the Illinois auction and were differentiated by distribution company, customer class, and contract duration. The products auctioned were specified as "full-requirement" contracts. Such a product definition is substantially different from other electricity auctions around the world in which a fixed quantity of either capacity or energy is auctioned. In a full-requirement contract, the seller has to follow × percent (i.e. his/her tranche) of the chronological load at each point in time over a specified commitment period. Depending on the technology offered by the seller, this product introduces a non-manageable risk, which is the ability to do load following.

Each of the eight products at the auction had a target number of tranches. The products were auctioned using a simultaneous descending clock auction, and each seller was allowed to offer one or more tranches of each of the products. The 2006 Illinois Electricity Auction was completed after 39 rounds, with 21 sellers bidding on it.

The product definition in the Illinois auction made it very difficult for bidders to price the load-following obligation (de Castro, L. et al. (2008)). As a result, high prices were observed and the auction was not considered to be a success. A year after the auction took place, it was annulled. A new mechanism to contract supply for short and mid-term periods is being implemented.[10]

Ontario—Replacement of Ageing Generation and Incentives to Foster Forward Markets

Power System Characteristics

The province of Ontario, with approximately 35,000 MW of installed generation and a peak demand of 29,000 MW, is the second largest manufacturing state in North America after California. The province relies heavily on nuclear generation (51 percent), but also has other sources at its disposal: hydro (22 percent), coal (18 percent), and oil and natural gas (9 percent). The transmission grid is connected to Manitoba, Quebec, New York, Michigan, Minnesota, and Ontario, and is capable of importing or exporting approximately 4,000 MW.

Ontario was experiencing a fast-growing demand for electricity, aggravated by an ageing generation fleet and delays in the refurbishment of nuclear plants. The government had promised to phase out all coal plants over the next few years, but this action would result in very thin reserve margins. Confidence among investors was shaken due to policy/regulatory flip-flops. In October 2003, the new government determined that the private sector would not build new capacity on its own. An RFP process was hence launched.

Use of Auctions

The initial RFP was for 300 MW of renewable energy generation. Bidders had to meet technical and financial criteria on a pass/fail basis. Thereafter, bids would be assessed solely on a $/MWh basis. In parallel, the government prepared a separate RFP process for 2,500 MW of new generation or demand-side management.

In 2006, the Ontario Power Authority voiced its concern over future supply shortfalls. It decided to facilitate the organization of auctions for forward energy contracts so as to create long-term price signals in order to foster the development of new capacity. The first auction was carried out on February 28, 2006 and two types of baseload contracts were sold: five-year terms in blocks of 25 MW for a total of 325 MW and one-year terms in blocks of 5 MW for a total of 25 MW. The chosen format was a simultaneous ascending clock auction[11], in which trading companies and industrial and commercial users acted as the bidding parties. Given the positive results of the first auction, a second one was carried out soon after, selling similar products for a total of 550 MW. In December of the same year, a third auction was held involving both baseload and peak products in a competitive multi-seller/buyer process.

Multi-country Auctions

The concept of cross-border auctions for energy procurement has yet to be explored. Global experiences are very limited, and most cross-border projects developed thus far are backed either by international treaties or by the local support of transmission system operators. The success of the limited number of private experiences has been mixed at best.[12]

There has been some experience with establishing auctions for day-ahead markets at the international level, such as in Central Europe, Scandinavia (Nord Pool), and across US-Canada interconnections. There has also been some experience with "selling" a plant capacity to multiple buyers in different countries, such as the VPP scheme described earlier.

A number of experiences with bi-national hydro plants located at the border of two countries that share the plant's production capabilities and electricity is also available. This type of sharing is usually backed by bi-national treaties, supported by the national congresses of the two countries, as is the case, for example, of the Itaipu (Brazil—Paraguay) and Yaciretá (Argentina—Paraguay) power plants.

One of the more relevant experiences worldwide in cross-country procurement schemes is the back-to-back 2,200 MW interconnection between Argentina and Brazil. This is one of the first privately owned international independent transmission interconnection projects in the world that permits both countries to utilize electricity resources more efficiently and cost-effectively. Interestingly enough, this interconnection is supported by a long-term energy contract that establishes a firm capacity of 2,000 MW to Brazil. Unlike the different cross-country interconnections worldwide—which are used for reserve exchanges on a spot basis—the Argentina-Brazil interconnection through the contract design was expected to be seen in Brazil as a generator that has a firm obligation with multiple private distribution companies and federal companies to deliver energy up to the contracted 2,000 MW through 20-year contracts. The interconnection is dispatched when a buyer requests the energy, which is assumed to be when the market prices in Brazil are higher than the contract energy price. The initial 1,000 MW contract was procured through an international bid organized in Brazil in 1998. Electricity and gas shortages in Argentina in 2004 and 2005, however, interrupted the power flows from Argentina to Brazil and dismantled the business structure. It became clear that a private investment between two countries without a government-supported treaty is risky. Today, the interconnection is idle.

The full-fledged concept of multi-country electricity auctions for long-term contracts involving green field plants has yet to be implemented. They may be potentially applicable for the development of generation resources on a multi-country basis, taking advantage of economies of scale and facilitating the use of the energy produced by a large number of countries on a regional basis. However, institutional arrangements have been lacking and opportunities for regional projects and interconnections have not been explored. In the absence of a transmission infrastructure in place, it has been difficult to implement multi-country projects, let alone entertain the idea of the competitive procurement of energy via auctions.

A very interesting institutional arrangement found in West Africa is the case of the Felou hydropower project, which is currently under construction. It does not involve auctions, since the energy quotas are pre-defined, but it is a step in the right direction in terms of a collaborative institutional arrangement, and may be the precursor of multi-country competition if other power pools in Africa follow similar steps.

The Felou hydropower plant is located in Mali in the Senegal River basin, which is managed by the Senegal River Development Organization (OMVS, French acronym), and owned by the governments of Mali, Senegal, and Mauritania. The ownership and respon-sibility for the operation and maintenance of the 200 MW Manantali Hydropower Plant, as well as the main transmission system supplying bulk power to the national utilities of Mali (EDM), Mauritania (SOMELEC), and Senegal (SENELEC), has been transferred to SOGEM.[13] This is a commercially oriented company jointly owned by the governments of Mali, Senegal, and Mauritania in equal shares. The responsibility for operation and main-tenance has been contracted out to a private operator through a management contract. While the three governments have agreed to share the cost of construction equally, the energy generated from the Manantali power plant is sold through contracts to the three national utilities. The volume of energy for each utility is determined through negotiations and not shared in the same proportion as the construction cost. The 60 MW Felou Proj-ect, which is downstream from Manantali, is being constructed by SOGEM. Energy from Felou will be sold through contracts that have been mutually agreed upon by SOGEM and the three national utilities. There has been no formal auction process. However, the collaborative arrangement lends itself to further potential development of hydro sites in Africa, which, due to their sheer size, are only economically justifiable if the energy can be shared among multiple off-takers. Joint ownership is a way of achieving economies of scale, channeling resources, and mitigating risks among multiple potential off-takers, including state-owned companies, private utilities, and possibly large end-users.

This collaborative institutional arrangement could set an example for the harnessing of still untapped hydro resources in the Southern Africa Power Pool (SAPP). Abundant, yet undeveloped hydro resources can be found primarily in the Democratic Republic of Congo, Angola, Mozambique, and Zambia, and there is a huge demand for electricity in the region, particularly in South Africa. There is currently no mechanism that enables those countries to compete against each other in offering energy via long-term contracts (PPAs) to potential off-takers, with ESKOM in South Africa being by far the most impor-tant. Needless to say, the lack of a transmission backbone makes competition virtually impossible today. A competitive procurement mechanism could be put in place, taking into account the combined cost of generation and transmission. Multilateral institutions could play a key role in designing those procurement mechanisms and in providing financing to expand the backbone to link the most competitive sources of generation. So far, most of the support to the Southern Africa Power Market has been for the develop-ment of indigenous resources to be used by local markets—and in some cases to support bilateral agreements between contiguous countries.

Latin America also has several similar cases of untapped potential across borders, as is the case for hydro resources in eastern Peru for example. The eastern side of the Peruvian Andes presents hydro potential of more than 20,000 MW that are economically viable. Peru cannot absorb all of its power alone because of its "lumpiness" and the relatively small size of its own market (no more than 6,000 MW today). Brazil could act as a partner in these projects by absorbing all the energy not used by Peru. The techni-cal merit of this solution is that the Peruvian hydro plants have storage capacity and are located upstream from the run-of-the-river plants located in the Brazilian Amazon. This could provide immediate benefits for the Brazilian plants.

Nord Pool: The "Do-nothing" Approach—The "Market Will Deliver"

POWER SYSTEM CHARACTERISTICS. Nord Pool is one of the oldest power pool arrangements in Europe. It covers the four Nordic countries (Norway, Denmark, Sweden, and Finland), with an aggregate installed capacity of about 100 GW and energy consumption of 400 TWh/year. Figure 5.3 shows the capacity split by country and technology.

REFORM PROCESS AND MARKET STRUCTURE. The four countries that make up the Nord Pool have been restructuring their power markets for over a decade, but at different paces. Norway was the first mover in the early 1990s, while Denmark had a full market operating in 2000. Nord Pool has been touted as a benchmark for multi-country power pooling capable of operating the system in a quasi-integrated fashion. Each country manages the power system within their borders and Nord Pool remains a voluntary pool operating a day-ahead spot market as well as a forward and futures market. It attempts to capture the benefits of pooling resources by sharing reserves, improving collective preparedness to shortfalls, organizing indicative planning, and managing cross-border congestion. With a long tradition of Nordic cooperation, and with the development of the jointly owned Nord Pool power exchange, the Nordic market is now *de facto* fully integrated, at least at the wholesale level.

AUCTION MECHANISMS IN THE NORDIC MARKET: THE RELIANCE ON MARKETS. Despite being lauded for its remarkable achievements in terms of power pool integration, Nord Pool has no specific procurement mechanisms like auctions for long-term contracts to buttress the development of new generation at either country or regional levels. The underlying assumption is that, given the efficiency of the market and regulatory framework, the "market" itself will provide the correct signals for contracting and expansion. The system has been working well, since supply has met demand requirements satisfactorily, assisted by a comfortable reserve margin. The stable Nordic economy,

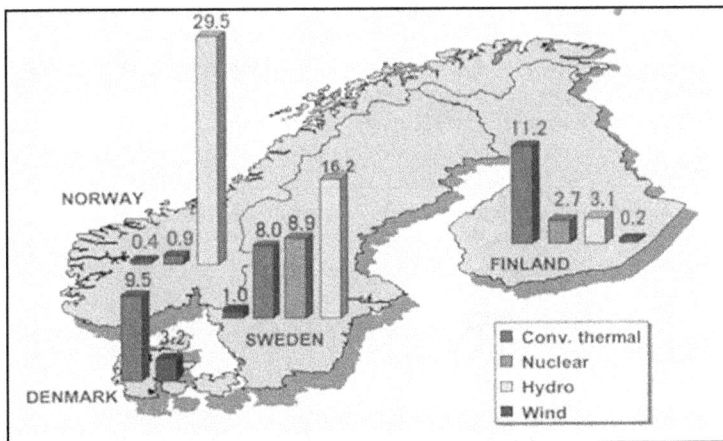

Figure 5.3. Characteristics of Nordic Countries

Source: SINTEF, Nordic Market Report, 2009

with its associated low electricity demand growth, contributes directly to the system's implementation.

A supply shock that hit the Nordic market in 2002–2003 put it severely to the test. As discussed by van der Fehr et al. (2005), as a result of an exceptionally low inflow period to hydro plants the second half of 2002, reservoir levels were at a record low at the beginning of the low-inflow/high-demand winter season of 2003. Electricity prices had risen to unprecedented levels and the (daily average) spot price peaked at 850 NOK/MWh (approximately US$125/MWh) in January 2003, or two to three times the normal level. High spot prices were fed through to consumers, who in some cases faced increases in electricity bills of 50 percent or more. There was speculation that the high prices were the result of the abuse of market power, as well as a lack of investment in both generation and transmission in earlier years, and that rationing on a massive scale would be required. As it turned out, no such drastic measures were needed, as responses from consumers and thermal power producers balanced the market.

Some saw the events of 2002–3 as a warning sign, or indeed as outright proof that the electricity market was flawed. Others considered its performance through this period evidence that the market had reached maturity, and is robust enough to withstand even rather extreme shocks. Nevertheless, the supply shock brought to the surface a number of potential weaknesses that warrant careful analysis and may eventually lead to further improvements in the regulatory framework, as well as in other market institutions. The introduction of multi-country auctions for long-term contracts has not been considered, but should not be overruled.

Notes

1. CESUR stands for "auctions for the provider of last resort".

2. After 2001, new market arrangements, called NETA, were put in place.

3. OFGEM, (2010).

4. They are: (i) need for unprecedented levels of investment to be sustained over many years under difficult financial conditions; (ii) uncertainty of future carbon prices is likely to delay or deter investment in low-carbon technology and lead to greater de-carbonization costs in the future; (iii) short-term price signals at times of system stress do not fully reflect the value that customers place on supply security; (iv) interdependence with international markets exposes the UK to a range of additional risks that may undermine security of supply; (v) high cost of gas and electricity may mean that increasing numbers of consumers are not able to afford adequate levels of energy to meet their needs and that the competitiveness of industry and business is affected.

5. This document has been subject to criticism. It is alleged that OFGEM has exceeded its regulatory role and preempted energy policy responsibilities.

6. The resource adequacy requirement is set at a level that can be expected to avoid the loss of load more than once in 10 years as a result of insufficient resources.

7. A capacity zone is an area whose locational capacity need is determined as a result of the forward capacity auction models and studies conducted by the ISO-NE.

8. The capacity of the physical resource is measured in terms of certificates of available capacity.

9. More complete information on the New Jersey auction can be found at www.bgsauction.com.

10. Negrete-Pincetic et al. (2007).

11. This design is comparable to the descending clock auction, but in the case of standard auctions (i.e., where the auctioneer is the seller).

12. Armar, (2009).

13. French acronym for Manantali Energy Management Company.

CHAPTER 6

Auctions and Renewable Energy Sources

This chapter discusses experiences in the use of auctions to support the development of renewable sources of energy. First, it describes the relevance of renewables in the generation mix of many countries. Second, it briefly explains the more traditional approaches to promoting the development of renewable generation, namely the use of feed-in-tariffs and renewable portfolio standards. Third, it describes the experience of auctions in trading renewable energy contracts. Appendix D details experiences with renewable energy development, focusing on feed-in-tariffs and renewable portfolio standards.

Overview: An Increasing Role for Renewables

Interest in renewables has been growing in light of concerns with climate change and with the environment. Together with energy efficiency, non-conventional renewables (which exclude large hydro) have been praised as the "most benign" form of energy. More recently, the unexpected and unfortunate massive oil spill in the Gulf of Mexico has exposed the US consumer to yet another dilemma—energy independence versus environmental protection. For all of these reasons, we thought it appropriate to dedicate a special chapter to the development of renewable sources of energy, particularly given our understanding that auctions can contribute to the development of those sources in a more cost-competitive and therefore sustainable way.

Some case studies and examples that reflect the use of renewable sources of energy were borrowed from previous sections of this report. They were supplemented by countries where the development of renewables has been remarkable, such as Germany, Spain, and some states in the US, such as Texas and California. This chapter aims to explore the subject further and attempts to structure the relevant issues in such a way so as to make it easier for those readers who are only interested in competitive procurement for renewable sources to find information. The discussion focuses on grid-connected renewables, but some of the basic concepts of competition might be of value to off-grid applications as well.

Renewable sources of energy include wind, solar (PV or CSP), biomass/bioelectricity, geothermal, methane (e.g. from landfills), wave and tidal power, and hydro generation. Green energy (or non-conventional renewables) represents a sub-set of this definition, and according to the EPA excludes large hydro plants due to their alleged social and environmental impact.

With the exception of large hydro, most of the other sources of renewable energy are not [yet] considered cost-competitive for supplying power to the grid. Their unit costs are above those of large-scale plants, such as thermal-based generation. Therefore, in most cases, non-conventional, grid-connected renewables are considered "out of the money" options from a purely financial standpoint. Needless to say, this situation may change if a cap-and-trade scheme is established or a carbon tax is imposed on CO_2 emissions. If the cost of CO_2 is internalized, some forms of energy that are currently on the verge of becoming competitive, such as wind, may become financially more advantageous than fossil fuel baseload generation. For the time being, it will be assumed that non-conventional renewables are not yet fully competitive.

In most cases, the development of non-conventional renewables has required some form of energy policy commitment and support. The two most common and explicit policy instruments to support the development of renewables have been feed-in-tariffs (henceforth FiT) and Renewable Portfolio Standard (RPS)—also called Renewable Obligations in the UK. FiT, in its basic format, is not considered to be a competitive mechanism, since the government sets a price for the energy to be acquired by utilities, and all bidders should be able to get a contract to sell renewable energy at that price. There may be some competition among equipment suppliers, but not among the suppliers of energy *per se*. Conversely, the Renewable Portfolio Standard sets a quota for renewables as the ultimate goal. Providers of renewable energy will compete in price to get a market share of this pre-established quota.

Feed-in-Tariffs and Other Mechanisms to Support Renewables

Renewable energy has thus far been promoted through the use of feed-in-tariffs or mandated production quotas/targets. These are alternatives to the auction approach, as described below.

Feed-in-Tariff (FiT)

In most countries, FiT (feed-in-tariffs or feed-in law) is the primary energy policy mechanism designed to encourage the emergence and development of renewable sources of energy. Under a feed-in-tariff, an obligation is imposed on regional or national electric grid utilities to buy renewable electricity from all eligible participants.

FiTs typically include three key provisions: 1) guaranteed grid access; 2) long-term contracts for the electricity produced; and 3) purchase prices, usually above market prices that are based on the specific costs of each renewable energy source.

The cost-based prices therefore enable a great diversity of projects to be developed (wind, solar, etc.), and allow investors to obtain a reasonable return on renewable energy investments.

Rates may vary between the different sources of power generation, depending on the place of installation (e.g. rooftop or ground-mounted), the size of projects, and sometimes the technology employed (solar, wind, geothermal, etc.). They are typically designed to ratchet downward over time to track technological change and overall cost reductions. This is consistent with keeping the payment levels in line with actual generation costs over time.

FiTs usually offer a guaranteed purchase for electricity generated from renewable energy sources within long-term (15–25 year) contracts that are typically offered in a non-discriminatory way to all interested renewable electricity producers.

As of 2009, feed-in-tariff policies have been enacted in 63 jurisdictions around the world, including Australia, Austria, Belgium, Brazil,[1] Canada, China, Cyprus, the Czech Republic, Denmark, Estonia, France, Germany, Greece, Hungary, Iran, Republic of Ireland, Israel, Italy, the Republic of Korea, Lithuania, Luxembourg, the Netherlands, Portugal, South Africa, Spain, Sweden, Switzerland, and Turkey, in about a dozen states in the United States, and is gaining momentum in other countries such as China, India, and Mongolia. In a few other places, such as in LAC countries and many states in the US, FiT is losing some of its momentum and is being replaced by other policy instruments leveraging on competitive procurement schemes such as auctions.

Renewable Portfolio Standard (RPS)[2]

A Renewable Portfolio Standard is a government policy whose objective is to increase the production of energy from renewable sources. Other common names for the same concept are Renewable Electricity Standard (RES) at the United States federal level, and Renewables Obligation or Renewable Energy Certificates in the UK.

The RPS mechanism generally places an obligation on electricity supply companies to produce a specified fraction of their electricity from renewable energy sources. It requires that electricity providers obtain a minimum percentage of their power from renewable energy resources by a certain date, which is made clear by renewable energy certificates. Certified renewable energy generators earn certificates for every unit of electricity they produce and can sell them along with their electricity to supply companies. Supply companies then pass on the certificates to some form of regulatory body to demonstrate their compliance with regulatory obligations. RPS relies almost entirely on the private market for its implementation.

RPS-type mechanisms have been adopted in several countries, including the UK, Italy, Belgium, and Chile, as well as in 30 out of 50 US States. Together these states account for more than half of the electricity sales in the US. Five other states, North Dakota, South Dakota, Utah, Virginia, and Vermont, have non-binding goals for the adoption of renewable energy instead of an RPS.

Regulations vary from state to state, and there is no federal policy. Table 6.1 presents the RPS goals for these states and the expected deadline for their achievement.

Table 6.1. Renewable Portfolio Goals for US States

State	Amount	Year	State	Amount	Year
Arizona	15%	2025	New Hampshire	23.80%	2025
California	33%	2030	New Jersey	22.50%	2021
Colorado	20%	2020	New Mexico	20%	2020
Connecticut	23%	2020	Nevada	20%	2015
District of Columbia	20%	2020	New York	24%	2013
Delaware	20%	2019	North Carolina	12.50%	2021
Hawaii	20%	2020	North Dakota*	10%	2015
Iowa	105 MW		Oregon	25%	2025
Illinois	25%	2025	Pennsylvania	8%	2020
Massachusetts	15%	2020	Rhode Island	16%	2019
Maryland	20%	2022	South Dakota*	10%	2015
Maine	40%	2017	Texas	5,880 MW	2015
Michigan	10%	2015	Utah*	20%	2025
Minnesota	25%	2025	Vermont*	10%	2013
Missouri	15%	2021	Virginia*	12%	2022
Montana	15%	2015	Washington	15%	2020
			Wisconsin	10%	2015

Source: US Department of Energy

Renewable Energy Auctions

Auctions do not represent a renewable energy policy *per se.* They are a mechanism that can be used to promote the development of renewable resources on a competitive basis.

Several countries have been expanding the non-conventional renewable base by using competitive procurement mechanisms. Those countries have not implemented energy policies that necessarily fit into the FiT or RPS, but have made long-term, albeit non-binding commitments to pursue a green agenda.

Auctions have been used in some nations to implement a government's stated policies to foster the development of non-conventional renewable energy (wind, small hydro plants, biomass, tidal, geothermal, and solar). Brazil, Argentina, Peru, and Uruguay are examples of some of the countries that have held auctions in Latin America[3]. Interesting examples in North America are Ontario (Canada) and California (US).

They have proven to be a viable alternative to the traditional, administratively set feed-in-tariffs used by most developed countries that have been responsible for the installation of thousands of MW of renewable energy worldwide. Actions foster competition and push prices down, thereby reducing tariffs for end-users and making the whole process more sustainable.

However, there are challenges to ensuring the effectiveness of auction mechanisms to promote any technology, including renewable. The first is the need to attract bidders in order to ensure competition. Simple auction processes with a clear set of rules help in this regard. The second and perhaps most important challenge is to ensure that auction winners will deliver the awarded projects, i.e., it is important to pre-qualify bidders to discourage speculators or financially insolvent companies from participating. Mitigation measures for this include the auctioning of projects that already have environmental permits and require an audited historical record of hydrology or wind measures from the bidders. Finally, it is important to have credible, effective enforcement and compliance mechanisms in place to ensure that projects are delivered on time and penalties are applied in the case of delays or improper behavior.

Renewable energy auctions can be bundled and auctioned in different ways, depending on the level of competition and specificity desired. Competition may be all encompassing, whereby all forms of renewables are eligible to participate in the same auction process. Alternatively, participation may be restricted to particular types of technologies or sites that take place at several levels, such as technology-neutral auctions, or renewable-specific, technology-specific, or technology and site-specific auctions, as described below.

All-Encompassing Renewable Auctions

All-encompassing (or technology-neutral) auctions entitle any generation source (and possibly demand-side bidders) to participate in the tender on a level-playing-field basis. The idea is to foster maximum competition, select the most efficient sources, and achieve a least-cost expansion plan. However, it is difficult for non-conventional renewable sources to compete head to head with baseload coal or large hydro, except under special circumstances. All-encompassing auctions are therefore seldom used. Governments prefer to establish auctions that target one or more types of technologies.

Renewable Specific Auctions

To enable an effective outcome in terms of least-cost procurement of electricity, different renewable technologies should ideally compete on a level-playing-field basis.

However, if governments have a preference for particular technologies driven by energy policy concerns, this element should be reflected in the auction design. The selection of a particular technology is often driven by energy or economic policy considerations.

Auctions cannot have the most efficient outcomes when underlying policies direct their design and implementation, and constrain the effectiveness of energy procurement at least cost. However, they can still provide the best results for a given set of technologies driven by policy decisions.

Some examples of countries that have implemented renewable specific auctions are described as follows.

PERU—AUCTIONS OF RENEWABLE SOURCES. Peru has tried twice to implement technology-specific auctions. The first time was in 2008, when the country organized an auction dedicated to hydropower, but without great success and with limited bidders. In February 2010, a similar mechanism was applied again in an auction to contract renewables under a specific law (Legislative Decree 1002). About 150 MW of wind power were competitively contracted at prices averaging US$80/MWh. Contracting of 160 MW of small hydro and 90 MW of solar plants was possible through contract durations of 20 years and delivery for three years ahead. Auction results are summarized in table 6.2.

THAILAND—IPPS PROVIDING FOR EXPANSION OF GENERATION CAPACITY. State-owned Electricity Generating Authority of Thailand (EGAT) has been carrying out several IPP programs from Independent Power Producers (IPP), Small Power Producers (SPP), and Very Small Power Producers (VSPP). EGAT is responsible for over 60 percent of the electricity generated in Thailand and also controls the entire transmission system and distribution to a few large customers.

In the case of IPPs, EGAT procured power from private power producers on a Build-Operate-Own (BOO) basis, whereby private power producers construct the facilities and become sole owners of the assets without having to transfer them to the government at the end of the contract period. The payment structure is output-based and is made under the Power Purchasing Agreements (PPAs), which are assigned to investors after a competitive tendering process following a first-price sealed-bid design. Payments resulting from these PPAs are divided into two components: (i) availability payment (intended to cover fixed costs), and (ii) energy payment (for the reimbursement of the costs of energy actually produced).

Table 6.2. Peruvian 2010 Technology-specific Auction Results

Source	Required volume of energy (GWh/year)	Contracted volume of energy (GWh/year)	Maximum price (US$/MWh)	Average contracting price (US$/MWh)
Biomass	813	143	120.00	63.35
Wind	320	571	110.00	80.35
Solar	181	173	269.00	221.10
Small hydro	500	161.71	74.00	59.90

Source: Osinergmin

The SPP program focused on smaller developments and defined requirements on the type of power plants that may be eligible. In particular, they are required to be nonconventional renewable sources such as wind, solar, small hydro, and biomass.

ONTARIO—REPLACEMENT OF AGEING GENERATION. In October 2003, Ontario's new government launched a RFP process to handle its growing demand for electricity amid delays in the refurbishment of existing nuclear plants and a phasing out of coal. The initial RFP was for 300 MW of renewable energy generation. Bidders had to meet technical and financial criteria on a pass/fail basis. Thereafter, bids would be assessed solely on a $/MWh basis. In parallel, the government prepared a separate RFP process for 2,500 MW of new generation or demand-side management.

In 2006, the Ontario Power Authority voiced its concern about future supply shortfalls. It decided to facilitate the organization of auctions for forward energy contracts to create long-term price signals in order to foster the development of new capacity. The first auction was carried out on February 28, 2006 and two types of baseload contracts were sold: five-year terms in blocks of 25 MW for a total of 325 MW, and one-year terms in 5 MW blocks for a total of 25 MW. The chosen format was a simultaneous ascending clock auction[4] in which trading companies and industrial and commercial users acted as the bidding parties. Given the positive outcome of the first auction, a second one was carried out soon after, selling similar products for a total of 550 MW. In December of the same year, a third auction was held involving both baseload and peak products in a competitive multi-seller/buyer process.

CALIFORNIA—MOVING FROM FIT TO AUCTIONS. Contrary to most regions in the world, which have relied on feed-in-tariffs to develop a strong renewable energy base, California has just introduced a "reverse auction market", specifically proposed to spur the development of in-state renewable sources. In September 2009, the California Public Utilities Commission proposed letting developers bid on contracts to install green energy projects. A solar company that offers to sell electricity to one of California's three big utilities at a lower rate than its competitors would win a particular power purchase agreement.

The system was dubbed a "reverse auction market" feed-in-tariff designed to avoid the pitfalls that have plagued efforts to encourage the development of renewable energy in Europe (by paying artificially high rates for electricity produced by solar power plants or rooftop photovoltaic projects). An auction would essentially let the market set electricity rates for photovoltaic projects that produce between one and 20 Megawatts in California, and can be built within 18 months.

"This mechanism would also allow the state to pay developers a price that is sufficient to bring projects online, but does not provide surplus profits at ratepayers' expense," reads a statement written by a utilities commission staff in its proposal. "Providing a clear and steady long-term investment signal rather than a pre-determined price can create a competitive market."

Technology-Specific Auctions

CHINA[5]. China has the largest renewable energy portfolio in the world, with an installed capacity of 42 GW as of 2005, comprised mostly of small hydroelectric plants. That year, the Chinese government announced an ambitious target to achieve 16 percent of energy consumption from renewable energy by 2020.

Until the enactment of the Renewable Energy Promotion Law in 2006, China had, among other things, adopted an auction system for wind generation—the so-called "concession" modality. The government introduced competitive bidding for wind farm development in 2003 to steadily ramp up new wind power capacity at the lowest possible costs. After years of high wind electricity tariffs, the government hoped that such a concession approach would drive down and reveal the cost of wind farms in China. Under the Wind Power Concession program, the National Development and Reform Commission invited international and domestic investors to develop 100 MW wind farms on a potential wind site. Winning bidders are granted approval to develop the selected project site, a PPA for the first 30,000 hours of the project operation, guaranteed grid interconnection, financial support for grid extension and access roads, and preferential tax and loan conditions by the central government. The central government's backing creates a comparatively lower-risk investment environment for wind farm developers in China.

The first round of bidding took place in October 2003, with two projects awarded 200 MW. While the winning bid prices were significantly lower than any previous wind farm price in China, they were below the long-run marginal costs. The selected developers had difficulty obtaining financing, and project construction was delayed. The subsequent round of bidding from 2004 to 2006 awarded an additional 2,000 MW of capacity. The winning bid price for the wind concession projects to date ranged from 4.6 to 6.2 US cent/ kWh, while the current average cost of wind power in China is estimated to be between 6.3 and 8 US cents/kWh.

The concession was of major concern to the wind industry in China because the bidding process resulted in prices that are too low to be financially viable. As a result, there are reduced incentives for developers to invest in this nascent industry. In addition, the number of companies attempting to bid for the concession projects actually fell from the first to the second round of concessions, contrary to expectations that the number of participants would grow with the program's increased visibility and the "success" of the first two concessions. Furthermore, better wind resource measurement is needed to decide on the selection of concession sites and bid prices.

The competitive process had the benefit of helping the government define a benchmark for the cost of wind power development in China. While feed-in laws have produced the highest renewable market penetration rates in the world and are relatively easy to administer, it is tricky to set up the feed-in-tariff level at the beginning, particularly when there are no reliable "real-world" cost benchmark data available on large-scale commercial wind farms or biomass power plants operating in the country.

Even with the promulgation of the 2006 Renewable Law, several wind power pricing policies still co-exist in China, which will be briefly described below. Some of them are typical auction processes, while others resemble feed-in-tariffs.[6]

- Tariffs determined by concession program at the central level. This is a competitive auction. The PPA has two terms. During the first term, the tariff resulting from the auction prevails, while in the second term (after 30,000 full-load hours) the average market grid price will be the basis for payment to the IPP.
- Bidding at local level and approved by central government. Also an auction process carried out locally and reported to central government for approval.

- Local government-approved tariffs. A project is submitted to the local authorities who agree on a tariff (on a cost-plus basis). The project is then submitted to NDRC to be included in the national surcharge level scheme.
- Fixed tariff at local level. Some provinces offer a kind of feed-in-tariff for new projects that are not part of the national concession program.
- Upper limit of tariff defined by central government. Some provinces have been taking advantage of the price convergence in a number of regions resulting from competitive processes and have set this as a tariff cap for new projects.

This combination of pricing policies in China has prompted the development of a remarkable wind capacity, but has also lead to some confusion. Moreover, it seems that inconsistencies in these policies are not beneficial to potential developers, particularly when they have to deal with bureaucracy at different levels of government. Most of the projects have been developed by state-owned companies. More regulatory clarity could be beneficial to further develop wind resources in China on a competitive basis.

BRAZIL—MOVING FROM FiT TO AUCTIONS. The first formal government support for a renewable energy program took place in 2002 with the creation of Proinfa, or the "Incentive Program for Alternative Energy." The objective was to scale up non-conventional renewable sources focusing on small hydro, wind, and biomass generation.[7]

Proinfa was not a competitive procurement process *per se*. When it was first launched, the auction mechanisms for power contracts had not yet been established. However, the program emerged to provide an allocation mechanism, similar to a beauty contest, to help the government implement its policy on renewables.

Its first phase established a differentiated feed-in-tariff to contract 3,300 MW of wind, biomass, and small hydro on an equal basis. The energy produced by participating plants was to be purchased by Eletrobras, acting in an ad hoc capacity for the system as a single buyer. Eletrobras then re-sold the energy to all electricity distribution companies in proportion to their actual market share. This tranche of renewable energy was added to other contract positions and worked as a credit for energy settlement purposes in the wholesale market.

The average price paid to each technology (2010) is shown in table 6.3 (actual prices depend on reference load factors).[8]

With the implementation of the market-based approach for wind auctions in 2009, the Proinfa feed-in-tariff scheme will no longer be utilized. Post-Proinfa, the government decided to use auctions to push the cost of renewables down and FiT is no longer utilized in Brazil. From an energy policy point of view, comparable sources should compete in order to achieve the ad hoc quotas for non-conventional renewables, which are to be set by the GoB from time to time. The decision was to hold separate auctions differentiated by technology source. So far, auctions for biomass (e.g. sugarcane co-generation) and wind energy have been carried out.

The main advantage of conducting auctions differentiated by technology (e.g. renewables) is the possibility of explicitly introducing energy policy concerns, such as the greening of the energy matrix, promoting regional economic development, or developing some forms of generation technology. Another advantage is that, given the similar features of a given technology, bids can

Table 6.3. The Proinfa Feed-in-tariff in Brazil

Technology	Price (US$/MWh)
Wind	154
Bioelectricity	77
Small Hydro	96

Source: ANEEL, 2010 figures

be compared on an "apples-to-apples" basis. On the other hand, its main disadvantages include the criteria from which the quotas for different technologies should be selected, and the fragmentation of the procurement process, which could possibly lead to the reduction of competition and increased costs for end-users.

To a great extent, technology-specific auctions are carried out in a similar fashion as a typical energy auction in order to meet the energy needs of distribution companies. However, there is a subtle, but important difference. In the case of renewables, the government has the prerogative to call an auction to contract a given volume of energy, even if it is not contemplated in the demand forecasts prepared by the distribution companies. These auctions, which are called "reserve energy auctions", are organized in such a way that they increase the reserve margin, and/or foster the development of particular sources of energy, such as renewables. They are fully specified by the government, including the definition of the technology (or project) and the portion of the demand to be contracted.

There is no requirement for a Firm Energy Certificate in a reserve energy auction model, and the product delivered is basically a 15-year energy contract (20 years for wind) that fixes a feed-in-tariff (which is auctioned). The total cost of the energy contracted is paid by *all* consumers (regulated and free) through a fixed charge (uplift). All energy produced by the plants is sold at the spot market on a merchant basis, and the revenue is used to offset the fixed payment by consumers. It is as if the consumers became investors of merchant plants (paying fixed amounts to remunerate for fixed costs, and collecting the resulting spot revenues). The Market Operator (CCEE) centralizes payments and clearings. The general process for these auctions follows the other typical guidelines set forth for regular auctions (e.g. prior environmental licenses required, hybrid auction mechanism, etc.).

The first technology-specific reserve auction for the regulated market was carried out in 2007 and only renewable energy could participate. With limited participation, results were disappointing. The main reason alleged was that prospective developers preferred to sell the energy to large end-users—that is, those customers willing to pay a higher price for the energy due to the fact that they were eligible for discounts on the use of the transmission and distribution system. This non-economic subsidy favored direct trading between the renewable source and the large, non-franchised user.

Apart from this initial setback, the "reserve energy" auction model has been considered successful. The fact that generators do not have to provide a "firm energy" requirement mitigates several risks, making those auctions very attractive for generators, which are basically selling their production for a fixed price. Many of the risks associated with wind energy are "pooled" and "socialized."

A short description of the recent biomass and energy reserve auctions is provided in the following section.[9]

BRAZIL—BIOMASS RESERVE ENERGY AUCTIONS. Sugarcane cogeneration occurs only during the harvest period, which coincides with the dry season in the Southeast of Brazil, where most consumption is concentrated. There is a natural *production synergy* between hydroelectric and bioelectricity generation. In economic terms, this means that energy produced by biomass power plants is more "valuable" because wholesale market spot prices are higher during that period than the annual average. The same counter-seasonal production behavior is observed for wind plants, whose production pattern is complementary to hydro storage levels in some parts of the country. Figure 6.1 illustrates this attribute by showing the historical hydro storage and a typical production

Figure 6.1. Historical Hydro Storage and Typical Wind and Bioelectricity Production in Brazil

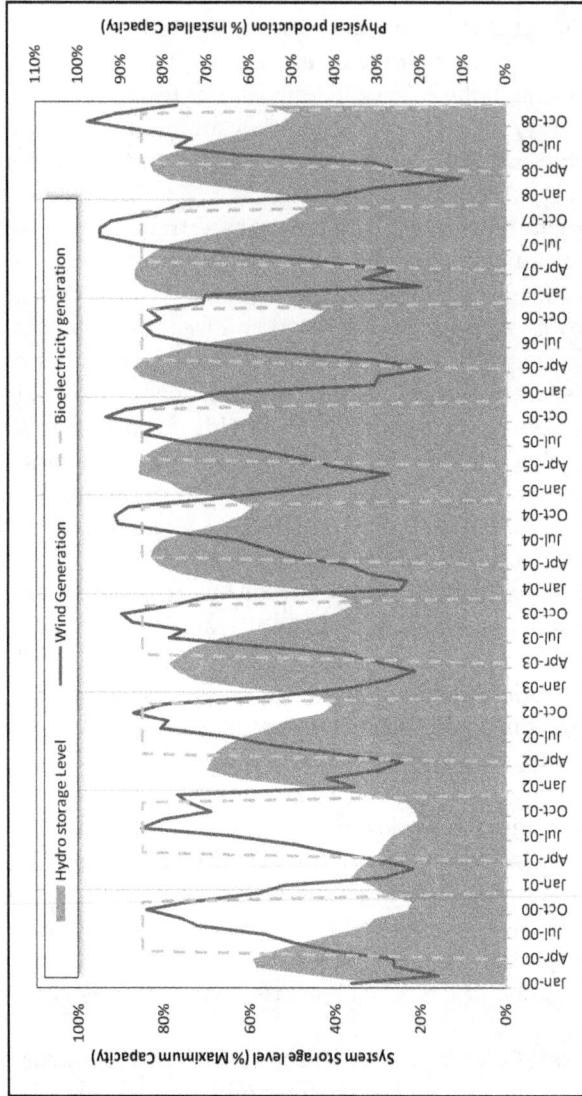

of a wind and a biomass plant. This counter-cyclical characteristic represents a significant competitive advantage to renewable sources. The benefits of portfolio diversity partially offset the higher unit costs of those technologies.

The first technology-specific "reserve energy" auction was carried out in August 2008 to contract new energy from the cogeneration of sugarcane bagasse ("bioelectricity") for delivery in 2011 and 2012. The motivation for this decision was the ethanol "boom" observed in 2006–2007 in Brazil, which fostered an expansion of sugarcane production and the installation of hundreds of new ethanol mills scheduled to start operations between 2009 and 2012. A special 'reserve' auction was carried out to contract new energy from these plants in order to use the expansion of ethanol production for the benefit of the power sector. The product design was a 15-year reserve energy contract with a flat amount corresponding to the yearly average of the plants' seasonal production profile (full production is available during the harvest only). Some 2,400 MW (gross capacity) of new bioelectricity plants will be built during 2011 and 2012 as a result of the auction.

About 60 percent of the gross capacity was sold at the auction (1,500 of capacity or 4,800 GWh/year) for an average price of US$80/MWh. The net energy cost for the consumer—which depends on the expected revenues in the spot market of these plants that will be assigned to consumers—might reach US$50/MWh if the yearly energy spot price of about US$30/MWh is observed during the contract term. Some 2,700 GWh/year are still available to be sold in future auctions or directly to free consumers.

Participation of biomass (and also mini-hydro schemes) has been very intense among non-franchised customers for the very same reason presented earlier, that large customers benefit from significant discounts on transmission and distribution use of system tariffs if they purchase energy through contracts that are backed up by non-conventional renewable energy up to 30 MW. The resolution also extends this mechanism to regulated consumers with loads greater than 500 kW (e.g., a supermarket or shopping center). Although they are not formally "free consumers," they can purchase energy directly from RE producers and are given discounts on wire tariffs if they do so. Because the wire tariffs paid by this special class of consumers are high, the benefit in contracting with a renewable producer can be substantial. These consumers may therefore offer attractive energy prices to RE. Some allege that this constitutes a non-economic incentive, reflecting distortions in the tariff structure across customer groups.

There have been cases where renewable developers preferred not to participate in formal energy auctions to sell to the captive market. Instead, they established bilateral contracts with qualified energy users. Regulations also allow renewable energy to be traded via marketers. This stimulates not only the establishment of contracts under this mechanism, but also the trading activity itself in the free market, given that a large number of trading companies will have access to these special consumers. Brazil currently has about 50 trading companies, but this number is increasing rapidly. Those marketers have played an important role in making the market more liquid and efficient, and in tailoring products that better meet the customers' needs.

BRAZIL—WIND ENERGY AUCTIONS. An important reverse auction to contract wind power for delivery in 2012 was carried out in December 2009. The motivation was to take advantage of the 2008–2009 world financial crisis that had lowered equipment costs, and to scale up the development of this technology in the country. The product offered to potential investors—a 20-year energy contract with delivery starting in 2012—has a very specific accounting mechanism designed to provide them with a fixed payment while managing the quantity-price risk and incentivizing/penalizing production above/below a given firm energy threshold. Basically, investors offer a certain MWh/year volume and consumers pay a fixed value for this production ex-ante. Monitoring helps to evaluate if this "reference value" is being achieved, and there are penalties/incentives for over and underproduction.[10]

The main challenge for developers of wind generation is to determine a firm energy certificate. A firm energy certificate (FEC) for non-dispatchable generation sources is defined as the maximum volume of energy that this source can commit to producing over the course of a year. These values are declared by the developer and become a binding commitment. The challenge for the developer is the fact that the actual energy production will be measured and compared to the FEC, which is not a typical procedure with other sources such as large hydro plants. In addition to the market settlement risk, the investor is subject to regulatory penalties if the verified energy production is lower than the declared values. Hence, this is a serious risk that cannot be easily mitigated, since portfolio bidding is not allowed in this kind of auction.

About 11,000 MW of wind projects signed up as sellers in the auction, most of them located in the northeast region, which has already exploited most of its hydro potential. Like in all other energy auctions carried out in Brazil, generators are the sellers and consumers are the buyers. During the auction, the consumers do not bid and are represented by a price cap, which means that only sellers make offers. The initial auction price was US$105/MWh and the uniform pricing phase finished at US$86/MWh after nine hours of bidding during 75 rounds, where some 1,800 MW of capacity was traded. After the final sealed envelope pay-as-bid round, the prices of the winning bidders ranged from US$85 to US$72/MWh. The final average price was US$82/MWh, a 22 percent discount compared to the initial price. The lowest price (US$72/MWh) was offered by Eletrosul, a state-owned generation company, to sell energy from three wind farms in the southern region. The auction results were a surprise, with prices lower than estimated by most, if not all, sector analysts. A diverse mix of investors (local and foreign private generators, manufacturers, and government-owned companies) won the contracts, and three new wind turbine factories are to be installed in the country.

Table 6.4 shows the winning bidders for the wind power auction and their corresponding capacity and energy contracted ranked in ascending order of price per MWh.

Some concerns have been expressed regarding the winning bidders' ability to bring these projects to fruition, in light of the low prices offered and apparent cut-throat competition. This remains to be seen, although the low prices may be masked by some indirect benefits and incentives offered to bidders. Some of the incentives include tax credits, which are available for several generation sources (including renewable), and are very attractive for increasing the competitiveness of a given technology, as well as a 75 percent income tax reduction during the project's first 10 years if it is installed in certain parts of the country. Further special financial conditions are offered by the Brazilian Bank of Development, including loans in domestic currency up to 80 percent of project investment, low spreads, and amortization periods of about 14 years.

Another renewable energy auction was carried out in Brazil in August 2010, resulting in an additional capacity of 2,900 MW. This includes 70 wind farms, 12 sugarcane

Table 6.4. Results of the 2009 Wind Energy Auction in Brazil

Developer	Installed Capacity (MW)	Energy contracted (average MW)	Price (US$/MWh)
Eletrosul	90	33	70.81
Desenvix	90	34	75.67
Focus	122	55	78.62
Renova	270	127	78.82
Elecnor Energin	96	35	80.58
Ineravante	42	19	81.06
Petrobras	101	49	81.08
CPFL	180	76	81.08
Impsa	211	83	81.62
Dobreve	144	66	81.64
Gestamp	48	16	82.25
Martifer	218	80	82.32
Coomex	30	10	82.43
Bioenergy	162	70	82.46
TOTAL	1,804	753	80.21

Source: Author's representation

cogeneration plants, and seven small hydro plants. Wind energy totaled 2,050 MW at an average rate of US$75/MWh. Biomass came in second with 713 MW of capacity at an average rate of US$82/MWh, and small hydro reached 132 MW at an average rate of US$81/MWh.

Site and Technology-specific Auctions

Sometimes governments want to develop technology-specific projects in particular locations. This is the case, for example, for the construction of very large hydro plants or wind farms in pre-determined sites that are considered to be of strategic importance to the country. For a number of reasons related to the sheer size, location, nature of risks, and complexity, it may be difficult for those projects to participate in all-inclusive auctions, competing head to head with other technologies. Under those circumstances, the government may carry out site- and technology-specific auctions. Examples include the development of wind farms in Egypt and large hydro plants in the Amazon region in Brazil.

Egypt[11]

Egypt is preparing the bid documents to launch the second round of bidding among firms that have been shortlisted to build its first private wind farm. In the first round, in November 2009, Egypt shortlisted firms for a 250-megawatt project consisting of a single wind farm whose location was previously selected by the government. The bidding process follows the World Bank procurement rules.[12] A second phase to be announced will be for 1,000 MW and will most likely include four farms.

In an attempt to diversify its energy sources, Egypt aims to generate 12 percent of its power from wind by 2020. The success of this bidding process is a key element for achieving a target to boost Egypt's wind capacity to 7,200 megawatts from the current 520 megawatts over the next 10 years.

The wind farm will be constructed on a Build-Operate-Own (BOO) basis, and is expected to start up in 2014. The private project developer will design, finance, construct, own, and operate the power plant for 20 to 25 years and will sell the power produced during that period to the Egyptian Electricity Transmission Company.

Brazil

Technology- and project-specific auctions can be carried out within the framework of the regular new energy auctions described earlier in this document. In this case, the selected projects or technologies do not compete with other potential technologies. Project-specific auctions to supply the regulated market have been carried out to develop large hydro plants in the Amazon region. Three hydro plants—Santo Antonio (3,150 MW), Jirau (3,300 MW), and Belo Monte (11,233 MW)—were auctioned in specific procurement processes carried out in 2007, 2008, and 2010, respectively.[13] Special conditions were created to tender these projects, including special financing conditions, granting of 30-year energy contracts, incentives for the formation of multiple consortia, tax incentives, etc.

More effort should be made to ascertain that the auction attracts a sufficient number of bidders to stimulate competition. Without this, the purpose of having an auction will be defeated. In the best case scenario, if there are interested bidders, the price resulting from the auction will be the reserve price set by the government. This would be tantamount to an FiT, which is not explicitly a government objective when preparing a competitive process via auctions. Box 6.1 illustrates a series of issues and challenges that had to be observed and managed by the government to guarantee some competition (albeit modest) for the granting of hydro concessions in the Madeira River. The clear trade-off in this case was to attract one more bidder with the expectation of pushing prices down, or to reduce the reserve price as a "fail-safe" procedure in case only one bidder were to participate in the tender.

Issues Regarding the Selection of Technologies and Site-specific Auctions

To enable maximum competition, in principle all technologies should be allowed to compete on a level-playing-field basis. As a corollary, there should not be technology-specific auctions. The underlying assumption for all-encompassing auctions is that the market would be able to price energy correctly in time and space. However, there are some energy policy objectives and other practical issues that need to be considered by policymakers who decide to steer the energy mix in a certain direction—that is, by selecting the type and relative participation of different technologies in the generation portfolio that will be allowed to participate in energy auctions.

It is sometimes difficult to open participation of all conventional sources in an energy auction, as is the case, for example, for very large hydro generation plants prioritized by governments due to their strategic role in a specific country. The capital expenditure of these projects is significant, which requires very special arrangements for financing and guarantees, and demands the formation of specific consortia to carry out project development. Environmental and construction risks may be high, requiring a careful and expensive due diligence when compared to smaller plants. These reasons have prompted the development of project-specific auctions. The objec-

Box 6.1. Reduce Reserve Price or Attract One More Bidder?[14]

The first large green field project auctioned in Brazil was the Santo Antonio hydro plant, with about 3.15 GW of installed capacity. It is located on the Madeira River, close to the Bolivian border. The macro-location includes two hydro sites, Jirau and Santo Antonio, with about the same installed capacity and about 100 km apart. The product of the auction included the right to dam the river and use the water to produce electricity, in line with a pre-approved technical design for which a preliminary environmental and social license had been granted. The "product" of the auction also included the obligation to sell most of the energy produced to the grid by establishing long-term energy-related contracts (PPAs) with the distribution companies who decided to procure energy from the plant. Only part of the energy produced (about 30 percent) could be sold to the non-franchised market on a freely negotiated basis. The combined product of the auction was awarded to the bidder offering the lowest price for the energy to be sold to the captive market.

The project itself presented many challenges. It was located in the Amazon region, far from major consumer centers. To minimize the area flooded and the ensuing environmental and social problems, the project entailed a low dam, and the adoption of bulb technology well suited to operate under those conditions. Given the small size of the turbines (about 75 MW), it was necessary to install many of them in a large stretch of the river. However, in absolute terms, those bulb turbines were among the largest ones ever produced. Silting and sedimentation issues had to be studied in great detail.

Non-technical issues were equally challenging. Even before the site was put up for bid, a consortium had already been established to participate in the auction. It included a large construction company, a state-owned generator, and potential large users. This consortium was in a very privileged position, as it had been carrying out inventory and pre-feasibility investigations for quite some time. Furthermore, it had negotiated exclusive supply agreements with three of the largest turbine manufacturers worldwide.

The subject was beyond the scope of ANEEL, the regulatory agency, which, however, decided to build a strong case that would involve CADE, the anti-trust agency.

The government's challenge was to mitigate some of the barriers to entry for new players as much as possible. At the outset, it was not clear how successful this attempt would be. It was difficult to overcome the asymmetry of information, since the consortium was more informed about the site than the GoB *per se,* let alone any other potential bidder. Given the relatively small manufacturing capacity worldwide to produce the specified turbines, it was necessary to challenge the exclusivity agreement between the consortium and turbine manufacturers.

The subject was again beyond the scope of ANEEL, but the institutions involved in the auction process decided to build a strong case to involve CADE, the competition authority, which normally seeks to detect anti-competitive behaviors and propose mitigation actions and penalties. However, this case required a preventive approach. It was understood that Santo Antonio should not set a bad precedent for many other good hydro sites in the pipeline that have yet to be auctioned. The competitive development of the remaining hydro potential was at stake, not only the success of this particular hydro plant.

After lengthy negotiations involving CADE, ANEEL, and the consortium, the GoB ruled that the exclusivity agreements needed to be revisited, as they would represent a major deterrent to an effective competitive process. In parallel, the GoB established a series of conditions to further reduce barriers to entry, thereby maximizing the number of players and competition. Five consortia expressed an interest in participating and four made binding bids.

(continued)

Box 6.1. Reduce Reserve Price or Attract One More Bidder?[14] (Continued)

Results were very encouraging, proving that one more bidder is better than controlling via reserve prices. The winning bidder price was R$ 78.9/MWh, significantly lower than the R$130/MWh original estimate prepared by the consortium that had carried out the initial pre-feasibility studies. Despite its success, the approach taken by the GoB may not necessarily be the best for every situation. In this particular case, there were indeed other potential bidders interested in the site and competition could be unveiled. However, other World Bank client countries may not be so amenable to this kind of competition. The second-best approach to challenge a well-entrenched bidder is to open the site for competition, with the caveat that this may not be enough. It would be necessary to set a reserve price that corresponds to the best available cost estimate for the site in question, including a prudent return on capital. In the case of Santo Antonio, the Brazilian Government calculated that a reasonable price would be approximately R$113/MWh to R$122/MWh. The latter was set as the reserve price.

Had competition been very limited, with only one bidder, this would likely have been the final price for the energy. A thorough technical analysis of the site prepared by the GoB, setting reserve prices at the above level, would have enabled savings of R$9 to R$17/MWh (vis-à-vis the information provided by the "best informed bidder"). However, the real benefit was achieved by fostering competition among multiple bidders, which made prices drop to R$70/MWh. This confirms a well-known principle in auction design—it is always preferable to add an additional competitor than to play with the reserve price to achieve the best outcome. It is worth mentioning that this is a case where all the institutions involved acted according to good practices of regulatory governance. This is the most important lesson, which shows the additional benefits of true competition.

tive in this case is to create conditions to maximize competition among a set of bidders for a given project.

Energy policy decisions are multi-faceted and should take into account cost, diversification, environmental objectives, and security concerns. This has gained importance more recently in light of the interest in promoting renewable technologies and cleaning up the energy mix. Promoting non-conventional technologies that are not yet economical to compete with traditional sources of energy requires specific government energy policy interventions.

As already discussed, an auction is a selection process whose award is solely based on a financial offer. If non-price objectives are legitimate and need to be considered, then the government has two alternatives: (i) first, forego the use of auctions for those out-of-the-money technologies, which are nonetheless strategically important for the power sector or the country; (ii) second, carry out auctions but with restrictions on participation—that is, by pre-selecting a range of possible technologies that meet the non-price objectives and restricting participation in the auction to only those technologies. After all, auctions can still be an efficient allocation mechanism, even when applied to a more limited portfolio of technologies.

Policy decisions will drive the mix of technologies that participate in energy auctions. Some examples of dedicated auctions and the rationale for their adoption are presented in table 6.5.

Energy policy should drive auction design, not vice-versa. Auctions cannot have the most efficient outcomes when underlying policies drive their design and implementation and constrain the effectiveness of the procurement of energy at least cost. They cannot ensure that energy will be procured at least cost if cost minimization is not the

Table 6.5. Rationale for Technology (and Site) Specific Auctions

Objective	Portfolio to be Auctioned	Rationale
Enhance the participation of non-conventional renewables to diversify the energy matrix.	Limit participation to available renewable sources in the region—e.g. wind, mini-hydro, others.	Most of those technologies are still out of the money and would not be able to compete with large baseload generation such as coal or large hydro (on pure financial terms).
Meet peak and baseload requirements in the most economic way.	Separate auctions for peaking and baseload units (e.g. diesel plants and hydro generation designed to provide firm energy).	It may be difficult to compare capacity and energy contracts in a common denominator such as $/MWh. It requires assumptions on supply-demand balance, hydrology, cost of fuel, and dispatch decisions.
Achieve seasonal diversification.	Separate auctions for sources that have different seasonal generation profiles, such as wind, biomass, hydro.	It may be difficult to compare the value of energy to be produced in different seasons.
De-carbonize the energy mix.	Restrict participation of fossil fuels.	Compliance with country or multi-country agreements to reduce GHG emissions (e.g. EU 20/20/20).
Take advantage of manufacturing industry booms and busts.	Single out some particular sources of energy to be auctioned (e.g. wind, solar).	In situations of excessive manufacturing capacity, bidders will try to squeeze margins from suppliers and transfer the savings to final users.
Develop nascent local manufacturing industry.	Exclude some technologies from the auction process (e.g. wind in China).	Adopt less competitive selection mechanisms such as FiT to transfer resources from customers to local manufacturers.
Increase system reliability during critical hydrological periods.	Restrict participation of wind energy in capacity auctions.	Government understanding that wind capacity is intermittent and cannot be called upon reliably.[15]
Site-specific auctions.	Only sources within the specified site are allowed to compete.	Objective of serving markets in transmission-constrained areas or off-grid developments.
Site-specific and technology-specific auctions.	Only selected technologies are allowed to participate in the auction, for that particular site.	Development of earmarked hydro projects in a particular site or joint development of coal mining and generation for a specific mine. Those projects are often considered a national or regional priority.

Source: Author's analysis

ultimate goal. However, an efficient outcome is still possible if a more limited portfolio of generation options is selected by the government.

If governments have a preference for particular technologies due to energy policy concerns, this element should be made explicit and transparently reflected in the auction design. There is a trade-off between those policy elements and allocative efficiency. Examples include the introduction of "out of the money" renewable energy contracts, environmental constraints, or de-carbonization of the power sector.

Notes

1. Recently switched to technology-specific auction mechanisms.
2. Based on Texas Energy Conservation Office—http://www.seco.cpa.state.tx.us/re_rps-portfolio. htm.
3. See Batlle, C., Barroso, L. A., (2011) for details.
4. This design is equivalent to the descending clock auction, but for the case of standard auctions (i.e., where the auctioneer is the seller).

5. This section was adapted from Wang (2010).

6. Based on the *Study on Pricing Mechanism for Renewable Energy.* Center for Renewable Energy Development. July 2009, China Renewable Energy Scale-up Program.

7. Sugarcane, rice crust, wood chips, landfill gas.

8. There has been no real increase in these values over the years; they have been basically adjusted according to inflation.

9. The World Bank, EWTEN (2010).

10. See Porrua et al. (2010) for details on the contract scheme.

11. Adapted from an interview with Mohab Hallouda, Senior Energy Specialist at the World Bank for Reuters Africa.

12. Therefore likely to be a FPSB following a pre-qualification stage.

13. These figures refer to the plants' installed capacity which, as already mentioned, is different from the plants' firm energy certificates.

14. Adapted from: Saraiva, J. Auctioning Hydro Concessions in Brazil. Presentation to the World Bank. Washington DC, June 2010.

15. Vergara (2010) challenges the government's assumption and proposes a determination of firm energy based on a stochastic assessment.

CHAPTER 7

Main Lessons

A number of lessons can be learned from the experiences with auctions, which can be organized according to the following themes:

1. Auction-related Procurement and Energy Policy Aspects
2. Market Context
3. Pre-conditions for a Successful Auction
4. General Auction Design Issues
5. Technology Choice and Renewables
6. Implementation Issues and Participants

Auction-related Procurement and Energy Policy Aspects

Auctions represent a competitive and efficient form of procuring electricity. They are far superior to single sourcing, "beauty-contests," or bilateral negotiations, which are not necessarily efficient and are more likely to be challenged when the political winds change.[1] Non-competitive procurement methods seldom provide a clear signal of the real cost of energy and are more vulnerable to corruption.

Auctions have established a credible market mechanism for the allocation of energy contracts, and in turn play a major role in attracting new generation capacity and helping to retain existing ones. Auctions have avoided some of the pitfalls and abuses related to single sourcing or direct negotiation between the contracting parties, which reduces the burden on the regulatory oversight process. Prices resulting from auctions have provided an elegant solution to the long-lasting regulatory challenge of defining what "prudent" costs of generation should be passed on to end-use customers.

An auction is not an end in itself, and should not be recommended or applied blindly. Auctions do not operate in a vacuum; rather they must be an integral part of a country's overall energy and procurement policies of reforming the power sector, introducing the participation of private generators, harnessing some endogenous sources of energy, and creating competitive pressure to push prices down to benefit the end-user. Governments have to make policy decisions before auctions are designed, such as assessing prerequisites for the implementation of a procurement policy, selecting the procurement mechanism, defining the type of product(s) that will be procured, and agreeing on the degree of centralization in the procurement process.

The incorporation of energy policy directives into procurement processes must be carried out in a clear and transparent way. The use of technology- or renewable-specific auctions, for example, must be thoroughly discussed in terms of their pros and cons—reduction in GHG emissions and possibly higher energy prices, to name a few—so that a consistent and long-lasting sustainable policy may be pursued. For example, Brazil has been successfully conducting specific auctions to contract renewable generation over the last few years.

However, the country does not have a specific renewable law that identifies targets to be met and these auctions are carried out at the government's sole discretion.

Market Context

Auctions of existing capacity foster competition "in the market," while **auctions for new capacity foster competition "for the market"** and the ensuing development of new power plants. When auctioning contracts to attract new capacity and retain existing resources, a key decision faced by policy makers is whether to hold separate auctions for each type of capacity or to carry out just a single auction.

An effective auction depends on competition. Competition or the lack thereof (e.g. market power, collusion) are usually structural issues, which depend, *inter alia*, on the number and nature of players, market concentration, types of products being offered, and specific regulations.

Developed power markets with a large number of buyers and sellers in sound financial standing are generally more conducive to competition. Those markets enable the trading of a great variety of energy-related products using more sophisticated electricity auctions. In addition to electricity contracts *per se* (capacity and/or energy), those markets trade a wider variety of products, including day-ahead bidding for dispatch, physical and financial transmission rights, virtual generation, and ancillary services, just to name a few.

Even in places where competition is modest and markets are small, countries can still benefit from the use of competitive auction mechanisms. Less sophisticated, vertically integrated power sectors in low or middle income countries may also benefit from a fresh look at the competitive procurement options at their disposal. One example is the granting of concessions to build and operate hydropower plants. Developing countries considering the participation of private capital in generation have been struggling with how to capture the economic rent of hydro sites to the benefit of the entire society. Many have postponed the development and monetization of those resources in the absence of good mechanisms or public funds to develop hydro plants, while others have considered the establishment of royalties, which are basically administratively set figures that are more subject to corruption and less efficient in terms of outcome. A solution to this issue can be the use of auctions for granting concessions to use the water resources, power generation included.

Auctions cannot materially change the structural conditions of the marketplace. However, some tailored auction design features can help mitigate some market imperfections. For example, governments may deal with potentially collusive behaviors or market power by specifying a reserve price that should be high enough to attract a bidder's interest and at the same time reflect particular costs for the power plant being auctioned, including a "prudent" rate of return on assets. However, there are limits to the effectiveness of reserve prices. Setting reserve prices for energy auctions is a difficult task, given the uncertainties involved. If a price is set too low, no bids will be received. If prices are set too high, the bidder will be capturing some extra rent, to the detriment of the consumer.

It is widely accepted that attracting one more player is always more effective than fine tuning reserve prices to increase competition.[2] Many auction practitioners therefore argue that governments should help create a competitive auction by facilitating the entry of as many bidders as possible. This requires good communication about the auction, elimination of barriers to entry, a clear definition of the product being auctioned, and a good monitoring system to detect abnormal bidding behaviors.

An auction should be designed in such a way that it does not discriminate against small-scale private investors by favoring large state-owned companies. A point of constant concern is the (mis)behavior of state-owned companies in the bidding process. Their economic rationale and political motivations are not always easy to understand and predict. This is further aggravated by the fact that the auctioneer is, in some cases, the sole owner of these companies, which has been a concern worldwide ever since auctions started being implemented. In Brazil and Colombia, for example, several auction mechanisms were thought to mitigate the possible use of market power by large, affiliated generation companies. Investors are primarily worried about the low rates of return (hurdle rates) expected by the public sector—sometimes alluded to as "patriotic" returns—that the government might impose on their SOEs.

Sometimes regulations may lead bidders to anti-competitive behavior. This was the case in Peru, where regulations determined that in the event of demand not being fully covered, the procurement process would be declared partially or totally cancelled and a new call for bids should be made to contract the shortfall. In this new call for bids, the auction price cap changes and the cap of the previous auction is disclosed. Having a new call for bids and disclosing the maximum price might create perverse incentives from the bidders' side, motivating strategic behavior to postpone bidding and jack up prices.

An efficient, albeit underutilized way of mitigating the generators' market power is to introduce demand response as an integral part of the auction process. Little activity has been seen in terms of the participation of demand resources in the auction design process competing with supply resources on a level playing field—and in developing countries, virtually none. Latin American auctions, for example, are one-sided, with multiple buyers and sellers, where just generators are active in the mechanism. The only exception is observed in Colombia, whose auctions use an elastic demand curve as a proxy to represent the consumer's willingness to pay. This price elasticity follows the experience of the US capacity auctions in ISO-NE and PJM. Appendix F presents four basic approaches to deal with demand-side participation in energy auctions. The two-sided auction is the most effective, whereby both demand and supply resources are allowed to participate in the same auction on a level-playing-field basis, but it is seldom used in the power sector.

Foundations for a Successful Auction

Robustness of the Institutions and Regulatory Framework

Designing and implementing any type of formal auction system requires a candid assessment of the robustness of the institutions and the regulatory framework in each country or state. Independent regulators are of great importance due to the need for regulatory oversight. However, some prior conditions need to be in place—such as rule of law and, in particular, enforcement of contracts. In restructured power sectors, contracts are a proxy for vertical integration. Experience has shown that even in countries where the legal framework is solid, the enforcement of PPAs resulting from auctions depends on the existence of cost-reflective tariffs and commercial discipline. Where cost-reflective tariffs are not the practice, or non-payment is perceived as high risk, auctions for new generation tend to fail or require government support (thus increasing government-contingent liabilities).

Regulatory Stability

Regulatory stability is a key element to attract investors to participate in competitive auctions. One of the greatest worries of current and potential investors with regard to auctions is related to regulatory stability and the fact that in some cases the auction rules are constantly changing—sometimes even during the bidding process itself. Occasional changes to improve the auction process are common and welcome. However, frequent and expected changes are a cause for concern. Although some of the changes announced by auction promoters represent improvements to the auction process itself, potential investors feel uncomfortable establishing consistent long-term strategies for actively participating in the generation market in uncertain scenarios. Participants know that once a plant is built, assets become sunk and investors are in a difficult position to negotiate contract changes with governments. In this sense, transparent and robust auctions, with a clear definition of the product, have been welcomed by most market participants.

Transparency and Fairness

Other necessary conditions for the success of an auction process include its transparency, as well as investors' perception of the fairness of the process. Lack of transparency in the process is related to the dissemination of information among auction participants before, during, and after the auction. For example, leaving the auctioneer (whose role is often confused with that of the government) with a great deal of flexibility in establishing parameters and formulas in a not-so-transparent way jeopardizes the perception of transparency and fairness.

Auditing the Process

A way to increase transparency is to have a publicly available independent ex-post audit of the process. This practice is common in some power markets, such as PJM in the United States for example, where two independent consulting firms are contracted. The first is responsible for the design and preparation of the auctions, and the second for the follow up and subsequent preparation of the audit report. The second firm should provide an unbiased, candid report with any design problems that may have impacted competition. Peru has also started contracting independent companies to supervise and monitor its energy auctions. In 2010, the Peruvian regulatory energy authority appointed a "supervising company" to monitor the auction process, verify if rules were being correctly followed, analyze conditions for competition, identify market power abuse, and prepare monitoring and evaluation reports. Brazil has not adopted approaches similar to those observed in PJM or in Peru, despite requests from market participants.

General Auction Design Issues

Basic Characteristics

There is no "one-size-fits-all" type of auction as a competitive procurement mechanism for electricity-related products. Details do matter when preparing auction rules. Generally speaking, the best auction format for any given situation achieves the following objectives:

- Creates/awards incentives to attract new entrants in an efficient way;
- Provides a mechanism for price discovery and to facilitate bidders' expression of economic values;

- Procures the product(s) at the lowest cost;
- Provides a fair, objective, transparent allocation of the products;
- Mitigates collusion among bidders.

Nature of the Auctions

Most of the energy auctions conducted as part of the first generation of power sector reforms have been designed as sealed-bid auctions. This methodology was the basis for the development of PPAs supporting capacity expansion. It is still used extensively, particularly in places with many sellers and one buyer. However, alternatives such as the descending clock auction design have demonstrated many advantages over traditional sealed-bid auctions. A clock auction enables an efficient price discovery and is therefore conducive to more aggressive behavior among bidders, resulting in lower prices.

Sealed-bid and clock auctions are often combined in hybrid designs to achieve "the best of both worlds." Each auction design has advantages and disadvantages that need to be considered when selecting the option that is best suited to the specifics of each power sector and products to be traded.

The type of auction depends, *inter alia*, on the objectives set forth by the government. For example, one of the main concerns for the Colombian regulator when designing its firm energy auctions was to attract as much participation as possible. It was decided that a descending clock auction was the ideal design given the features of the power sector in Colombia. On the other hand, the Brazilian regulator decided that a descending auction phase followed by a pay-as-bid phase was better suited to their auctions for new and existing generation. It was thought that competition could be a problem in those auctions, while having a sealed-bid phase at the end would take care of that issue. Along the same lines, participation in auctions for large hydro plants tends to be weak and sealed-bid auctions are commonly used in those cases, either as a stand-alone auction, or as the first phase in a hybrid auction.

Clock auctions are not necessarily more complex than sealed-bid auctions. This may be the case as countries start designing a new unknown mechanism. However, experience has shown that once this learning curve and fear are over, countries consider the implementation of clock auctions a straightforward process. Moreover, benefits have ended up offsetting implementation costs in many instances.

Typical Electricity Products

The electricity contract auctioned is the main pillar for the allocation of trading rights and risks. Contract sanctity should include, *inter alia*, mechanisms for dispute resolution, enforcement schemes, and penalties for non-compliance. Wherever markets exist, electricity contracts must be read in conjunction with Grid Codes, which specify how power is dispatched, how generation units are committed, and how system service charges are paid for. Contract enforcement is also essential in order for the power pools to function efficiently, given the multi-party nature of the Grid Code agreements. If one piece fails, the whole system may be in jeopardy. All buyers in the auction process have to demonstrate credit worthiness for the volume of contracts they aim to procure.

It is essential to fully specify the products (contracts) to be auctioned and eliminate any ambiguities with regard to what auction participants are bidding on and how risks are to be allocated between the contracting parties. The product definition stage should answer at least the following questions:

- Are demand and supply conditions conducive to competition?
- Who are the counterparties?
- What is being procured? Energy, capacity, both?
- What are the fully specified terms, conditions, fuel-price indexation, guarantees, allocation of transmission risks, general obligations, duration, force majeure clauses, and liabilities?
- If different products are auctioned, will they be standardized?

Supply Adequacy

Long-term electricity contracts have been used to provide a price hedge to both buyers and sellers by allowing the trading of energy to be settled at a pre-agreed price for the duration of the contract. By entering into those agreements, the contracting parties do not have to trade energy at the volatile prices observed in spot markets. Long-term contracts play a major role in ensuring supply adequacy to the power systems as a whole. In this case, the auctioned product links the payments received by generators to certain adequacy services provided to the system. These "reliability products" can take many different forms. Examples include requirements of installed capacity, firm capacity, and firm energy (for energy-constrained resources). Despite those products being financial contracts, regulators require that they be backed up by physical assets, thereby contributing to strengthening the supply adequacy of the power system.

Centralization vs. Decentralization

In a centralized auction scheme, demand is pooled and procured jointly. Governments usually play a key role in defining the processes to aggregate demand and in designating an auctioneer to conduct the auction *per se*. Centralized auctions seem to be more efficient for fostering competition. The advantages of centralized auctions include: (i) Increasing competition and international interest (since a larger demand is auctioned, thus attracting more bidders); (ii) Allowing small distribution companies to benefit from economies of scale, which might result in cheaper contracting; (iii) Mitigating the market power that some gencos can use when negotiating with each disco individually in a situation with high market concentration; and (iv) Including a few standardized products, likely attracting a larger number of participants for each product. Hence, auctioning an aggregated amount of demand emerges as a preferred alternative vis-à-vis carrying out various smaller auctions when demand blocks from different distribution companies are similar.

Centralized auctions are not tantamount to a formal 'single buyer' scheme (which is also a type of centralized auction). The government does not have to take the title for the energy, nor does it have to provide guarantees for the contracts. These are signed directly between sellers—generation companies—and buyers, which are distribution companies. In this sense, it is of the utmost importance that distribution companies are perceived as creditworthy players so that sellers do not factor high-risk premiums into their prices.

Other Procedural Issues

Auction Administration. **Drafting of the various auction documents should start early in the process.** This should allow serious potential bidders a sufficient period of time during which they can analyze the documents and provide comments. Bidder qualification requirements and criteria should also be determined while the products to be auctioned are defined. Pre-auction bid guarantees (deposits), as well as all documentation from qualified bidders, should be properly handled.

Bidders should be trained on the workings of the auction mechanism to be implemented, and it is advisable to conduct a mock auction (sometimes called a dry run or trial auction) before holding the actual auction. It is also advisable to deal with the signing of all documents, completion guarantees, and payment transfers promptly after the auction has ended to ensure security of supply. Finally, it is highly recommended that the entire process be screened by independent experts on an ex-post basis.

Auction Promotion. **Marketing and promoting the auction through several channels in order to attract sufficient interest** and participation in the auction are necessary ingredients for its success. Also, reasonable timing is critical for promoting symmetrical information and the entrance of new bidders, to allow a sensible analysis for the construction of new capacity.

Communication. **Well-specified and communicated auction rules are critical for the success of the auction,** which requires: (i) Providing comprehensive, complete, unambiguous auction rules with no loopholes, that take into account all possible scenarios and avoid unintended consequences; (ii) Informing bidders of the rules early on, and providing sufficient time for them to evaluate those rules, giving them the opportunity to comment, validate, and provide inputs, thereby conveying a message that the rules are "for real"; (iii) Explaining auction objectives and operations (seminars and workshops), including informative training sessions and dry runs, to all stakeholders and market participants.

Frequency of the Auctions. **In the case of new capacity, it is important that the rules define when and how often auctions are to be held**—either as required by the identification of a forecast gap or, alternatively, on a regular basis to provide buyers with a risk management instrument. For example, in the case of Brazil, two auctions for new energy are conducted yearly on a mandatory basis for delivery three and five years ahead, although these may be complemented at the government's discretion by other project-specific auctions or auctions to contract reserve capacity. This is a risk-management instrument for distribution companies to mitigate the risk of buying an uncertain volume of energy to meet their load growth expectations five years before if just a single five-year auction was in place. With the two auctions, distribution companies can buy a reference volume in the five-year auction and supplement the difference in a subsequent auction, following a wait-and-see strategy.

In the case of existing capacity, auctions should be held frequently enough to provide generators and consumers with a risk management instrument to hedge against load growth uncertainty. The frequency of the auctions for existing capacity is also related to the duration of the contracts for that type of capacity.

Distributed Auctions. **If auctions are designed and managed by distribution utilities and contract prices are passed directly to end clients by means of a pass-through mechanism** (as is the case in Chile and Peru), distributors have a constant yield for their assets regardless of auction results. This discourages proper design, which minimizes prices. In that case, a stronger regulation is needed at the design stage and it is important that buyers have incentives to procure power at the lowest possible cost.

Other Contractual Issues

Terms and Conditions of Contracts. **The duration of contracts being offered to attract new capacity should be long enough (e.g. several years) to recover the costs of financing**

the project. Contracts for existing capacity should have a short duration, since the fixed costs of existing resources are already sunk and they should be used as instruments to pass short-term price signals to the consumer. This is done in order to avoid decoupling the price signal for regulated users from short-term marginal generation costs: if energy is contracted for the long-term in the auction, consumers do not perceive changes in market prices. They thus don't adjust their consumption to the real value of energy at any given time.

VOLUME OF LONG-TERM CONTRACTS TO BE AUCTIONED. **The volume of long-term contracts to be auctioned, which will be the basis for expansion, has to take into account the aggregate supply and demand balance** a few years ahead (e.g., 3–5 years). The forward time interval depends on the shortest lead time to enable low-cost generation to be built, and may vary for different auctions depending on the type of capacity required and available for bidding. In the case of new contracts to retain existing capacity, the volume to be procured is determined by the installed generation capacity.

The responsibility for load forecasting and accountability for over/under investment should ideally be under the same umbrella. The responsibility for load forecasting in some cases falls on the government (or system planner), while in other cases, consumers (either by themselves or represented by distribution companies) are required to inform their load forecasts in a distributed way in each auction. Distribution companies tend to be more rigorous and realistic when they prepare their own forecasts and are obliged to pay for their short or long positions in the market. This behavior, in turn, leads to more adequate investment levels.

STANDARD VS. NON-STANDARD ELECTRICITY PRODUCTS. **The tradeoff between auctioning standardized and non-standardized energy products should be carefully analyzed.** Although auctioning standardized products increases competition and facilitates trading, they may be disadvantageous for distribution companies with very distinct consumption patterns and load factors. Aggregating dissimilar blocks and trading one single product may be too rigid a procedure, since there might be a significant mismatch between the energy profiled in a standard contract and the load shape of a particular distribution company. An option would be to develop several different contracts by aggregating only similar demand blocks, and to procure them through smaller auctions. However, the drawback of this option is that competition could be weak in smaller auctions because some contracts might not attract a lot of interest. Those generators could avoid competing among themselves by participating in different auctions in a kind of collusive agreement. Therefore, when blocks are dissimilar, the choice of product(s) has to consider the trade-off between increasing competition and tailoring the products to the distribution company's unique market requirements.

Auctions and World Bank Procurement Guidelines

The World Bank has encouraged its client countries to procure energy competitively. The primary modality recommended by the WB for the procurement of goods and services is equivalent to the FPSB auction. However, when the Bank finances the cost of a project procured under a BOO, BOT, or BOOT concession, the procurement rules are flexible enough to accommodate auctions, provided that the mechanism used for awarding the concession is satisfactory to the Bank and is approved on an ex-ante basis.

Technology Choice and Renewables

INTEREST IN RENEWABLES. **Interest in renewables has been growing in light of concerns with climate change and the environment.** Together with energy efficiency, non-conventional renewables (which exclude large hydro) have been praised as the "most benign" form of energy. When conducting auctions for renewable sources, regulators face the challenge of establishing dedicated auctions for renewables or alternatively blending them with conventional sources of energy, thereby fostering "fuel-to-fuel" competition to the maximum extent possible.

With the exception of large hydro, most of the other sources of renewable energy are not [yet] considered cost-competitive for supplying power to the grid. Therefore, the development of those sources has in most cases required some form of energy policy commitment and support. The two most common and explicit policy instruments to support the development of renewables have been feed-in-tariffs (henceforth FiT) and Renewable Portfolio Standard (RPS)—also called Renewable Obligations in the UK. FiT, in its basic format, is not considered to be a competitive mechanism, since the government sets a price for the energy to be acquired by utilities, and all bidders should be able to get a contract to sell renewable energy at that price.

PROMOTING RENEWABLES VIA AUCTIONS. **Auctions have proven to be a viable alternative to the traditional, administratively set feed-in-tariffs.** While they do not represent a renewable energy policy *per se*, they have been challenging the firmly entrenched feed-in-tariff mechanism, which has been responsible for the installation of thousands of MW of renewable forms of energy worldwide. Actions foster competition and push down prices in the entire supply chain, thereby reducing tariffs to end-users, making the whole process more sustainable.

Auctions have been used in some countries to implement a government's stated policies to foster the development of non-conventional renewable sources of energy. Brazil, Peru, and Uruguay are examples of some of the countries that have held auctions in Latin America. Ontario (Canada) and California (US) are interesting examples in North America.

All-encompassing (or technology-neutral) auctions entitle any generation source (and possibly demand-side bidders) to participate in the tender on a level-playing-field basis. The idea is to foster maximum competition, select the most efficient sources, and achieve a least-cost expansion plan. However, it is difficult for non-conventional renewable sources to compete head to head with baseload coal or large hydro, except under special circumstances. Furthermore, governments may have a preference for particular technologies driven by energy policy concerns or economic policy considerations. For this reason, all-encompassing auctions are seldom used. Governments prefer to establish auctions that target one or more types of technologies. Auctions can still provide the best results for a given set of technologies driven by policy decisions.

Implementation Issues and Participants

Implementation Challenges

Moving from auction theory to real-life implementation is not an easy task. This holds true particularly when auctions are implemented in markets that are not fully functional, or where institutions are not strong enough to support any formal competitive electricity auction procurement schemes. Furthermore, individual markets' peculiarities may call for very specific auction design and implementation challenges.

Making the right core policy decisions is a prerequisite for a successful procurement process, but it is not enough to guarantee its success. If the implementation is not properly done, the decisions made at the policy level will end up being only good intentions. It is therefore essential to carefully design the product(s) to be procured, who is (or is not) allowed to participate, and the auction rules that will govern the procurement process.

It is of the utmost importance to ensure that new generation projects procured through electricity auctions are built and have adequate operating performance so that long-term system adequacy and reliability is assured. This depends, inter alia, on the proper design of project completion guarantees and penalties for delays and underperformance.

The "devil is in the details" also holds true for auction implementation. As noted before, there is no single auction format that is best for all situations. Moreover, the difficulty of developing detailed interdependent auction rules must not be underestimated. Clear auction rules are critical for the success of the auction, and include:

- Comprehensive, complete, unambiguous rules with no loopholes that take into account all possible scenarios, and avoid unintended consequences;
- Specifying what is and what is not allowed, and credible penalties for violating the rules;
- Informing bidders of the rules early on, and providing sufficient time to evaluate them. It is not only important to give bidders all the relevant information on the auction process but also to grant them time to process this information;
- Giving bidders the opportunity to comment, validate, and provide inputs for the rules;
- Explaining auction objectives and operations (seminars and workshops) to all stakeholders and market participants;
- Providing informative training sessions and conducting tests.

Auction participants

Governments have to specify at the outset who should be allowed to participate in the auctions among all potential buyers and sellers in the market. This depends, *inter alia,* on the market design, number and nature of participants, and the need to foster competition among different energy sources or, in some cases, a stated government policy to favor some kinds of technologies such as non-conventional renewables.

PARTICIPANTS ON THE BUYERS' SIDE. **for distribution companies to acquire electricity contracts on behalf of regulated users.** Alternatively, they can be extended to free consumers or marketers, who may be allowed to participate. Participation of distribution companies can be mandatory or voluntary, depending on the overall procurement policies. Two-sided auctions also need confirmation as to who is allowed to bid with demand/energy reduction programs.

The choice of potential buyers is an important decision, as it may affect overall system reliability and stimulate "free riding." Free riders are those who do not commit themselves to signing long-term contracts and count on the system reliability provided by a more limited group of customers who participate in the auctions and sign long-term power purchase agreements. One way of dealing with this challenge is to simply implement auctions for the franchised market, letting the non-franchised market (free customers) negotiate energy on a bilateral basis or implement their own auction mechanisms.

The problem of ignoring the non-franchised market has to do with the overall reliability of the power system. Free customers, who have more latitude in signing (or not) long-term power purchase agreements, are less likely to enter into long-term contracts with generators to support the development of new plants, which may lead to a capacity shortfall in the longer term. From a financial standpoint, the captive market will be hedged, while the non-franchised market will be heavily exposed to high spot prices in times of scarcity. However, from a physical standpoint, if load shedding happens to occur, it will affect both market segments equally. On the other hand, since the lack of a secure energy supply does not discriminate between consumers (i.e. regulated versus non-regulated), the lack of contracting on the non-regulated market could have ramifications on the regulated market as well, thus jeopardizing the security of supply as a whole, which is perceived to be a public good. The system should be designed in a way that fosters responsible contracting, thereby paving the way for a robust expansion of the power system.[3]

PARTICIPANTS ON THE SELLERS'S SIDE. **Participants may include plants that already exist, those under construction, or green field plants.** An important design and implementation choice regarding policy is to conduct separate or joint processes for existing and new (green field) capacity. One issue when auctioning contracts to attract new capacity and retain existing resources is whether to have separate auctions for each type of capacity or to carry out just a single auction. Auctions of existing capacity foster competition "in the market," while those for new capacity foster competition "for the market", and the development of new power plants.

Different approaches have been used by different countries. Brazil, for example, conducted separate auctions for new and existing capacity, while Chile, Panama, Peru, and PJM put all capacity into a single auction. Colombia and New England follow another approach, where new and existing resources are offered in the same auction, but the clearing price is determined only by new capacity.

There are advantages and disadvantages to conducting separate energy auctions for new and existing generation. The main advantage of segmenting auctions between existing and new capacity is to clearly state the objectives of each procurement process. If new and existing generation assets compete jointly, the latter will likely set prices at long-run marginal costs, despite being depreciated and already paid by the consumers.[4] This is a controversial empirical question, which, broadly speaking is part of the long-standing debate of pricing electricity on an average marginal cost basis.

Notes

1. A well-known example is the Dabhol plant in India. It was initially developed as a non-solicited, non-competitive project. The project never came to fruition for a variety of reasons. Tariffs agreed upon between the developers (Enron as the consortium leader) and the State of Maharashtra were considered extremely high—close to US 24 cents/kWh, and were therefore challenged when a new government took office.
2. See reference to the design of energy auctions for the two Madeira River hydro plants in Brazil.
3. The omnipresent expectation of an industry-wide bail-out unfortunately distorts incentives for responsible contracting and expansion. This was observed in Brazil during the 2001 power crisis. Players knew far in advance that the crisis was around the corner, but did too little too late to promote a more aggressive expansion of the system. When the crisis erupted, both generators and

distributors jointly approached the government requesting compensation for their losses. Since the bail-out culture is so ingrained and difficult to change overnight, particularly for public services, when the crisis was over, the government's second-best alternative was to impose strict limits on contracting obligations and mandated procurement via auctions for the captive market. However, the same obligations were not applied to the free market, which in principle does not have the same incentives to expand the system. On the other hand, in times of shortage, an unreliable supply will impact both customer groups (free and captive) equally. To some extent, the free customer segment is perceived to be "free-riding" the power sector regulations. For a detailed analysis, see Maurer (2002).

4. An area of concern is when the power sector moves from a cost-plus regulation to a deregulated regime. Allowing amortized plants to sell at market prices creates a perception that the consumer is paying twice for the same asset base.

CHAPTER 8

Conclusions

Auctions are an interesting and potentially effective form of procuring electricity. If successfully designed and implemented, they may lead to far superior results than other selection alternatives such as accepting unsolicited proposals, direct negotiations, Swiss challenge, or different forms of first-come first-served basis such as feed-in-tariffs, as auctions increase transparency and foster competitiveness.

The subject of auctions of electricity contracts is of increasing interest among a growing number of countries. Some have been trying to learn more about the possibility of introducing competition in the procurement of energy, while others, which have been using traditional competitive methods for selecting IPPs (e.g. first-price sealed bids), are looking at more sophisticated methodologies that can further enhance competition and reduce energy costs to the end-user.

Relevant experiences have been assembled on the implementation of electricity auctions over the last few years as a mechanism to competitively attract and/or retain generation resources. While this report is not a how-to manual, it contains a wide range of auction experiences and highlights the main issues and options to be considered when a country decides to move forward towards more competitive, market-driven auction processes. Practical results constantly make it clear that each country's issues and objectives must be carefully evaluated as part of the auction design process.

Latin America has been leading the effort to introduce energy auctions as an instrument to promote competition in energy procurement. Dozens of auctions have been carried out to date, with most being aimed at contracting new capacity. Results have been very satisfactory more often than not, in terms of entertaining competition, attracting a large number of private players, and ensuring lower costs for consumers. The region has conducted a wide range of auctions both "in the market" and "for the market," encompassing a great variety of products—from standard forward contracts to sophisticated energy call options. Overall, about 30 energy auctions have been conducted in Brazil, Chile, Peru, Colombia, and Panama. Brazil, for example, has successfully conducted a total of 31 auctions for existing and new energy. As of April 2010, approximately 57,000 MW of new capacity have been contracted for delivery dates between 2008 and 2015.

Moving from auction theory to real-life implementation is, however, not an easy task. This holds true particularly when auctions are implemented in markets that are not fully functional, where institutions are not strong enough to support any formal electricity procurement schemes, or where contract sanctity is often challenged. Most of the time, the basic product of an auction is an energy contract, the proxy for vertical integration in restructured power systems. An auction requires legal and regulatory mechanisms that can bind participants to their offers. In a broader sense, it requires rule of law contract sanctity. Those are prerequisites to any de-verticalization of the power sector and the introduction of Independent Power Producers.

Several design and implementation challenges have been observed. Design issues are related to the goals of the auction, the products to be procured, the country's characteristics, the stability of the regulatory framework, and country-specific requirements in terms of steering its energy policy. Implementation issues have to do with the degree of centralization of the procurement process, the role of the auctioneer, and a rigorous communication process to ensure maximum transparency and interest from multiple bidders.

The use of auctions is not tied to a specific market arrangement, to a regulatory and institutional framework, or to the degree to which market reforms have been carried out. They can be used across a wide range of institutional and regulatory frameworks from the power sector and the benefits have offset the implementation costs overall in many cases.

An electricity auction is able to: (i) increase the transparency needed in the procurement process in order to reduce risks; (ii) foster competition; (iii) provide economically efficient outcomes that are unlikely to be challenged in the future as the political and institutional scenarios change; and (iv) establish an objective, market-driven criterion for the thorny regulatory issue of pass-through of generation costs to a utility-franchised market. Auctions can also be used to procure energy contracts among a sub-set of technologies, such as wind, biomass, or even site-specific hydropower plants.

While there is no "one-size-fits-all" formula for successful auctions, some lessons are applicable to different cases. The analysis has grouped them into three different categories, namely procurement policy, incorporation of energy policy decisions, and the auction implementation *per se*. The first and second groups include lessons regarding the underlying energy and procurement policies, while the third group includes lessons on the design and implementation of the auction itself.

There is a great deal of potential for furthering the use of auctions in the power sector, even in small, unsophisticated markets. For example, they may be used as a mechanism to grant the use of water rights, thereby enabling the development of new hydro sites. They can also be used to select preferred projects or to allocate long-term energy contracts competitively in multi-country power pools. Multi-product, discriminatory price auctions are potentially applicable to select small, modular units of emergency power generation. Two-sided auctions may entertain demand response, increasing competitiveness, reducing market power, and paving the way for a more energy-efficient economy.

Finally, auctions can be an efficient alternative to develop non-conventional sources of energy, as a substitute for or complement to the traditional feed-in-tariff schemes. A number of experiences have shown that, despite the existing skepticism, auctions for renewable sources can work to expand the energy portfolio and push costs down. The list of options goes well beyond the first-price sealed-bid auction, the primary mechanism in the World Bank procurement rules. Auction design and implementation must be adapted to fit the individual country and market circumstances. A great deal of flexibility in the use of auction instruments is also necessary for the numerous reasons mentioned above.

Appendixes

Electricity Procurement

I. The Role of Procurement in Ensuring Security of Supply

A common element in developed and developing countries is the need to ensure resource adequacy (i.e., attract and retain generation capacity) at the least possible cost. In developed countries, the primary objective has been to replace/retain plants that are being retired and new capacity requirements have been driven by concerns over carbon emissions. Hence, in developed countries, the need to attract new capacity *substitutes* is the primary objective in order to ensure load supply.

In developing countries, the pressure to meet an increasing growth in demand is much more intense than in developed countries. An annual load growth of 5 to 6 percent requires that the existing generation capacity doubles in about 15 years. In these countries, the primary objective is to ensure the emergence of an *adequate* volume of new generation.

II. Adequacy Mechanisms[1]

Different market-based arrangements for handling the resource adequacy problem have emerged, ranging from the government's "do-nothing" approach (relying on the market to ensure the efficient long-term outcome) to mandated quantity requirements (where the purchase of a particular product in certain quantities and terms is imposed on consumers), or price mechanisms (pre-determined extra payment is provided to generators in exchange for a certain product).

The main approach has been to provide capacity owners with an extra income to foster new investments in generation and retain existing resources. Developers receive payments associated with certain services that are provided to the power system, sometimes referred to as "reliability products" (Battle and Rodilla (2009)). These products can take many different forms. Some examples include installed capacity made available, firm capacity or energy (for energy-constrained resources), options to buy energy at a certain price, and reserves that can be called upon by the system operator when needed. All of these products can be procured competitively.

The most common adequacy mechanism is the calculation and assignment of a certificate of *firm capacity or energy* assigned to all generators. These certificates reflect the generator's contribution to the overall adequacy and reliability of the system supply, which is in turn a function of the country's planning criterion. The computation of capacity or energy certificates depends on the country's supply mix (especially whether hydro and/or thermal is a dominant resource). It can range from a very simple "available capacity certificate" that represents the plant's nameplate capacity adjusted by forced and expected maintenance rates, to more complex computation schemes that include energy constraints, probabilistic outages, and stochastic inflows.[2] A project certificate represents its incremental contribution to the overall system supply and can be used to allow a direct comparison between the contributions of different technologies to the system's reliability. The sum of the certificates is a practical and transparent *measure* that can be weighed against the system's requirements (either peak load or average energy demand over a fixed horizon, depending on the country's specific characteristics) in order to assess the need for new generation resources. If the total firm capacity or energy is greater than or equal to the total load, security of supply would be considered adequate. Otherwise, it would be necessary to procure new generation resources to meet load requirements reliably.

In some countries, such as Chile, Peru, Colombia (until 2008), Panama, the UK (before NETA), and the US, capacity payments are offered to generation plants in proportion to their capacity certificates. As discussed in Oren (2005), the underlying motivation for capacity payments is to provide extra income to incumbent generators who would be unlikely to recover their fixed costs in an energy-only market due to the suppression of energy prices as a result of political or regulatory intervention. Capacity payments are meant to keep such generators from going out of business. Advocates of this approach also infer that direct payment for capacity will lead to over-investments, particularly when those payments exceed the amortized cost of the plant. Capacity payments may be administratively set—as is the case of Peru, Chile, Colombia (before the reliability options mechanism implemented in 2008) and in the UK system before NETA—or traded in a market such as the capacity markets developed in the US in New England, PJM, and New York in the early 2000s.

Considering all the factors and uncertainties involved, calibrating the capacity payment so as to attract the targeted level of reserves is a challenging task and, depending on the value set, could result in over or under capacity. As will be discussed later on, this is the same challenge faced by feed-in-tariffs, which have recently re-emerged as a support mechanism for the procurement of renewable forms of energy. Where capacity markets were implemented, capacity prices alternated between very low, during the long periods when the system's reserve margin was large, and extremely high, when not enough capacity resources were available.[3]

Another way to link firm capacity certificates and security of supply is to require that consumers 'back' their loads with the equivalent volume of firm certificates. This is known as a quantity obligation. The capacity obligation approach is more direct in the sense that, once the target quantities of generation capacity are determined by technical considerations, the firm certificates are allocated to the load-serving entities (LSEs). Basically, if the total firm capacity is lower than the total load, penalties will be applied, thus creating incentives for consumers who are 'short' on certificates to procure new capacity. This approach has been used in Brazil.

In other countries, such as Colombia, the total firm energy requirement is also used as a trigger for the 'last resort' procurement of new capacity. Typically, if the firm fore-casted energy is less than the forecasted load,[4] a procurement auction to contract new energy is carried out to bridge the gap. Finally, some other countries, such as Peru and Chile, operate a capacity market where administratively set capacity payments are distributed to generators in proportion to their firm capacities.

III. Forward Contracting

New generation investments involve large capital outlays and require long-term commitment from the developers. Financing in developing countries is generally obtained through project finance, where the project's cash flows are relied upon to repay the long-term debt incurred within a given comfort level required by the lenders. The objective of investors when building new generation is to minimize project risks in order to ensure its bankability.

A long-term electricity forward contract provides revenue stability to investors and protects them from many of the effects of government interference. For example, a new investor with a contract is less vulnerable to disturbances in spot prices due to the government-sponsored construction of excess capacity or the strategic, collusive behavior of existing generation companies. Electricity contracts also play a key role in providing *financial security* for newcomers. If a country has a solid distribution sector with a commercial discipline, a bilateral contract between a generation and a distribution company is very reassuring to investors. However, if the distribution companies have a poor credit rating, perhaps due to political pressures to keep tariffs artificially low, it may be necessary to adopt some type of government guarantee in a procurement scheme backstopped by the government, which is typically known as a single buyer model.[5]

Contracts that enable the development of new generation capacity are usually custom-made forward electricity contracts and are different from the more standardized future contracts traded in the commodity markets. Hence, a mechanism, ideally a competitive one, must be implemented to procure long-term forward electricity contracts.

Box A.1 illustrates the basic differences between forward and future energy contracts. Future contracts play an important role in making the electricity markets more liquid and can therefore provide incentives for developers to build without necessarily resorting to long-term contracts. This can be viewed as an intermediate solution between the construction of merchant plants and a heavily hedged investor with a long-term PPA. Market liquidity gives investors more comfort in that the energy generated by their plants may be traded in the market. However, only a few developing countries—Colombia being the most relevant case with a recently created organized market for trading electricity contracts—have active liquid markets for future contracts.

For the purposes of this report, a forward contract will be the typical financial instrument between a buyer and a seller to hedge against price volatility and make the projects

Box A.1. Forward x Future (Financial) Energy Contracts[6]

A common error among non-finance specialists is to interpret forward contracts as future contracts and vice-versa. Both are products for future delivery but with distinct characteristics, particularly with regard to the guarantees for clearing.

A forward contract is a contract for the delivery of some asset at an agreed price and in a defined location at a specified time in the future. The contract price is paid only at the time of delivery, when the asset is received. The contract is a financial instrument that guarantees the asset price for buyers and sellers. The difference between the asset market value and the contract price at the delivery date represents a profit or loss for the buyer/seller of the asset. For instance, if the forward contract price is $100 but at the delivery date the asset spot price is $110, then the buyer will have a profit of $10, either by using the asset at a lower price than if he would have to buy it in the spot market, or by taking delivery of the asset and immediately selling it for $110. The seller who has to deliver the asset will have a loss of the same value. Forward contracts can be standardized but are not obliged to be, and therefore involve counterparty credit risk.

A future contract is similar to a forward contract in that it specifies a price and a future date for the delivery of an asset. However, futures contracts are highly standardized and are offered by and traded on a futures exchange. Changes in the value of the contract are settled daily (marking to market) and futures contracts do not normally result in physical delivery. These features make futures contracts easy to trade. Each futures contract is issued by a particular commodity or financial exchange. The contract usually requires both the buyers and sellers to deposit funds called a *security margin*, or deposit, with the exchange, to insure against default. In other words, the exchange ensures the clearing.

bankable. This contract can be for energy or capacity, profiled over a certain period of time (day, season, year, etc.).

IV. Constraints and Challenges for Developing Countries

Many developing countries face obstacles that hinder the efficiency of their procurement process. The key *constraints* in the procurement of new capacity for these countries have been:

(i)   Limited access to financing: Resources are generally obtained through project financing, where the project cash flows are relied upon to repay the long-term debt incurred within a given margin of comfort required by the lenders. This source of financing limits access to credit and is also typically more costly than other options.

(ii) Lack of a hedging mechanism to guard against price volatility: An inherent characteristic of energy markets is the price volatility caused by factors such as weather. As liquid future markets are not well developed to hedge against price volatility, obtaining long-term financing for new generation becomes difficult or more costly.

(iii) Barriers to entry: Local (incumbent) generation companies may artificially decrease spot prices to discourage entry by new capacity, thus creating barriers to entry.

(iv) High, but uncertain, load growth: Creates asymmetric incentives for generators and consumers. Private generators will invest based on low demand forecasts because this ensures their remuneration. If load growth increases, they will accrue additional revenues from higher spot prices. In contrast, consumers would like capacity to be planned for the high demand forecast or they risk experiencing energy shortages.

(v)   Economies of scale: In a small country, the load forecast increase for an individual distribution company may not be enough to justify the construction of, for example, mid-sized hydroelectric plants, which are usually cheaper than a small hydro plant (per MW installed). However, the *aggregate* load of many distribution companies might allow the contracting of a larger—and more economical—plant, thus reducing consumer tariffs. The economy of scale argument has been used to justify the need for centralized procurement processes.[7] However, it is important to determine explicit responsibilities for demand forecast.

(vi) Weak institutions and regulatory instability: In some developing countries, institutions are not strong enough to support any formal electricity procurement scheme. In addition, some do not have creditworthy distribution companies, perhaps due to political pressure to keep tariffs artificially low.

(vii) Exposure to government policies, either directly or through state-owned companies: A typical example would be government-sponsored "extra" investment in new capacity because of a perception that GDP growth will be much higher than that predicted "by the market." As a consequence, energy spot prices may become artificially low, thus decreasing the returns of private investors.

These constraints result in a set of challenges that must be considered in the design of a procurement scheme. Box A.2 summarizes key *challenges* for the design of an efficient procurement scheme for new capacity in developing countries.

**Box A.2. Key Challenges for the Procurement of New Capacity in
             Developing Countries**

✓ Ensuring *security of supply*, i.e., the procured resources should provide supply reliability according to
   the country's planning criteria;
✓ *Protecting investors from risks* that they cannot control or hedge. One example is transmission congestion or pricing: developing countries are expanding the network at a rapid pace and new congestions are
   appearing or disappearing all the time. Because transmission planning is out of the investor's control,
   this is an uncontrollable risk. Another example is hydrological risk due to excessive energy spot price
   volatility. Investors should bear the risk from activities related to project development, such as construction costs and project delays;
✓ Procuring energy *at least cost* for a given capacity and technology choice;
✓ Capturing *economies of scale* of large generation projects in the procurement process. This is intimately
   connected to the need for a centralized procurement scheme (with individual or multiple ownership);
✓ Ensuring that there are alternatives that allow market participants to *manage uncertainties associated
   with volatile load growth rates*;
✓ *Reducing barriers* to entry by new players;
✓ *Ensuring the delivery of the auctioned energy* by allowing the participation of projects with environmental
   permits already issued and by designing an effective and enforceable scheme of project completion
   guarantees and penalties for delays; and
✓ Selecting the *contracting and guarantees schemes* in line with the country's institutional characteristics
   and economic conditions of demand representatives. For example, in some cases, it may be necessary
   to have some type of treasury guarantees.

V. Procurement Mechanisms

V.1 Negotiation is a mechanism whereby buyers freely negotiate the terms and commercial conditions of the procured product. *"Auctions may perform poorly when projects are complex, contractual design is incomplete, and there are few available bidders. Ex-ante design is hard
to complete and ex-post adaptations are expected.[8] Ex-post adaptations may be better administered
with cost-plus, rather than fixed-price contracts. Furthermore, auctions may stifle communication
between buyers and sellers, preventing the buyer from utilizing the contractors' expertise when
designing a project. The product is not well defined and needs to be customized to client's needs.
The choice of product and contract influence the choice of award mechanism. In negotiations, the
buyer decides to forgo the bidding process altogether and picks a contractor directly. Negotiation
may save time, as there is no need to advertise and consequently a contract can be signed with
considerably less delay."[9]* Despite those particular circumstances, a non-competitive process such as direct negotiation is more prone to corruption and nepotism, and therefore
more likely to be challenged subsequently as the political winds change. Bulow and
Klemperer (1996) show that, in most cases, a seller would prefer using a simple (no
reserve price) auction to the best possible negotiation with one less buyer. Direct negotiations are still used to acquire energy products, but it has several drawbacks: it lacks
transparency, makes entry by new investors more difficult and, where distribution companies procure energy on behalf of regulated users, it requires that the regulator define
the "prudent" costs of negotiation that should be passed on to final customers. The definition of "prudent" costs is sometimes arbitrary and based on technocratic inputs, which
are often disassociated from the market reality.

V.2. First-Come First-Served Basis. Countries have used first-come first-served
basis schemes to expand generation capacity or to promote energy conservation. Many

countries have used a feed-in-tariff (FiT) process to foster the development of renewable sources of energy. By means of this mechanism, the government mandates utilities to procure energy from renewable producers at an administratively set price. Oftentimes countries may set a total quota for each renewable technology. Bid selection follows a first-come first-served basis until this quota is completed and there is no direct competition among bidders. Competition is somewhat limited to the extent that the low-cost producers are the ones most likely to bid. Chapter 8 provides a detailed description of FiT and other mechanisms for procuring renewables. On the demand side, Standard Offers are the analogue version to FiT. The regulator specifies a minimum price that utilities have to pay to energy users or load aggregators when submitting projects with the objective of promoting energy savings or demand-side management. The price often depends on the type of proposed energy savings (e.g. lighting, motors, air conditioning, etc.). The State of New York has been implementing Standard Offers successfully. The mechanism is under consideration in South Africa.

V.3. Beauty Contest (or Administrative Allocation). *In this case, a government agency proposes outlines and criteria to be followed in the selection process. Typically, a set of guidelines and some measurable criteria are presented, leaving some room for subjective evaluation. Participants present their best case on why they should be awarded the products, covering a variety of aspects (e.g. including business plans). This is typically a subjective, non-transparent selection process that involves a great deal of time, effort, and documentation. Also, it is normally difficult to assess the credibility of participants' claims. Due to its lack of transparency, administrative allocation is more prone to corruption and kickbacks. A beauty contest was used by Sweden to allocate mobile phone frequency spectrum and will be summarized as follows:*

> "*Most licensing processes of mobile telephone frequency spectrum (3G) that took place in Europe have been centered on auctions. However, Sweden decided to adopt administrative processes, also called beauty contests or administrative licensing. It was believed that a rapid development of 3G would be an essential part of the development of Sweden as an IT notion. The Swedish Regulator (PTS) focused on two main criteria when choosing operators. The first was rapid roll-out and the second nationwide coverage. Credits were awarded for every complete unit of 10,000 inhabitants and coverage of 30 km². Four competitors failed in terms of technical feasibility and one failed in terms of financial capacity. In the final phase of the selection process, all five remaining competitors obtained the maximum score for the area coverage. Four companies promised 100% coverage of the population by the year 2003. Therefore, four licenses were awarded. The decision was challenged in court, resulting in a very complex, multi-party proceeding. Doubts were also raised on the transparency of the process, since not all information exchange during the selection process was made public. The court noted that the contest between the applying companies, although allowed by the telecommunications law, contained particular procedural rules, which deviated from the constitutional law's instructions that should have been formulated in law or regulation. The court's final decision did not overturn PTS decision, which helped mitigate the effect of the trial proceedings on the launch of the 3G network.*"[10] Borgers and Dustmann (2003) criticize beauty contests due to their lack of transparency, driven by a vague selection process, unclear final decision, and bias towards the incumbent. The latter, called "National Champions" by Klemperer (2000), was not an issue in the Swedish process, but is certainly a major drawback in other beauty contests, which may end up limiting the number of interested players.

V.4. Output-Based Aid. *There are many variations in this kind of performance-based pro-curement. "Some schemes have introduced an element of competition, with the subsidy linked to the number of new connections that a utility company or service provider is able to provide in a certain area. Competition has been based on either the smallest grant to supply a given number of customers or the largest number of customers for a given grant.* In some cases, the competition gives the winner a concession to supply all potential customers in an area (an exclusive concession). *In others, such as in Chile, competition for grants does not offer exclusive rights in a given jurisdiction."*[11] Exclusive concessions in power distribution seem to provide a reasonable, practical balance among the objectives of maximizing competition, reducing costs to expand the network, and enforcing the obligation to serve.

V.5. Swiss Challenge[12] is an attempt to introduce some form of competition to unsolicited proposals. *"Swiss challenge is a form of public procurement in some (usually less developed) jurisdictions that requires a public authority (usually a government agency) that has received an unsolicited bid for a public project (such as a port, road, or railway) or services to be provided to the government, to publish the bid and invite third parties to match or exceed it. The original proponent gets the right to match any superior offers given by the third party"*.[13] An example of Swiss challenge adopted by the Philippines BOT Law is illustrated as follows:

"Under the Philippines BOT Law, unsolicited proposals for BOT projects are acceptable if: (i) the project involves a new concept of technology and is not listed on the roster of prior-ity projects by the government; (ii) there is no government guarantee, subsidy or equity required; and (iii) the project is submitted to a price test or "Swiss challenge" from com-petitors. Once the government receives an unsolicited proposal, it must invite comparative proposals from other bidders, following a transparent process. If a lower-priced proposal is received, the original proponent has 30 days to match it and win the contract. Otherwise the award goes to the lower bidder. This challenge has been used, for example, in the case of a New Zealand developer who submitted a proposal to the National Power Corporation to rehabilitate and maintain a 350 MW hydro plant, challenging an unsolicited proposal by an Argentine company."

Notes

1. The reliability of a power system usually refers to its capability of supplying today's and tomor-row's load even in the event of unanticipated circumstances. The concept involves both a struc-tural viewpoint—in the sense of having adequate capacity to meet expected demand over a given horizon—and a short-term viewpoint, involving the system's ability to withstand a critical com-bination of events. In the context of electricity procurement, reliability is mostly concerned with the adequacy aspect of a power system.
2. The certificates are calculated through planning studies in line with reliability standards.
3. See Battle, Rodilla (2010) for details.
4. This estimate takes into account all new generation contracted or under construction.
5. Arizu et al. (2006).
6. Adapted from J.C. Hull, Options, Futures and Other Derivative Securities, Prentice Hall, NJ, 1993.
7. At this point we warn the reader not to confuse a centralized procurement process, where buyers might define the auctioned demand and contracts have no government involvement, with a single buyer scheme, where government is involved. Experience shows that central planning and cost-plus tariff setting may encourage the building of over-capacity. There are alternative procurement schemes that allow for economies of scale while avoiding "optimistic" forecasts of load increase. Those will be addressed later in this document.

8. This may be the case, for example, in the procurement of energy efficient services, where the definition of the "product" being procured is not always straightforward, and may include goods, works, and services. Services may include project design, operations and maintenance, training, and measurement and verification. Works may involve revamping existing systems, construction of stand-by power and cogeneration facilities and the like. Sometimes the specifics of the work to be executed are known only after a detailed audit is carried out. See Singh et al. (2010).

9. Adapted from Bajari et al. (2008).

10. Adapted from Andersson et al. (2005).

11. Adapted from Brook et al. (2001).

12. Based on Kerf et al. (1998).

13. See example of a Swiss Challenge scheme on the Philippine Built-Operate-Transfer-Bidding at Kerf (1998).

The Use of Auctions in the Electricity Industry

There has been a growing interest in the use of auctions in the electricity industry as a way to promote efficient procurement and foster competition in all sectors: generation, transmission, and distribution. Auctions have been employed throughout the world in diverse situations ranging from the hourly dispatch of generators in day-ahead markets to long-term contracts for concession rights to build and operate hydroelectric plants or transmission assets.

The following sections will examine different situations in which auctions have been chosen as the mechanism for the competitive procurement of power in all senses, either from existing or future generation plants. Examples discussed include: day-ahead dispatch, balancing and ancillary services, short, mid and long-term energy contracts, concession rights, and Financial Transmission Rights.

I. Day-ahead Dispatch

One of the first types of auctions established in the electricity industry was devised to enable an efficient dispatch of the power system. In most formal wholesale markets, generation unit owners and loads submit price/quantity bids to supply and consume energy for each hour of the following day. Based on those bids, the market operator sets day-ahead prices at every location in the network and day-ahead commitments and schedules for generation units. Different markets use a variety of mechanisms to pay for and charge for imbalances between day-ahead schedules and real-time output or consumption. The basic outcome of this type of auction is the energy *spot* price, which is the price of the most expensive unit scheduled and reflects the price of electricity for each settlement period of the system (usually hourly). This is the basis of the spot market settings of many electricity markets worldwide, including those in the US, Europe, Oceania, and some in Latin America (Colombia, Guatemala).

This kind of auction mechanism has been important for coordinating the operation of the transmission network when there are many different owners of generation units. Another justification for its use is that bidding schemes generate an efficient use of system resources in a competitive environment. In addition, it is also claimed that spot pricing schemes theoretically provide efficient economic signals for system expansion. Early electricity market designs, pioneered by Chile and the UK, were centered on competition in the short-term energy spot market, and not so much on long-term contracts. The expectation was that short-term spot prices would provide a correct signal for capacity expansion. In theory, if investors were able to forecast an increase in energy spot prices, they would have an incentive to build new capacity. Consistency would be assured because long-term energy contracts could be priced in relation to the futures market.

While the straight application of spot pricing theory may be conceptually correct and lead to efficient results, international experience has shown that investors do not always respond to scarcity signals such as price spikes in energy-only markets because they are not strong enough. As a consequence of the lack of demand response in spot markets, regulators and governments intervene in periods of high spot prices to keep them at socially acceptable levels. Accordingly, spot prices and the trading of energy only on a short-term basis have not ensured system expansion.

II. Balancing and Ancillary Services

Since the dispatch of generators is determined based on forecasts of consumption and availability of units made 24 hours prior to the actual events, real-time operation will always be at least slightly different than scheduled. Moreover, the quality and reliability of electricity delivered requires that some units be at the system operator's disposal performing services such as operating reserve, voltage control, and Automatic Generation Control (AGC). Since at any given point in time, the volume of electricity generated must correspond exactly to that which is consumed, such provisions for demand and supply mismatches and system disruptions are the focus of the so-called balancing and ancillary services markets, respectively.

Auctions have also been a preferred alternative as a way to allow bidders to compare the opportunity costs of providing such ancillary services. These auctions basically function according to the same principles as those for day-ahead scheduling. Each bidder submits price and quantity bids that should reflect their willingness to increase or decrease supply during a given interval, or to keep their plants running and ready to go live, for example.

Switzerland, the US and the Nordic region are examples of markets where these auctions have been implemented. Other markets, such as in the UK, also use auctions for network constraints (Balancing Market) during the real-time operation so as to alleviate the system from congestion.

III. Electricity Contracts

There is a great variety of electricity contracts auctioned in different markets around the world, which differ from each other in the way they are structured. For example, they may be structured as call options or forward contracts. Physical delivery of energy may (or may not) be required, and their duration may range from a few weeks to many years.

Most of the contracts traded in the worldwide energy market are standard financial forward contracts with a fixed price. In these contracts, the seller must supply a predetermined volume of energy to the consumer. The holder of the contracts has to compensate the generator (seller) at the fixed price agreed upon in the contract. In case there is a positive (negative) difference between energy physically produced and energy sold in contracts, such a difference is sold (purchased) at the spot market.

An energy call option is a financial instrument that specifies quantity, delivery time, location, and strike price ($/MWh) for energy. It gives the holder the right but not the obligation to obtain the specified energy at the specified strike price and can be exercised physically or financially. A call option acts as price insurance, guaranteeing that the buyer will not pay more than the strike price for the energy it insured. To obtain such insurance, the buyer pays a fixed premium ($/kW-month or $/year) to the generator (or to a marketer).

Short and mid-term energy contracts usually serve as instruments for risk hedging against price uncertainty. For example, industrial consumers may be interested in locking the price they will be paying for energy some time in advance so that they are not exposed to market volatility and possible price spikes. The same instruments may also be used as balancing mechanisms in markets where regulation requires distribution companies and/or large consumers to hold contracts that back up their market requirements. Uncertainty in demand poses a challenge for the purchase of long-term contracts that match consumption far into the future. This is where short and mid-term contracts may play a key role.

The introduction of auctions for electricity contracts has helped increase the liquidity of markets for energy contracts, consolidating their efficiency, which has the benefit of:

- Allowing owners of power stations to mitigate price risk (e.g. these instruments can be used as a way for governments to retain ownership of the plant without having to engage in the risky and volatile wholesale electricity market, thus protecting the taxpayer by providing government with stable revenue streams);
- Allowing private generators to compete with state-owned generators in a more level playing field;
- Enabling private investors to manage issues of competitive neutrality raised by the operation of public and private sector generators in a single market;
- Attracting private sector investment in new plants to ensure reliable power supplies without placing pressure on the government budget.

IV. Concessions

The construction of large projects such as long transmission lines and hydroelectric plants is usually carried out through concessions, in which a company is given the right to use the water, and to build and operate the assets for a specified amount of time so as to recover investment costs and provide a return to investors.[1] When the concession involves the use of a public good (such as a river) a concession fee is usually paid to the government. Concessions are also typically adopted for services commonly referred to as natural monopolies, such as electricity distribution.

Auctions are usually organized in these settings so that investors bid the amount of money or the percentage of revenue they are willing to pay to the granting authority for the right to undertake the activities in question. In other contexts, bidders make their offers with respect to the amount of money they will charge consumers for providing a given service.

International experience has demonstrated that substantial benefits may be obtained from the adoption of these mechanisms, resulting in greater revenue collection by governments and a reduction in fees paid by the public. Auctions of concessions have been used worldwide in the privatization of distribution assets, and in the granting of hydro sites and rights to build transmission facilities, etc. New uses of auctions to grant hydro concessions are promising, particularly in countries where these resources are abundant, and where they are considering the participation of private capital to develop the generation potential due to constraints on public capital. Box B.1 highlights the dilemmas faced by those countries, and how auctions can help introduce an efficient and transparent mechanism with significant social benefits.

Box B.1. Granting Hydro Sites and Oil Fields—Any Common Denominators?

A challenge faced by many World Bank client countries is how to extract economic rent from hydro sites. If the government grants those sites for free to state-owned utilities, the economic rent presumably stays with the community and will benefit a wide range of customers, from the poorest rural household to large industrial end-users, who will promote economic growth and create employment.

The problem of granting concessions gets complicated when the developer of a particular site is a large private energy user (e.g. aluminum plant or mining facility) that intends to use the generation primarily for captive consumption. Oftentimes, those investors are interested in the most favorable sites, preferably those whose water flows have been regularized upstream and whose dams have been built using government funds. Governments may genuinely be concerned with attracting private capital to develop hydro generation, which would otherwise remain dormant for many years due to the government's budgetary constraints. However, giving those sites away to large, captive users may be politically unacceptable. It would be tantamount to transferring a country's economic rent equivalent to the potential energy of the site without receiving proper compensation. An analogy would be to transfer oil fields to the private sector without any payment to the host country. The latter is obviously unacceptable, but the granting of a hydro site is not intuitively so. Oil fields have traditionally been granted through competitive procurement mechanisms, but this has been the exception rather than the rule for hydro sites.

Countries have been struggling with the issue of how to capture a fair rent from hydro sites. In the absence of satisfactory mechanisms, some prefer to wait and develop the sites using government funds and own the associated assets. This is not necessarily the best solution, since lack of government funds may go on for many years before sites can be developed and economic rent be captured. Many countries are considering charging royalties and have gone through a negotiation process to define the amount of royalties to be charged to prospective developers. Those amounts are administratively set, and therefore may lead to corruption, nepotism, and kickbacks.

One possible approach is to grant the concession (which includes the right to use the water to produce electricity) on a competitive basis, using auctions. It is a practical solution if there is some competition for the hydro site from potential energy users, such as aluminum industries, mining facilities, and private utilities operating in the country, or even imports from neighboring countries. This could be an option to be further investigated for the development of large hydro sites in Africa, such as the Inga project in the Democratic Republic of Congo, or perhaps for the development of the huge hydro potential in Ethiopia or Angola, which can be harnessed to export power to countries such as Egypt, Sudan, Kenya, Uganda, Tanzania, and others. The establishment of an effective power market, with third party access, facilitates the emergence of competition for the sites and therefore gives the host country the possibility of receiving fair compensation for the generation developed by the private sector or utilities from neighboring countries.

Auctioning hydro sites under those circumstances has seldom been done, but it may turn out to be a transparent and efficient way of allocating valuable natural resources to potential hydro developers. It is a paradigm shift, with potentially huge transformational impact. Although its analysis goes beyond the scope of this paper, the subject deserves further investigation by development institutions supported by auction practitioners.

V. Virtual Power Plants

The expression virtual power plant (VPP) auctions refers to auctions for the sale of electricity supply contracts that give the holder the right to the output, or a share of the output, of a power plant. These sales, rather than physical divestitures, are virtual divestitures by one or more dominant incumbents. The contracts usually sold in VPP auctions are sold as divisible goods of varying durations, and offered in periodic open and transparent auctions. Details about VPP auctions will be provided in Appendix C.

VI. Transmission Lines and Interconnectors

Brazilian auctions for the concession of transmission lines under a Build-Own-Operate (BOO) scheme have been using a first-price sealed-bid mechanism. In this situation, the value of the item (the cost of building, operating, and maintaining a transmission line) is very much standardized and well established among bidders. According to the regulations, there is no market risk, since owners of transmission assets are paid based on their availability, not on the energy transported. It is a very stable, predictable cash flow stream.

Brazilian auctions for the construction, operation, and maintenance of transmission lines follow a sequential multi-unit auction design in which each individual item is auctioned through a FPSB phase followed by a contingent second phase that takes place as an oral descending auction. Between 1998 and 2009, about 32,000 km of new high voltage transmission facilities (230 kV and above) were awarded, with strong participation from both local and foreign investors, and with an increasing number of competitors in the auctions over time.

Figure B.1 presents the detailed results for all 500kV circuits auctioned from 2000 to 2006. The figure shows (i) the discount offered by the winning investors for each circuit with respect to the reference annual allowed revenue (set by the regulator as the initial cap in the auction, which is calculated based on the standard investment and O&M costs of the related equipment and capital structure for the transmission business), and (ii) the investment cost per kilometer for the transmission facility (i.e., circuit and substation) implicit in the offers made. The efficiency of the auction design to award concessions for new circuits has been remarkable: with the increase of competition in the auctions, discounts have increased and the US$/km for the 500kV circuits has decreased substantially.

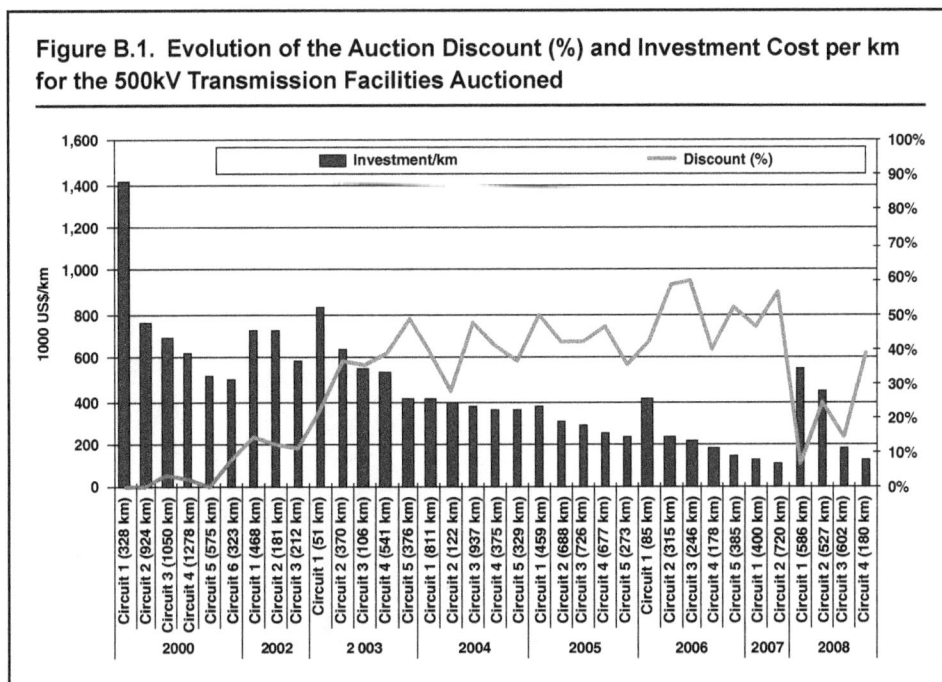

Figure B.1. Evolution of the Auction Discount (%) and Investment Cost per km for the 500kV Transmission Facilities Auctioned

Source: PSR Analysis

VII. Financial Transmission Rights

Financial Transmission Rights (FTRs) are purely financial instruments (i.e. they function whether or not physical transmission of energy occurs) designed to provide hedging against the risks arising from congestion in transmission systems. Whenever generators and loads are exposed to the possibility of different marginal prices at the points in the network where power is injected and withdrawn, congestion fees may be charged. FTRs represent a hedging against those charges. This is a very important financial instrument for promoting competition and enabling the development of locational marginal pricing.[2]

In its simplest form, an FTR is characterized by an amount in MW (also called the reservation level) and by a pair of nodes in a transmission network where the power is injected and withdrawn (source and sink nodes), respectively. Its liquidation is done at a value given by the difference between the marginal prices in the sink and source nodes multiplied by the reservation level. For example, an FTR from node A (source) to node B (sink) for 100 MW pays $100 (P_B - P_A)$, where P_A and P_B are the marginal prices of electricity in nodes A and B, respectively.

Acquisition of FTRs is generally done via auctions in which FTRs corresponding to the transmission capacity of the system are sold in monthly, annual, and longer-term contracts. This scheme was first developed in the early 1990s and some variations of it are currently being implemented across deregulated markets in the US (e.g. PJM, New York, and New England), Italy, and the Nordic region. Other markets used similar auctions to grant access to cross-border transmission capacities, such as the market in Central European countries.

Notes

1. And the right to use the natural resources, in the case of a hydro plant.
2. Locational marginal pricing has the potential to optimize the use of resources, by conveying price signals to new plants and by operating the system according to least-cost, security-constrained principles.

Virtual Power Plant Auctions Around the World[1]

Introduction[2]

Virtual power plant (VPP) auctions refer to auctions for the sale of electricity supply contracts that give the buyer the right to the output, or a share of the output, of a power plant. These sales, rather than physical divestitures, are virtual divestitures by one or more dominant incumbents. Virtually all VPP auctions have followed the simultaneous ascending clock auction design with discrete rounds.

The products typically sold in VPP auctions are essentially option contracts with four basic elements:

- Option price: the price ($/MW-month) that gives the buyer the right to a certain amount (MW) of energy during a specific time period;
- Strike price: the price ($/MWh) that should be paid by the buyer when he exercises the option;
- Duration: the time frame during which the contract is valid;
- Energy: the energy (MW) the buyer has the right to buy at the strike price.

VPP auctions have been used to promote competition by boosting the development of wholesale electricity markets and providing potential investors with an easier way into the markets. As Ausubel and Cramton (2009) state, at least three arguments have been put forward by observers through which VPP auctions may promote competition and liberalization:

- They may facilitate entry into the electricity market by assuring the availability of electricity supplies on the high-power grid to new entrants.
- They may promote the development of, and add liquidity to, the wholesale electricity market.
- They may reduce market power in the spot electricity market.

The experience of VPP auctions shows that they are a good instrument for facilitating market entry and promoting the development of wholesale power markets. For example, the French wholesale market is considered to be the third most active wholesale electricity market in Europe today. However, in 2001, there was barely a wholesale electricity market in France, to the point that data from the German wholesale market had to be used when setting reference prices for the early Electricité de France (EDF) auctions. Also, European utilities have been expanding their operations outside their principal markets partly due to the access to generation afforded by VPP auctions.

With less concentrated markets in generation, the market power of dominant firms may reduce spot prices. Some authors argue that VPP auctions are not as effective as physical divestiture, since the contracts are relatively short-lived in some of the auctions. Schultz (2005) would therefore prefer long-term, non-staggered contracts or physical divestiture. Ausubel and Cramton (2009) argue that the VPP auction should be viewed as simply the wrong choice of instrument for remedying market power in the spot market. The reason is that VPP auctions involve a relatively small fraction of total installed generating capacity in the given market. For example, in France, VPP auctions account for no more than 10 percent of generating capacity, while in 2001, EDF accounted for over 80 percent of the French market. In Spain, while Endesa and Iberdrola had the obligation to divest less than 6 percent and 5 percent, respectively, together they had a market share of around 60 percent. This is not a matter of merely increasing the capacity available through VPP auctions, because even at current levels, clearing prices have reached the reserve prices in many of the VPP auctions outside of France.

Several regions throughout the world have used such auctions. VPP auctions were first introduced in France in 2001 when EDF (Electricité de France) was required by the European Commission to sell part of its generating capacity to potential entrants into the French market. France still runs the longest series of VPP auctions to date. At the time of this writing, EDF had conducted over 30 VPP auctions. The same concept has also been used in Belgium, the Netherlands, Denmark, Spain, Portugal, Germany, and in the US. The Canadian province of Alberta conducted an auction in 2000 that was not formalized as a VPP divestiture but has similar characteristics. France was the first country to formally start VPP auctions in 2001. Examples from Spain and the Netherlands are also described below and some of the other experiences will be discussed in turn.

I. Alberta, Canada

Alberta, located in western Canada, has significant reserves of coal (approximately 60 percent of the country's reserves) and natural gas (accounting for over 80 percent of the country's production). Its electricity industry supplies 1.5 million customers in Canada's fourth most populous province. Peak demand in 2009 was about 10,000 MW and installed capacity is approximately 13,000 MW at the present time. Generation primarily comes from coal- and gas-fired plants. Alberta imports power from the neighboring provinces of British Columbia and Saskatchewan.

The electricity market reform process in this Canadian province was first initiated in 1995 through the Electric Utilities Act. Reform was mainly driven by the need to attract private investments in the generation sector and to induce greater competition. The following year, the Power Pool of Alberta was created and started operations as a marketplace for all wholesale electricity transactions. It is considered to be an efficient power market, with participation from both the supply and demand sides.

Concerns over the possibility of incumbent utility companies exercising market power and driving prices higher than expected led the government to implement Power Purchase Arrangements. These agreements were to be between generating units owned by the three electricity utilities and buyers who would acquire the right to sell the output of these plants in the Power Pool, with contract durations of up to 20 years.

In 2000, the government auctioned Power Purchase Arrangements (PPAs) for the output from the province's 12 thermal generating plants to new players. The selling process was an initial approach to what has later become a VPP divestiture. It was established that the sellers (i.e., the generators) would retain ownership of the plants and remain responsible for maintenance and operation activities, while the buyers would be entitled to the output of the plants. Buyers would pay for the associated fixed and variable costs incurred. Plant capacities ranged from roughly 20 MW to 800 MW, totaling 6,400 MW, and consisted of a mix of baseload coal and peak gas-fired units.

The auctioning process in Alberta was highly structured, with (i) PPA contracts and auction rules finalized and published well before the auction, (ii) a bidder qualification process to ensure necessary financial strength, and (iii) bidder information sessions to educate bidders and answer questions. The auction was run through the internet and used the simultaneous clock auction design. Finally, contracts were executed shortly after bidding finished.

The success of the auction was due to its openness, transparency, certainty, stability, and care taken to ensure that the auction design and rules were a good fit with the characteristics of the PPAs being traded. Eight of the 12 PPAs were sold, and the auction raised US$780 million. There were 70 rounds of bidding over an approximately two-week period. Some controversy arose as to product definition through the auction process, particularly on the form and content of the PPA contracts. However, the government agency and auction participants praised the auction design and implementation, and the objective of creating new entrants in the marketplace was achieved.

II. France

EDF, the French national integrated utility company and one of the largest state-owned energy companies in the world, produces, transmits, and distributes about 95 percent of the electricity used in France. It controls an installed capacity of about 100 GW with an energy production of around 500 TWh/year. Its generation mix is mostly based on nuclear energy, establishing France as one of the leading countries in the area of nuclear technologies.

VPP auctions were first pioneered by EDF in 2001 as part of a regulatory quid pro quo, whereby EDF would be allowed to proceed with the acquisition of a joint controlling stake in Energie Baden-Württemberg AG (EnBW), the fourth largest electric utility company in Germany. The European Commission (EC) noted that EDF would be gaining joint control of one of the potential competitors that was particularly well-placed to enter the French market. The EC required EDF to create room for other potential entrants in the French market, with a significant generating capacity. At the same time, given EDF's status as the largest nuclear energy producer in the world, the regulator recognized that physical divestitures of EDF's nuclear baseload plants would be undesirable in several respects. In particular, EDF had demonstrated a strong track record in the safety and security of its nuclear plants, and the public clearly benefited from economies of scale in EDF's joint management of the portfolio of nuclear plants. Consequently, the undertaking agreed upon by the regulator and EDF in early 2001 prompted a virtual divestiture by EDF of 6 GW of generation capacity located in France.

The VPP contracts offered in the EDF auctions were divided into two groups: baseload products and peak-load products.[3] There were six baseload products with durations ranging from three to 48 months, and five peak-load products. The price differentials among the different products in a given group were determined by the seller before each auction. Each VPP product is an option contract for energy. Buyers pay an option premium to the sellers (the value of which is decided during the auction process) and whenever the electricity spot price exceeds the strike price, the option is exercised. The strike prices approximate the variable cost of the respective energy. The VPP auctions follow the simultaneous ascending clock auction design with discrete rounds.

The first EDF auction was conducted in September 2001, and there have been 32 successful auctions held on a quarterly basis as of this writing. In the meantime, the VPP auction has proven popular with regulators throughout Europe. The basic mechanism has been replicated: Electrabel in Belgium, Nuon in the Netherlands, Elsam in Denmark, Endesa and Iberdrola in combined auctions in Spain, REN and EDP in combined auctions in Portugal, and E.ON and RWE in separate voluntary auctions in Germany. A similar structure was used in the Texas Capacity Auctions in the US, and was planned in connection with the Exelon-PGE merger, again in the US.

III. Spain

The Spanish power system has an installed capacity of 91,000 MW. The capacity mix includes hydropower (18 percent), natural gas (30 percent), coal (13 percent), nuclear (8 percent), and renewable sources (32 percent). Most of the expansion in renewable sources is comprised of wind generation, where Spain has made remarkable progress, albeit at a very high cost to be paid by customers. Yearly load growth is around 2.5 percent per year, considered a high figure by European standards.

In 2005, the government published the *White Paper* of the Spanish Electricity Market, which set forth directives and proposals aimed at reducing market concentration and increasing the competition and efficiency of the electricity market. After a process of mergers and acquisitions, the Spanish market was dominated by only two companies (Iberdrola and Endesa) which together represented around 80 percent of all electricity generated in the country. In order to increase competition, the two dominant market players were required to hold Virtual Power Plant (VPP) auctions so that a wider range of companies and investors had access to the existing generation capacity. There have been seven auctions so far in which two products were available—one for peak hours and the other that could be exercised on a 24×7 basis. Both products are option contracts for energy, and were offered with durations of three, six, and 12 months. The Endesa-Iberdrola auctions were initially held quarterly, like the EDF auctions, but they later became semi-annual. These auctions also follow the simultaneous ascending clock auction design with discrete rounds.

IV. The Netherlands

In approving Nuon's purchase of assets from Reliant Europe, the Dutch competition authority declared that 900 MW of generating capacity had to be put at arm's length for five years through the use of a virtual power plant (VPP) auction. The 900 MW was divided into 90 identical blocks of 10 MW, with an imposed cap of 23 blocks (230 MW) for any one bidder. There was also a bidder qualification process to ensure financial and technical capability.

The auction followed a hybrid design. It started with an ascending clock auction phase, whereby bidders had to stipulate the number of blocks they would buy at a specified price. The price rose ("ticks" up) by an increment round by round. Once excess demand had reached a "trigger level", a final sealed-bid uniform price round was held. At this stage, bids were ranked block-by-block in descending order in terms of price, and the top 90 bids were the winners.

Notes

1. Although the goal of VPP auctions is not perfectly in line with the major objective of this report (i.e. auctions to increase capacity), they also involve the sale of electricity supply contracts. The objective, in this case, is to auction a contract that gives the holder the right to the output, or alternatively a share of the output of a particular power plant.

2. This introduction is based on Ausubel and Cramton (2009).

3. In the early EDF VPP auctions, there was a third product group: Power Purchase Agreement (PPA) products. The PPA product was a firm baseload product from November to March.

Additional Experience with Renewables: FiTs and RPS

As described in Chapter 6, renewables promotion has relied on feed-in-tariffs and RPS. This appendix provides complementary information regarding: (a) success with FiTs and (b) examples of RPS.

I. FiTs: Results and Lessons Learned

Feed-in-tariffs have had an excellent track record in promoting the development of renewable resources. Countries like Denmark, Germany, and Spain have witnessed tremendous growth in the installed capacity of renewable generation. The European Commission concluded that "well-adapted feed-in-tariff regimes are generally the most efficient and effective support schemes for promoting renewable electricity." A comparison between the development of wind energy in Germany (FiT) and the UK (RPS) shows that whilst installed capacity has remained low in the UK, it has increased significantly in Germany, despite the better conditions (wind speed) observed in the UK. Spain is one of the most successful cases in Europe. The FiT incentive has proven to be very successful—at least in building some new technologies—with Spain having become one of the world leaders in renewable energy installed, particularly for wind and solar. Renewable electricity plants (solar, wind, biomass, waste, and small hydro) currently produce over 56,000 MWh in the country per year (over 20 percent of the total electricity demand).

However, the success of FiT and the development of wind and solar energy have of course come at a substantial financial cost to consumers.[1] In Spain, the considerable support received by solar, and the large amount of wind energy produced, have both contributed to a relevant fraction of the total electricity tariff. In 2009, total support for renewables was 4,600€ million, and over half this figure corresponds to photovoltaic projects.[2] Germany and Spain have recently announced their intention to reduce the level of FiT. The case of Spain, described in box D.1, is emblematic, as it illustrates the different issues and powers at play related to the decision to cut FiT levels.

Feed-in-tariffs are very much dependent on the prices set for the energy to be procured under long-term contracts. This presents a similar challenge to administratively setting capacity payments as discussed earlier in this report. If prices are set too high, it will lead to over-investments and tariff increases. If they are set too low, no bidder will participate and the program will be considered a failure. To get the renewable program off the ground, policy makers prefer to err on the conservative side, that is, over-estimating the price paid, including a premium for risks. This mechanism undoubtedly increases the comfort level of investors and other decision makers. Once a price is posted, it entails a steady stream of revenues for the life of the project.

Box D.1. Clouds Over Spain: Solar Feed-in-Tariff to be Slashed by up to 45 Percent[3]

Spain's Ministry of Industry issued a press release yesterday announcing that it has sent the National Energy Commission a proposal for a Royal Decree to cut current feed-in-tariffs for solar photovoltaic energy by up to 45 percent.

Since the start of the summer, the Spanish solar photovoltaic sector has been involved in talks with the country's Ministry of Industry regarding the government's plans to cut feed-in-tariffs for solar energy. At times, the process has been more like a soap opera than a rational dialogue between government and industry, where considerable uncertainty, rumors, and unsuccessful meetings abound.

Yesterday, however, the final chapter of the saga came to an end as the Ministry of Industry responsible for overseeing the energy sector in Spain issued a press release revealing that it had sent a proposal to the National Energy Commission for a Royal Decree introducing cuts to the feed-in-tariffs for solar photovoltaic energy, in addition to the previously announced cuts to the wind and solar thermal electric feed-in-tariffs agreed upon with the latter two sectors earlier this year.

The Ministry of Industry has officially proposed a 45 percent reduction in the feed-in-tariff for future ground-based solar photovoltaic installations, a 25 percent cut for large rooftop arrays, and a 5 percent cut for small rooftop systems. According to the Ministry of Industry press release, "these cuts respond to technological improvements and cost reductions in the photovoltaic sector".

The Ministry of Industry said in its press release that the proposed measures "will enable these technologies [wind, solar photovoltaic and solar thermal electric] to contribute over time to reducing electricity costs and create a more visible and stable framework in the future".

As a result, comments from the industry have been hard to come by, although Spain's solar photovoltaic trade associations have described the proposed 45 percent cuts as "madness". In earlier meetings with the sector, the Industry Minister, Miguel Sebastián, was also quoted as saying that his government "did not want ground-based solar arrays" any longer. These significant cuts, which considerably exceed similar measures announced in Germany earlier this summer, will certainly have put a damper on the holidays of those making a living from solar photovoltaic in this Mediterranean country.

II. Renewable Portfolio Standards (RPS)

Unlike FiT, RPS does not guarantee the purchase of all renewable energy regardless of cost. RPS programs tend to allow more price competition between different types of renewable energy, but can be limited in competition through eligibility and multipliers for RPS programs. Those supporting the adoption of RPS mechanisms claim that market implementation will result in competition, efficiency, and innovation that will deliver renewable energy at the lowest possible cost, allowing it to compete with cheaper fossil fuel energy sources. Conversely, some of those who propose FiT claim that competition may lead to depressed prices, thereby decreasing the chances of projects actually being built. In China, the shift in direction from competitive procurement (via auctions) to FiT was primarily due to the lack of success in terms of completion rates for projects awarded under the auction schemes.[4] Some examples of RPS are described below.

a) Texas RPS

The Texas RPS is believed to be one of the most effective and successful in the US, and is widely considered a model mechanism. It has had one of the greatest influences on the rapid growth of the Texas wind energy industry, and is currently presenting the largest installed capacity in the US.

When Texas produced its first Renewable Portfolio Standard as part of the state's electricity industry restructuring legislation in 1999 (Senate Bill 7), it mandated the construction of certain volumes of renewable energy and prompted the renewable energy industry to rapidly accelerate its production on Texas sites. The Texas Public Utility Commission implemented the program.

The RPS mandated that electricity providers (competitive retailers, municipal electric utilities, and electric cooperatives) collectively generate 2,000 megawatts (MW) of additional renewable energy by 2009. The 2005 Texas Legislature increased the state's total renewable energy mandate to 5,880 MW by 2015, with a target of 10,000 MW in 2025. Each provider is required to obtain new renewable energy capacity based on his/her market share of energy sales times the renewable capacity goal. For example, a competitive retailer with 10 percent of the Texas retail electricity sales in 2009 would be required to obtain 200 megawatts of renewable energy capacity.

The Texas RPS has been very successful. Its 10-year goal was met in just over six years. The current cost competitiveness of wind power has Texas five years ahead of its renewable construction schedule. Wind power development in Texas has more than quadrupled since the RPS was established. After the RPS was implemented, Texas wind corporations and utilities invested $1 billion in wind power. Due to its competitive pricing, available federal tax incentives, and the state's immense wind resources, wind power is expected to remain competitive with coal and gas-fired plants. The policy stimulated the construction of some of the world's largest wind power projects in the state of Texas.

In an effort to diversify the state's renewable generation portfolio, Senate Bill 20 also includes a requirement that the state must meet 500 MW of the 2025 target with non-wind renewable generation. This provision indirectly promotes solar power and biomass in Texas and provides farmers and ranchers with new revenue sources from the use of crops and animal waste to produce energy.

b) Renewable Energy Credits (REC)

One REC represents a volume of qualified renewable energy that is generated and metered. In Texas, this corresponds to one megawatt hour. To meet the RPS targets, utility companies may buy or trade RECs.

The RPS provides for a Renewable Energy Credit (REC) trading program that will continue through 2019. The REC trading system generated great flexibility in the development of renewable energy projects. The renewable energy capacity required by the electricity sellers can be provided directly or through the REC market. If a utility earns extra credits, it can sell them to others in need of credits to meet their RPS requirements. This enables electricity providers that do not own or have enough renewable energy in their portfolio to supplement the requirements by purchasing credits instead of capacity.

Renewable Energy Credits are issued quarterly, based on meter readings. The REC market is administered by ERCOT, the Texas electric grid operator. Penalties for non-compliance with RPS requirements are enforced by the Public Utility Commission of Texas (PUCT), which has the authority to cap the price of RECs and may suspend the standard if necessary to protect the reliability and operation of the grid.

An increasing number of states and municipalities has been introducing renewable portfolio standards. Furthermore, as there are a large number of high-profile companies looking to improve their image and reduce their environmental impact, the market for green tags in the US has been growing significantly.

c) United Kingdom RPS Equivalent—From NFFO to REC[5]

In 1990, the UK started to develop renewable energy sources through the Non-Fossil Fuel Obligation (NFFO) program. It was administered as a series of competitive orders in which renewable energy developers submitted bids specifying the energy price at which they would be prepared to develop a project and deliver energy. The Department of Trade and Industry determined the level of capacity for different technology bands and the bids that should be accepted, and offered contracts to meet this capacity.

Local distribution companies had to purchase all NFFO generation offered to them and pay the contracted price for this generation. The difference between the contracted price and the pool-selling price, which represented the subsidy for renewable generation, was reimbursed using funds from a Fossil Fuel Levy.

The NFFO order ended in 1998 and was replaced by the Renewable Obligation Certificate (ROC). Similar to the case of Texas described earlier, eligible renewable generation facilities receive ROCs corresponding to 1 MWh of energy produced. Distribution companies are obliged to buy ROCs corresponding to a fraction of total energy sales, set at a quota of 3 percent of generation in 2002/2003. If the distribution company is not able to obtain sufficient ROCs, it has to make buy-out payments (30 UK Pounds in 2002/2003). Those payments are recycled to suppliers that have presented ROCs, thereby increasing the value of producing renewable energy for competitive generation if the quota is not achieved.

A shortage of renewable energy resulted in a levy on electricity bills that was paid by all electricity consumers. The administrative body for this system was the Non-Fossil Purchasing Agency (NFPA), which was set up and owned by the distribution RECs. Like other Green Certificate schemes or Renewable Portfolio Standards, the ROC is based on market principles. Shortage of renewable generation increases the value of the ROC, thereby encouraging market entry and causing a decline in the price of renewable energy. The aim is the deployment of renewable technologies according to national targets at least cost (see Jensen and Skytte, 2003). The ROC will therefore encourage the deployment of the cheaper and more well-established renewable technologies unless additional support policies for newer technologies are adopted.

III. Policy Decisions

One important aspect to be taken into account when countries choose a certain renewable policy has to do with the stage of development of the market. In fledgling markets, with inexperienced players and a lot of uncertainty, FiTs provide the necessary comfort level for those players to consider investment decisions and lead a project to fruition. Other schemes that involve some form of competition (on the sale of RECs or in the case of auctions) may deter investors from participating, given their apparent complexity, their need to establish his/her own price without knowing the business well, and the chances of underbidding in a competitive process, which may lead to the well-known "winner's curse." PURPA is an interesting example where initially prices were set based on the avoided cost, which was the basis for the development of the industry. Later on, once the road was paved, uncertainties were mitigated, and a good track record in terms of development was observed, it was possible to consider the introduction of competition.

The jury is still out. FiT has undoubtedly accelerated the development of renewable sources—but perhaps at very high costs. These issues are now being revisited by a few countries, such as Germany and Spain, which have been considered models in terms of pushing the renewable agenda forward. On the other hand, some places that are adopting RPS, such as the state of Texas, have also experienced significant growth.

Needless to say, the success of renewable energy development depends on a series of other factors, in addition to the pricing and contracting policies discussed before. Some of the lessons learned include:

- Inadequate transmission is frequently cited as the most significant obstacle (to wind power development) in Texas.
- The lack of a coherent environmental policy (in Brazil), often leading to delays in the licensing of such large hydro plants, may tilt the table towards the development of more oil and coal-fired plants. Paradoxically, more than 10,000 MW of such technologies have been awarded via auctions over the last few years.
- In contrast, renewable generation is usually spread out over several plants with easier environmental licensing (in Brazil) and smaller capacities, which also contributed to providing a *"portfolio" effect* and thus a *hedge against larger project delays*.
- The *"not-in-my-back-yard"* approach has been intensely observed, even for supposedly benign non-conventional renewables. Problems in licensing and public outcry have delayed one of the most important off-shore windmill projects in the US, on the coast of Massachusetts.

Looking forward, one expects that some of the positive features of FiT and RPS may be combined in such a way so as to introduce competition, foster innovation, and push prices down to final users. However, there is always some tension between significantly scaling up renewable sources and keeping costs down, particularly when the available renewable options are far from being cost competitive. Despite this consideration, the following examples, which describe the use of auctions, demonstrate that a reasonable trade-off between a policy of reducing costs and greening the matrix can be achieved. Competition via auctions represents a good mechanism for striking a balance between these two apparently conflicting goals.

IV. California

California's installed capacity is about 58,000 MW with an all-time peak demand of 50,270 MW (July 2006). The marginal fuel type is natural gas. Contrary to most regions in the world, which have relied on feed-in-tariffs to develop a strong renewable energy base, California has just introduced a "reverse auction market", specifically proposed to spur the development of in-state renewable sources.

The feed-in-tariff mechanism was first adopted in California under the Public Utility Regulatory Policies Act (PURPA 1978). It was meant to promote greater use of renewable energy and reduce oil dependence.[6]

Under this act, utilities were required to purchase power from 'Qualifying Facilities', especially small renewable generators, at 'avoided cost' rates. These rates, which reflected the marginal cost of acquiring the same volume of energy from an alternative source, were determined by the state utility commissions. State Regulatory Commissions were required to establish procedures according to which electric power should be purchased by electric utility companies. Many commissions pegged the rates to high oil prices, resulting in highly favorable guaranteed payments and stimulating renewable development. A further stimulus to deployment was given by the Investment Tax Credit, implemented in 1979. Despite not being PURPA-generation specific, it did set in motion the further development of these facilities.

Qualifying facilities were not necessarily renewable sources of energy. A QF could be a fossil fuel plant, since qualification in this case was by virtue of a significant gain in thermal efficiency, enabled, for example, by the simultaneous production of steam and heat (co-generation facilities). Qualifying facilities were typically smaller than the typical baseload generation and peaking units built by public utilities.

The avoided cost to the utility was determined based on technical parameters, but it was essentially an administratively established figure. In retrospect, cost estimates used to set PURPA contract prices proved to be excessive. Most of the states established that the power-contracting scheme should be characterized as a "price-posting" procedure— that is, once the price was announced, the utility was obliged to take all the power it was offered at the avoided cost.[7] This was acceptable at the early stage of PURPA. However, when the mechanism started to gain momentum, the interest from the non-utility sector increased, as did the supply sources of renewable generation. The utilities would end up receiving more offers than their own market required. Some coined the expression "PURPA Machine" when alluding to the perverse incentives that the mechanism created, leading to an oversupply and excessive prices being transferred to the consumers.[8]

V. Brazil

Brazil has had experience both with FiT and with competitive mechanisms to procure renewable sources of energy. Table D.1 summarizes prices, volumes, and costs resulting from the two main Brazilian renewable energy support mechanisms implemented thus far, namely Proinfa and renewable energy auctions. The annual costs of both programs are practically the same (about US$1 billion), but the energy auction scheme is meant to deliver about 20 percent more total capacity. The average energy cost and an expected tariff impact were about 25 percent and 60 percent lower when auctions were used. In the case of bioelectricity, more efficient plants were acquired through the auction scheme

Table D.1. Overall Results of the Main Renewable Support Mechanisms in Brazil

	PROINFA			Technology-specific ("Reserve energy" auctions)		
	MW	GWh/year	US$/MWh	MW	GWh/year	US$/MWh
Wind	1423	3740	154	1800	6596	80
Small Hydro	1191	6260	96	—	—	
Bioelectricity	779	2661	77	2379	4800	84
Impact on costs						
Total capacity (MW)	3,393			4,179		
Total energy (GWh/year)	12,661			11,397		
Average cost (US$/MWh)	109			80		
Total cost (million US$/year)	1,381			911		
Net impact on tariffs (US$/MWh)	3.8			1.6		

Source: Eletrobras, EPE, ANEEL, ONS and PSR. April 2010, prices include taxes.

and not all new plants contracted have sold their total surplus capacity in the auction, leaving some quantity to be sold in future auctions or directly to free consumers.[9]

The experience of FiT and the recent renewable energy auctions in Brazil are revealing. Auctions have proved to be an interesting way to support the implementation of renewable energy at minimum cost for a given portfolio of technologies and renewable quotas defined as part of the energy policy agenda. It is an indirect way to ensure feed-in-tariff price discovery. As in the case of FiT, long-term contracting reduces risk aversion and facilitates project financing. In principle, auctions maintain the advantages of feed-in-tariffs (income certainty) and are also capable of minimizing costs to consumers by entertaining competition and pushing costs down to the end-user.

Notes

1. This of course should be balanced against the reduction in system costs because of reduced fuel consumption, and also against non-monetary benefits such as security of supply and environmental or R&D improvements.
2. Barroso et al. (2010).
3. Source: Renewable Energy Magazine. August 02, 2010.
4. Personal conversation with Xiaodong Wang, Senior Energy Specialist, World Bank.
5. Butler, N. and Neuhoff, K. Comparison of Feed-in-Tariff, Quota and Auction Mechanisms to Support Wind Power Development. MIT and Center for Energy and Environmental Policy Research. CMI Working Paper 70.
6. The Support Renewable Energy Act of 2010 (Bill S.3021/111th Congress) amends the Public Utility Regulatory Policies Act of 1978 to authorize the Secretary of Energy to promulgate regulations to allow electric utilities to use renewable energy to comply with any federal renewable electricity standard.
7. In some cases where transmission constraints were present, a rationing scheme evolved into a first-come, first-served procedure. Developers had the prerogative to build their own access lines.
8. Some states, such as California and Massachusetts, considered alternative schemes based on a procedure of first announcing the quantity of PURPA power utilities expected to use in the future and then accepting bids from QFs to supply this quantity. The former mechanism was similar to a "feed-in-tariff" procedure, while the latter had elements of a competitive procurement of energy, sometimes referred to as auctions. The typical contract was of a physical nature. Despite the fact that the QFs were being embedded within the utilities, there were many factors beyond energy costs that were taken into account when a bidder was awarded a contract, such as *inter alia*, environmental impact, "dispatchability," (that is, to what extent the utility had the prerogative to dispatch the plant), type of fuel, location, etc.

Therefore, the product offered by the bidders was complex and diverse. Some states believed that this complexity should be reflected in the bid evaluation schemes to rank offers. Others, such as the California Power Utility Commission (PUC), had an auction design that reduced the price issue to a single variable. According to the pure definition of auctions used in this paper, most of the competitive procurement of energy proposed under PURPA was not an auction per se, since the selection was based on price and non-price factors.

PURPA basically traded physical contracts encompassing a great variety of technologies. According to this scenario, the selection process was relatively complex, oftentimes multi-dimensional, with different weights assigned to price and non-price factors. It should be understood that PURPA preceded power sector reform in the US (and to some extent contributed to it). Therefore, there was no way to implement pure financial contracts to play a role of price hedge instruments, whereby sellers have a guaranteed price for a certain volume of energy. When PURPA was enacted and implemented, there were no power markets or wholesale competition in the US, which explains the complexity of the contractual relationships and selection processes.
9. Adapted from: *"Implementation of Renewable Energy Market Development Policies in Brazil"*. Energy and Water Department, the World Bank. Washington DC. Forthcoming (2011).

Issues Related to Descending Clock Auctions

I. Starting Price

For the descending clock auction to work as intended, it is important that the starting price be set in a way to create excess supply. It is competition among the bidders that determines the clearing price. The starting price will quickly be bid down, unless there is insufficient competition. A low starting price potentially lowers the expected cost of buying the products, but it does so at the expense of possibly reducing the number of bidders. One additional bidder is more valuable to the auctioneer than a lower starting price.[1] Hence, this trade-off must be handled carefully when the starting price is selected.

Setting the starting price is an art. Its value directly introduces a cognitive bias on bidders—known as anchoring or "focalism"—that describes the common human tendency to rely too heavily, or "anchor," on a piece of information when making decisions and then adjust to that value to account for other elements of the circumstance. Once the anchor is set, there is usually a bias toward that value. Although a very high starting price has the potential to stimulate more supply to join the auction, it poses the risk of a poor and expensive outcome if collusion is observed and/or there is less supply than demand. The "anchoring effect" might distract participants to reference their bids to, and compare the auction results with, the starting price. In contrast, setting too low a starting price can limit the effectiveness of the price discovery impact of the auction. There are several methods available to determine the starting price. The most common one is to base the starting price on market fundamentals, cost of new energy, price indexes, and recent experience. There is, however, a trade-off that must be carefully taken into account: lowering the reserve price may discourage some bidders from participating, thereby leading to less competition. With limited competition, the product is likely to be traded at the reserve price. In general, it is usually thought to be more valuable for the auctioneer to have one additional bidder than to have a lower reserve price.

II. Auction Mechanism (rounds)

The clock auction is run in discrete rounds. In each round, the auctioneer announces just the round price. Each bidder submits a quantity bid and the auctioneer determines the total excess supply at the end of the price round. As long as there is excess supply, the price decreases. The price decrement is determined by best practice methods, essentially in relation to the extent of excess supply. If there is no excess supply, the clearing price is determined.

In the descending clock auction for the Firm Energy Market in Colombia, the auctioneer discloses the total excess supply at the end of the prior round, the start of round price, and the end of round price. Each bidder submits a supply curve at all prices between the start and end of round price.

III. Activity Rule

An activity rule in a dynamic auction is intended to enhance price discovery by motivating each bidder to bid throughout the auction in a manner that is consistent with the bidder's actual value(s) for the product(s). The most common activity rule is that a bidder cannot bid in a subsequent round if he has failed to bid in the previous round, and bids must be consistent (i.e. the successive quantities must be the same or lower). To the extent that bids better reflect each bidder's true values, the price is more apt to progress in a manner consistent with the final competitive price.[2]

IV. Information Disclosure Policy

The information disclosure policy determines who knows what in the auction. A well-known result in auction theory is that bidders reduce their price discount (to their estimated maximum value of the product) to a minimum when they have maximum prior information on the product. Different practices have been observed elsewhere. In some approaches, auction demand is announced beforehand, and at the end of every round the auctioneer reports the total excess supply at the end of the prior round, the start of round price, and the end of round price. This is a silent (and anonymous) auction in the sense that no individual offers are reported.

The disclosure of only the current price and total offered quantity is enough to foster competition, provided the product and market context have been described prior to the start of the auction, and adequate time has been allowed for the bidders to carry out their due diligence.

V. Clearing Rule

The auction ends when there is either no or minimal excess supply. The clock ticks down while excess supply remains. Thus, the auction will conclude when excess supply is (close to) zero or negative at the end of round prices. The auctioneer then backs up the bids made to determine the clearing price where supply and demand are balanced.

With "lumpy" bids, it is generally not possible to have precise market clearing, where supply is exactly equal to demand. The full quantity bid is usually allocated to the marginal generator, and other bids scaled pro rata to their bids and the clearing quantity.

VI. Information Technology

In order for a descending price clock auction to be applied, especially to multiple items, a computational system (software) must be developed. In the experience of the countries that have implemented this type of auction design, the development timing of the system is small and costs are negligible compared to the benefits of transparency and competition.

Notes

1. See Bulow and Klemperer (1996).
2. See Cramton (1998) and Cramton (2006).

Approaches to Entertain Demand-Side Participation in Energy Auctions

A uctions can indeed be used to trade "Nega-watts"[1], that is, commitments made by certain industries and consumers (or distribution companies acting on their behalf) to reduce their load and help bridge the supply-demand gap. Demand reduction becomes the product being procured by the utility. In this case, demand is playing the role of a resource, and may as well be procured via auction mechanisms.

Demand-side management programs can be divided into two main areas: energy efficiency programs and demand response programs. Energy efficiency generally refers to the suite of actions geared towards optimizing the ratio between the volume of energy consumed and the end products and services obtained from it. It is usually attained through technology-related investments and behavioral changes to increase end-use energy. Demand response programs aim to either directly or indirectly manage consumption by shifting part of the demand to off-peak hours or when electricity costs are lower. Demand-side options have not received a lot of support as part of power sector reforms worldwide. On the one hand, generators and distributors fear that demand-side options, particularly those that boost energy efficiency, may undermine their revenues and profits. On the other hand, regulators are reluctant to remunerate demand bidders for the megawatts reduced, since it is difficult to meter. Measuring energy conservation efforts requires an ex-ante agreement on a baseline or counterfactual demand, and a well-established monitoring system.[2] The challenge is to determine what would be the energy consumption in the absence of the demand-side intervention, which cannot be metered as objectively as the production of a new power plant. This "what-if" scenario creates fear and uncertainty among policy makers and regulators.

Experience with auctions for demand reduction or energy efficiency is still very limited. They are not as mature as supply-side options to help bridge the supply-demand gap. A few examples of competitive procurement of demand resources are available in Brazil, India, Europe, and the US. In some places, the concept of "standard offer" is applied, whereby ESCOs offer energy-saving programs at pre-established prices, usually differentiated by technology.[3] The US has been leading the demand response efforts. A small number of power markets in the US have been able to accommodate short-term demand response, competing head to head with supply resources. The challenge is to enable long-term energy efficiency gains to compete on a level playing field with generators, since most of the energy auctions involve short and medium-term contracts (e.g. two years, like in BGS auctions in New Jersey, USA). Experience in the US has also shown the need for end-user education prior to making significant changes, and protection for those who cannot change their electricity utilization patterns.

There are four basic approaches for dealing with demand-side participation in energy auctions:

- **The first approach** assumes that the energy and demand forecasts already take all possible efficiency gains into account. Therefore, EE and DSM are perceived as passive elements of the market, as opposed to active participants. Price elasticity is not considered, or for the sake of simplicity, it is assumed that demand for electricity is virtually inelastic and price response can be ignored. Therefore, there is not much room left to treat demand response as an active participant in bridging the supply-demand gap. The underlying assumption is that expanding capacity, as opposed to rationalizing consumption, is part of the least-cost solution. In this scenario, auctions for demand-side participation make little sense. This has been the approach in most countries. All auctions held in Brazil thus far assume that demand is inelastic and represents an aggregation of inelastic demand curves informed by all distribution companies interested in participating in a particular energy auction.

- **The second approach** consists of building a demand curve that embeds some price elasticity. The calculation of the reserve price takes into account the supply sources and this elastic demand curve. Nonetheless, demand resources are not allowed to bid in the same auction as supply sources. It is therefore still a one-sided auction, which has been the approach adopted in PJM and in Colombia.

- **The third approach** consists of establishing dedicated auctions for demand-side resources, which are willing to bid MWh of energy to be saved. However, there is no supply-demand resource competition, as auctions are carried out separately. It is also a one-sided auction.

- **The fourth approach** enables supply and demand resources to compete on a level-playing-field basis. This is the least common type of demand response auction. Two-sided auctions are rare. They have been encouraged by FERC (US) in the competitive procurement of energy-related products. FERC's decision to include demand resources in any competitive procurement for electricity resources is a paradigm shift. Developing countries still have a long way to go in this regard, particularly those that do not have a formal electricity market where demand resources could be brought to the table on a level-playing-field basis. Things may change, as regulators and stakeholders entertain more demand response, partly in reaction to power crises—but it may still take some time to surmount barriers and reduce regulatory uncertainties regarding the monitoring and evaluation of the demand-side gains.

Despite the fact that demand-side auctions have lagged behind, there have been a number of recent and encouraging experiences in some places in the US that have adopted reverse auctions for the allocation of energy efficiency grants. Usually those grants have been allocated. Energy efficiency and demand-side management grants have typically been allocated on a first-come first-served basis, using the traditional standard offer model, which is a consolidated process in some states, such as New York. Missouri, on the other hand, recently tried an alternative mechanism, using online reserve auctions to successfully award US$ 3 million in energy efficiency grants resulting in 75 GWh of energy saved. On July 28, 2010, sixteen grants were awarded in three consecutive one-hour auctions with 23 pre-qualified bidders. A summary of this auction process is shown in box F.1.

Box F.1. Online Reverse Auctions to Award Energy Efficiency Grants[4]

The Missouri Department of Natural Resources utilized the Procurex, Inc. online reverse auction engine to successfully award $3 million in energy efficiency grants. Procurex, Inc. structured three consecutive one-hour auctions with 23 pre-qualified bidders. A total of $3,000,000 in grants were awarded with grant values of $100,000 (10 grants), $250,000 (4 grants), and $500,000 (2 grants)

The online reverse auction allowed pre-qualified providers to bid on $3 million in incentives on a $/kWh-saved basis for expected energy efficiency projects. Available incentive dollars were allocated based on the lowest price obtained, thus increasing the cost-effectiveness of the program and allowing the Missouri Department of Energy to spread each grant dollar further.

When all the winners fully implement their programs, Missouri could save up to 75 million kWh. As one participant in the process put it, *"That is a powerful use of reverse auction technology."*

Ian Ayres, the William K. Townsend Professor of Law at Yale Law School and writer for the New York Times blog Freakonomics, covered the historic event and said, *"Overall, across three different auctions, the average promised price-effectiveness was 3.97 cents per kilowatt-hour of saved energy."* This compares favorably *"to recent point estimates of the average cost of other utility energy efficiency programs, which range from 4.7 to 13.3 cents per kilowatt-hour."* (Auffhammer, Blumstein, and Fowlie, 2008).

He continued, *"For now, the great state of Missouri has shown that competitive auctions are a feasible way to get the most out of our stimulus money."*

Bret Grady, CEO of Procurex, Inc. said, *"I was quite pleased with the results that we delivered with this auction. A process that has worked so well in other categories such as energy, commodities, and services was applied very successfully for the State of Missouri. I would expect given these results that we will be running similar events for other states and municipalities looking to replicate these savings."*

Box F.2 provides evidence of the difficulties faced by developing countries in creating a level playing field for the participation of demand resources in the design of wholesale markets, and consequently for the implementation of demand-side resources in the future.

Box F.2. Demand Response—An Orphan in Wholesale Market and Auction Design

Demand response has not had many supporters. The design of wholesale markets seldom takes into account the active participation of demand, due in part to the fact that competitive wholesale markets were drafted by the same professionals who had been working with least-cost planning for many years. In most planning exercises, demand was considered or was assumed to be virtually inelastic, and the market design simply muted demand response, corroborating a self-fulfilling prophecy. Most of the auctions implemented thus far have been one-sided procurement processes, whereby only generators are allowed to bid, and the demand is assumed to be a vertical line.

Over the past 10 years, demand response in power markets has been gaining importance—in part due to the 2001 California crisis and similar events in many other developing and developed countries. There was a realization that the absence of demand response led to spikes in prices in the spot market. Had more demand response been present, some of the rolling black-outs that annoyed California customers for so long could have been easily avoided. The design of the power rationing in Brazil in 2001 also proved the point. By using demand response via price and quantity rationing schemes, the country was able to save

(continued)

Box F.2. Demand Response—An Orphan in Wholesale Market and Auction Design *(Continued)*

about 20 percent of energy for nine months almost on a national scale, and, what is even more impressive, without a single black-out or brown-out. It is oftentimes touted as a best practice and has been considered by many countries ever since. Economists proved to be right in encouraging the power sector to look at the supply and demand side to make energy more affordable and reliable.

This learning experience does not happen overnight. The construction of the wholesale market in Brazil in 1997, for example, highlights this point. In the original conceptual design, as prepared by a consortium of consultants led by Coopers & Lybrand from the UK, there was a specific market rule on Demand Side Bidding (DSB), one form of demand response that could be immediately implemented by the system operator in defining the merit order and the necessary generation for least-cost dispatch.

Unfortunately, during the detailed phase of wholesale market design, the DSB rule, a precursor of demand participation, suffered a premature death. The reasons were manifold. Perhaps the most significant one was the complete lack of support from the stakeholders involved. Generators perceived DSB as a competitor, while distribution utilities viewed it as a threat that could slash revenues and profits. The system operator was still working under the old culture with its obligation being to meet the needs of the demand (as an exogenous variable). Government and regulators were not sufficiently convinced about the benefits of demand participation, and expressed skepticism that this market rule, in the absence of a reliable demand baseline (counterfactual), could lead to windfall profits.

Notes

1. This expression was coined by Amory Lovins.
2. A good discussion on procuring energy efficiency services can be found at Singh, J. et al. Procuring Energy Services. The World Bank. 2010.
3. The Standard Offer, used in many jurisdictions, is not considered a competitive procurement *per se*, but a mirror image of the feed-in-tariff used to attract energy efficiency and demand-side participation.
4. http://procurex.blogspot.com/2010_10_01_archive.html

Competitive Electricity Procurement—Key Attributes

	Brazil	Colombia	Chile	Peru	Spain	PJM	New England	Mexico	Panama
Capacity mix	Hydro 75%, Thermal 25%	Hydro 67%, Thermal 33%	Hydro 40%, Thermal 60%	Hydro 60%, Thermal 40%	Hydro 15%, Thermal 55%, RES 30%	Thermal-based	Thermal-based	80% thermal, 20% hydro	45% thermal, 55 % hydro
Load growth (per year)	5–6%	2–4%	4–6%	5–8%	2–6% (–5% in 2009)	0.5–2%	0.5–2%	2.5–4%	5–7%
Year of first reform implementation	1998	1996	1982	1992	1998	1997	1996	1992	1997
Institutional arrangements	Competitive market (wholesale competition)	Competitive market (wholesale competition)	Competitive market (wholesale competition)	Competitive market (wholesale competition)	Competitive market (full retail)	Competitive market (full retail) in some states	Competitive market (full retail)	Vertically-Integrated	Competitive market (wholesale competition)
Main objectives of the auction-based electricity procurement	Attract new capacity	Attract new capacity	Attract new capacity	Attract new capacity	Define energy price for POLR	Retain (and attract) new capacity	Retain (and attract) new capacity	Attract new capacity	Attract new capacity
Wholesale electricity market	Cost-based energy spot market with financial contracts	Bid-based energy spot market with financial contracts	Cost-based energy spot market with financial contracts and nodal prices (LMP)	Cost-based energy spot market with financial contracts and nodal prices (LMP)	Open bilateral trading market with a voluntary day-ahead and intra-day market, and an OTC market	Bid-based energy market with physical and financial contracts	Bid-based energy market with physical and financial contracts	Cost-based dispatch, no energy market	Cost-based dispatch & financial contracts
Specificity of the electricity procured through contract auctions	Specific project; specific technology and "any energy"	All technologies and projects compete	All technologies and projects compete	All technologies and projects compete	All technologies and projects compete	Any project; any technology and demand resources	Any project; any technology and demand resources	Project-specific, defined by central planning	All technologies and projects compete
Degree of centralization in the auction-based electricity procurement process	Joint auctions by distribution companies organized by the government	Joint auction to ensure reliability, closing gap between supply and demand organized by a government agency	Distribution companies organize and manage their auctions, possibility of joint auctions	Distribution companies organize and manage their auctions, possibility of joint auctions	Joint but voluntary auction for the suppliers of last resort organized by the market operator	Joint auction to ensure reliability, closing gap between supply and demand organized by the market operator	Joint auction to ensure reliability, closing gap between supply and demand organized by the market operator	Single buyer, planned and organized by the government	Joint auctions by distribution companies organized by state-owned transmission company

Why auctions?	Move away from benchmark prices & stimulate price discovery with efficiency	Replacement of a regulated capacity fee by a market price	Move away from benchmark prices & stimulate price discovery	Move away from benchmark prices & stimulate price discovery	Define a competitive price for the providers of last resort	Replacement of capacity markets and definition of market value for capacity	Replacement of capacity markets and definition of market value for capacity	Stimulate price discovery with efficiency	Stimulate price discovery with efficiency
Mandated (M) or voluntary (V)	M	M	M	M	M	V	V	M	M
Buyers	Regulated users	All consumers	Regulated users	Regulated users, but free consumers can be included	Providers of last resort	All consumers	ISO New England buys for the region, then the cost is allocated to load after the fact	All load, defined by central planner	Regulated users
Sellers	Separate auctions for existing and new capacity	New energy (existing energy is price taker)	All existing and new generation (in the same auction)	All existing and new generation (in the same auction)	Generators and traders	All existing and new generation capacity, demand response and energy efficiency (in the same auction)	All existing and new generation capacity (in the same auction)	IPPs	All existing and new generation (in the same auction)
Load forecast responsibility	Distribution companies are required to inform their load forecasts in each regular auction to supply regulated market	Regulator and planner provide demand, auction bridges the total system gap	Done by distribution companies, auction supplies the regulated market	Done by distribution companies, auction supplies the regulated market	Done by Providers of last resort	ISO reliability committee, auction bridges the total system gap	ISO reliability committee, auction bridges the total system gap	Central planner, auction bridges the total system gap	Provided by distribution companies and approved by Transco, auction supplies the regulated market
Demand side bidding	No demand response, the regulator's reserve price in the auction has this role	No demand response but slope demand curve used in the auction	No demand response. Reserve price fixed by the regulator and published before auctioning	No demand response. Reserve price fixed by the regulator	Out of the regulated auctions, large industrial interruptible contracts signed with the TSO	Allowed, both in the auction mechanisms (sloped demand) and as a resource	Allowed to participate and treated just like generation in the auction	No demand response	No demand response

(continued)

	Brazil	Colombia	Chile	Peru	Spain	PJM	New England	Mexico	Panama
Frequency	Yearly	When needed	When needed	When needed	Quarterly	Yearly (for the main auction, then several adjustment auctions in shorter time frames)	Yearly (for the main auction, then several adjustment auctions in shorter time frames)	When needed	When needed
Grace period	1–3–5 years ahead for 1,5,15 year contracts tied to energy certificates	3 to 7 years ahead	3 years ahead for any period up to 15 years	3 years ahead for any period up to 15 years	1 month	3 years	3 years	3 years ahead for any period up to 15 years	3 years ahead for any period up to 15 years
Total to date	31	1	3	3	11	7	4	8	2
Volume (MW)	57,000 MW of new capacity	3,000 MW	4.2 average GW	3.0 average GW	10,000 MW	31,000MW	31,000MW	11,500 MW	600 MW
Product	Short, mid & long-term financial firm electricity contract & reliability options, backed by firm energy certificates	Long-term firm energy reliability options	Mid & long-term energy contracts	Mid & long-term energy contracts	Short-term energy contracts,	Capacity certificates	Reliability options	PPA	Mid & long-term energy contracts
Base (B)/Peak (P) product	B	B&P	B&P	B&P	B&P	P	P	B&P	B&P
Auction Process	2-phase hybrid auction	Descending clock auction	Sealed-bid combinatorial auction with pay-as-bid rule	Pay-as-bid auction	Descending clock auction	Uniform price sealed-bid auction	Descending clock auction	Pay-as-bid auction	Pay-as-bid auction
Min purchase lot (MW)	1	1	Defined in each contract	Defined in each contract	1	1	1	Defined in each contract	Defined in each contract
Delivery	Physical	Physical	Physical	Physical	Physical	Physical	Physical	N/A	Capacity is physical, energy is financial

Market power mitigation	Regulatory monitoring (information policy, reserve prices, etc)	Regulatory monitoring (information policy, reserve prices, etc)	Expert Panel, reserve prices, Free Competition Tribunal	Regulatory monitoring (information policy, reserve prices, etc). External supervising company follows the process.	Regulatory monitoring (information policy, reserve prices, etc)	Regulatory monitoring (information policy, reserve prices, etc)	Regulatory monitoring (information policy, reserve prices, etc)	N/A	Regulatory monitoring (information policy, reserve prices, etc) & expert panel
Energy policy decisions	Specific auctions for technologies and projects	All technologies compete together	All technologies compete together	Separate auctions for renewable	All technologies compete together	All technologies compete together	All technologies compete together	Separate auctions for renewable	Separate auctions for renewable under evaluation
Planning the auction									
Who organizes the auction	Auction committee formed by sector institutions	Regulator defines rules and schedule, market operator is the managing body	Distribution companies supervised by the regulator	Distribution companies supervised by the regulator	National Energy Commission is the trustee, market operator is the managing body	System and market operator	ISO	Transmission Company	Distribution companies supervised by the regulator
Who decides how much is needed	Distribution companies for regular auctions and government for some specific auctions	Regulator and planner provide demand, auction bridges the total system gap	Done by distribution companies, auction supplies the regulated market	Done by distribution companies, auction supplies the regulated market	Done by Providers of last resort	ISO, auction bridges the total system gap	ISO reliability committee, auction bridges the total system gap	Central planner, auction bridges the total system gap	Provided by distribution companies and approved by Transco, auction supplies the regulated market
Who decides when to conduct an auction	Government	Planner and regulator	Disco(s)	Disco(s)	Regulator (the Ministry)	ISO	ISO	Transmission company	Disco(s)
How often are auctions organized?	There are regular auctions to contract new capacity, government can organize specific (additional) auctions whenever needed	At regulator's discretion, whenever there is a gap between total system future demand and supply	Disco(s) decide	Disco(s) decide	Quarterly	Yearly	Yearly (for the main auction, then several adjustment auctions in shorter time frames)	Transmission company decides	Disco(s) decide

Glossary

A

A-3 auction
Regular auctions carried out every year in Brazil to contract new generation projects. The contracts auctioned off determine that electricity delivery must commence in 3 years.

A-5 auction
Regular auctions carried out every year in Brazil to contract new generation projects. The contracts auctioned off determine that electricity delivery must commence in 5 years.

AGC
Automatic Generation Control

Average MW
Average MW is an energy unit and reflects the MW that can be continuously delivered by a project. 1 average MW = 8760 MWh over a year.

B

BGS
Basic Generation Service—refers to the service of customers who are not served by a third party supplier or competitive retailer in the state of New Jersey, USA.

BOO
Build-Operate-Own—a form of project financing, wherein a private entity receives a concession from the private or public sector to finance, design, construct, and operate a facility as stated in the concession contract. The private entity owns the project outright and retains it in perpetuity.

BOT
Build-Operate-Transfer—a form of project financing wherein a private entity receives a concession from the private or public sector to finance, design, construct, and operate a facility as stated in the concession contract. The facility ownership is transferred to the conceding entity at the end of the contract period.

C

Capacity payments
Payments made to generators in exchange for the availability of their generation capacity.

Captive consumers
Captive (or franchised) consumers are those who are obliged to acquire energy from the local utility.
Regulated users who are represented by distribution companies.

Captive market
Competition among existing market participants to provide services (e.g., electricity supply) to customers.

Competition "in the market"
Competition "for the market"
Competition among potential investors and market entrants for the right to provide services to customers (competition to enter a market).

Concession	A contract or license that grants the right to operate a business within a certain geographical area and is usually associated with some degree of exclusivity.
CESUR	Auctions for the provider of last resort (the English equivalent of *Compra de Energía para el Suministro de Último Recurso*).
CPI	Consumer Price Index
CPUC	California Public Utilities Commission
Cost-plus	A cost-plus contract, more accurately termed a Cost Reimbursement Contract, is a contract where a contractor is paid for all of its allowed expenses up to a set limit, plus an additional payment to allow for a profit.
CREG	Energy and Gas Regulatory Commission, the English equivalent of *Comisión de Regulación de Energía y Gas*—the Colombian energy regulatory agency.
CSP	Concentrated Solar Power
D	
Disco	Distribution company or any entity responsible for procuring energy and selling it to retail consumers. In this report, disco, distribution company, or distribution utility are used interchangeably.
E	
EMGESA	Generation and energy trading company located in Colombia
ENDESA	Empresa Nacional de Electricidad, S.A, the largest electric utility company in Spain.
ESCO	Energy Service Company
ESKOM	South African electricity public utility
ETESA	Panama's state-owned transmission company
F	
FCM	Forward Capacity Market, operated by the New England Independent System Operator.
FEC	Firm Energy Certificate—a certificate issued by the Brazilian regulatory agency to all power plants in the country in GWh/year and reflecting the sustainable energy production of each generator.
FERC	Federal Energy Regulatory Commission—US agency that regulates, monitors, and investigates energy-related matters.
FiT	Feed-in-tariff
Free Consumers	Free (or non-franchised) consumers are those who can freely choose their electricity supplier.
Firm Capacity	Volume of energy from a power plant that may be guaranteed to be available at a given time.
Firm Energy	A measure of a plant's sustainable production capacity, usually measured in MWh/year or the equivalent, and denominated in average MW.
FPSB	Auction mechanism known as *First-price sealed bid*.
G	
GDP	Gross Domestic Product
Genco	Generation company

I

IPP	Independent Power Producer
ISAGEN	Colombian public company involved in generation, construction and energy trading activities.
ISO-NE	Independent System Operator that operates in New England, USA.

L

LSE	Load Serving Entities—any entity that acts as load aggregator on behalf of a group of consumers (e.g., a distribution company).
Load Shedding	Cutting off the electricity demand when the existing supply capacity is not able to meet the load requirements and a minimum reserve margin.

M

Make-or-Buy	Make-or-buy usually refers to the process of deciding whether to produce an item internally (in-house) or buy it externally (from an outside supplier). In the context of the expansion of the generation capacity, it refers to a government's decision to build a project on its own or to outsource the construction and operation tasks to a private investor.
MER	*Mercado Electrico Regional*—Regional Electricity Market encompassing Panama, Guatemala, Nicaragua, El Salvador, Honduras, and Costa Rica.

N

NETA	New Electricity Trading Arrangements is the name of the system under which electricity is traded in the United Kingdom's electricity market, replaced in 2005 by the British Electricity Trading and Transmission Arrangements (BETTA), which introduced a single wholesale electricity market for Great Britain.

O

O&M	Operations & Maintenance
OEF	Firm Energy Obligations, the English equivalent of *Obligaciones de Energia Firme*
OFGEM	Office of the Gas and Electricity Markets—regulatory agency in the UK.
Old Energy	In energy auctions in Brazil, this refers to the energy produced by existing plants (as opposed to new or green field plants).
Out of the money	A call option whose strike price is higher than the market price of the underlying security, or a put option whose strike price is lower than the market price of the underlying security. In energy, a contract priced above market price.

P

PPA	Power Purchase Agreement (PPA) is a legal contract between an electricity generator (provider) and a power purchaser (the government, a distribution company, or another consumer). The power purchaser purchases energy, and sometimes also capacity and/or ancillary services, from the electricity generator. Such agreements

	play a key role in the financing of independently owned electricity-generating assets.
PJM	PJM Interconnection is a regional transmission organization (RTO) that coordinates the movement of wholesale electricity in all or parts of the states of Delaware, Illinois, Indiana, Kentucky, Maryland, Michigan, New Jersey, North Carolina, Ohio, Pennsylvania, Tennessee, Virginia, West Virginia, and the District of Columbia.
POLR	Provider of Last Resort
Procurement	Used in a broad sense in this report, encompassing activities ranging from product identification, terms of reference, bidding, selection, awarding, and contracting.
R	
REC	Renewable Energy Certificate
RFP	Request for Proposals
RPS	Renewable Portfolio Standards
S	
SIEPAC	Central American Electrical Interconnection System (the English equivalent of *Sistema de Interconexion Electrica para America Central*).
V	
VPP	*Virtual Power Plant*—used to refer to auctions for the sale of electricity supply contracts that give the holder the right to the output, or a share of the output, of a specific power plant.

References

Andersson, P.; Hulten, S.; and Valiente, P. 2005. "Beauty contest licensing from the 3G process in Sweden." *Telecommunications Policy* 29 (8). Elsevier.

Armstrong, M. 2006. "Price discrimination." Mimeo, Department of Economics, University College London.

Arizu, B.; Maurer, L.; and Tenenbaum, B. 2004. "Pass Through of Power Purchase Costs" Energy and Mining Sector Board Discussion Paper Series, Paper No. 10, The World Bank, Washington, D.C.

Arizu, B.; Gencer, D.; and Maurer, L. 2006. "Centralized Purchasing Arrangements: international practices and lessons learned on variations to the Single Buyer Model." Energy and mining Sector Board Discussion Paper, Paper No. 16, The World Bank, Washington, DC.

Armar, A. 2009. "Building Regional Power Pools. A Toolkit." The World Bank, Washington, DC.

Ausubel, L. M.; Cramton, P. 2009. "Virtual Power Plant Auctions." University of Maryland. Available at: www.cramton.umd.edu.

Bajari, P. et al. 2008. "Auctions Versus Negotiations in Procurement: An Empirical Analysis." *Journal of Law, Economics and Organization,* May 7.

Barroso, L.A.; Street, A., Granville, S.; Pereira, M. 2011. "Offering Strategies and Simulation of Multi Item Dynamic Auctions of Energy Contracts." *IEEE Transactions on Power Systems* 26 (3), August.

Barroso, L. A.; Rosenblatt, J.; Bezerra, B.; Resende, A.; Pereira, M. 2006. "Auctions of Contracts and Energy Call Options to Ensure Supply Adequacy in the Second Stage of the Brazilian Power Sector Reform." Proceedings of IEEE General Meeting 2006, Montreal.

Barroso, L. A.; Rudnick, H.; Seinsuss, F.; Linares, P. 2010. "Economic and market impacts of renewable integration in Europe and Latin America." *IEEE Power & Energy Magazine* 7 (4): 28–36. September-October.

Batlle, C. & Rodilla, P. 2010. "A critical assessment of the different approaches aimed to secure electricity generation supply." *Energy Policy* 38 (11), Pages 7169–7179. November.

Batlle, C., Barroso, L. A., 2011. "Support schemes for renewable energy sources in South America." MIT—CEEPR Working Paper 11-001. Short version appeared at 2011 Spring issue of IAEE Energy Forum.

Batlle, C., Barroso, L. A., Pérez-Arriaga, I, J., 2010. "The changing role of the State in the expansion of electricity supply in Latin America." *Energy Policy* 38 (11): 7152–7160. November.

Bezerra, B.; Barroso, L. A.; Pereira, M. V. 2011. "Bidding Strategies with Fuel Supply Uncertainty in Auctions of Long-Term Energy Call Options." *IEEE Transactions on Power Systems* 26 (2). May.

Binmore, K.; v.d. Fehr, N-H; Harbord, D.; Jewitt, I. 2004. "Comments on the Proposed Electricity Contract Auctions in Brazil." Available at: http://www.market-analysis. co.uk/PDF/Reports/brazilianelectricityauct.pdf.

The Boston Globe, "Editorial: Revolution in the power lines." February 20, 2009.

Botero S., Izasa, F., and Valencia A. 2010. "Evaluation of Methodologies for Remunerating Wind Power's Reliability in Colombia." *Renewable and Sustainable Energy Review.*

Brook, P. and Smith, S, editors. 2001. *"Contracting for Public Services. Output-based aid and its applications."* The World Bank, Washington DC.

Bulow, J. I. and Klemperer, P. D. 1996. "Auctions vs. Negotiations." *American Economic Review* 86: 180–194.

Butler, N. and Neuhoff, K. 2005. "Comparison of Feed-in-Tariff, Quota and Auction Mechanisms to Support Wind Power Development." MIT and Center for Energy and Environmental Policy Research. CMI Working Paper 70.

Camac, D.; Ormeño, V.; Espinoza, L. 2006. "Assuring the efficient development of electricity generation in Peru." Proceedings of the 2006 IEEE PES General Meeting, Montreal, Canada.

Center for Renewable Energy Development. 2009. "Study on Pricing Mechanism for Renewable Energy." CRED Task 3. Output No 13, China Renewable Energy Scale-up Program. July.

Cramton, P. 1998. "Ascending Auctions." *European Economic Review* 42: 745–756.

Cramton, P. 2006. "Simultaneous Ascending Auctions." in P. Cramton, Y. Shoham and R. Steinberg (eds.), *Combinatorial Auctions,* Chapter 4, 99–114, MIT Press.

Cramton, P.; Shoham, Y.; and Steinberg, R. 2006. "Combinatorial Auctions." MIT Press.

Cramtom, P. and Stoft, S. 2007. "Colombia Firm Energy Market." Proceedings of the Hawaii International Conference on System Sciences, January.

de Castro, L.; Negrete-Pincetic, M.; Gross, G. 2008. "Product Definition for Future Electricity Supply Auctions: The 2006 Illinois Experience." *The Electricity Journal* 21(7): 50–62.

Dutra, J. and Menezes, F. 2005. "Lessons from the Electricity Auctions in Brazil." *The Electricity Journal* 18 (10): 11–21. December.

Dutra, J. 2010. "Overcoming Barriers to Competition. The Evolution of Electricity Auctions in Brazil." Presentation at Harvard Kennedy School, Boston. April 6.

Eberhard, A. 2007. "Management Program in Infrastructure Reform and Regulation." University of Cape Town. Seminar, EPFL Lausanne June 26.

Eberhard, A. 2007. "Generating Power and Controversy: The Experience of Independent Power Projects in Africa." University of Cape Town. Seminar, EPFL Lausanne June 26.

v-d Fehr, N-H. M.; Amundsen, E. S.; Bergman, L. 2005. "The Nordic Market: Signs of Stress?" *The Energy Journal,* Special Edition on European Electricity Liberalisation. July.

ISO New England Inc. 2009. "Internal Market Monitoring Unit Review of the Forward Capacity Market Auction Results and Design Elements." Prepared by LaPlante, D.; Chao, H. and The Brattle Group (Newell, S., Celebi, M. and Hajos, A.). Available at: http://www.iso-ne.com/markets/mktmonmit/rpts/other/fcm_report_final.

Harbord, D.; Pagnozzi, M. 2008. "Review of Colombian Auctions for Firm Energy." Available at: http://market-analysis.co.uk/PDF/Reports/. November 25.

Herrera-Dappe, M. 2009. "Sequential Uniform Price Auctions." Working paper, University of Maryland.

Holt, E. & Associates et al. 2006. "Who Owns Renewable Energy Certificates? An Exploration of Policy Options and Practice." Lawrence Berkeley National Laboratory. Berkeley, CA. April 2006.

Hogan, W. 1996. "A wholesale pool market must be administered by the independent system operator: avoiding the separation fallacy." *The Electricity Journal*: 26–37.

Hull, J. C. 1993. "Options, Futures and Other Derivative Securities." Prentice Hall, NJ.

Humeyra, P. "Egypt eyes new wind farms." Interview with Mohab Hallouda, World Bank. Reuters Africa, March 2010.

Kahn, A. E.; Cramton, P.; Porter, R. H.; and Tabors, R. D. 2001. "Pricing in the California Power Exchange Electricity Market: Should California Switch from Uniform Pricing to Pay-as-Bid Pricing?" Blue Ribbon Panel Report for the California Power Exchange, January.

Kerf, M. et al. 1996. "Privatizing Africa's Infrastructure. Promise and Challenges." World Bank Technical Paper No. 337. Washington DC.

Kerf, M. et al. 1998. "Concessions for Infrastructure. A Guide to Their Design and Award." World Bank Technical Paper No. 399. Washington DC.

Klemperer, P. 2000. "Auctions: From Theory to Practice." Oxford Press.

Klemperer, P. and Bulow, J. 1996. "Auctions Versus Negotiations." *The American Economic Review*. March.

Lev S. Belyaev. 2007. "Electricity Markets: Comparing competitive and single buyer markets." *IEEE Power & Engineering Magazine* 5 (3): 16–26.

Loxley, C. and Salant, D. 2004. "Default service auctions." *Journal of Regulatory Economics* 26 (2): 201–229.

Lloyd, D. et al. 2004. "Competitive Procurement and Internet-Based Auction: Electricity Capacity Option." *The Electricity Journal*, Elsevier 17 (4). May.

Maurer, L.; Pereira, M.; Rosenblatt, J. 2005. "Implementing Power Rationing in a Sensible Way: Lessons Learned and International Best Practices." ESMAP. The World Bank, Washington DC.

Maurer, L. 2002. "The Electricity Insider." Equity Research, Latin America. Morgan Stanley. May 8.

Menezes, R. and Monteiro, P. 2008. "An Introduction to Auction Theory." Oxford University Press.

Migron, P. 2008. "Putting Auction Theory to Work." Cambridge University Press, New York.

Miller, Brad. 2003. "Energy Auctions in Brazil." CRA, The World Bank, PPIAF. Washington DC.

Mocarquer, S.; Barroso, L. A.; Rudnick, H.; Bezerra, B.; Pereira, M. V. 2009. "Energy policy in Latin America: the need for a balanced approach." *IEEE Power & Energy Magazine* 7 (4): 26–34.

Moreno, R.; Bezerra, B.; Mocarquer, S.; Barroso, L. A.; Rudnick, H. 2009. "Auctioning Adequacy in South America through Long-Term Contracts and Options: From Classic Pay-as-Bid to Multi-Item Dynamic Auctions." Proceedings of the 2009 IEEE PES General Meeting, Calgary, Canada.

Moreno, R.; Barroso, L. A.; Rudnick, H.; Mocarquer, S.; Bezerra, B. 2010. "Auction Approaches of Long-Term Contracts to Ensure Generation Investment in Electricity Markets: Lessons from the Brazilian and Chilean Experiences." *Energy Policy*.

Negrete-Pincetic, M. and Gross, G. 2007. "Lessons from the 2006 Illinois Electricity Auction." Proceedings of the IREP 2007, Charleston, SC, USA.

NERA Economic Consulting. 2006. "Public report presented to The Illinois Commerce Commission." Available: http://www.illinoisauction.com.

Ofgem. 2010. "Promoting choice and value for all gas and electricity customers. Project Discovery. Options for delivering secure and sustainable energy supplies." Consultation Document. February.

Oren, S. 2005a. "Ensuring Generation Adequacy in Competitive Electricity Markets." Ch. 10 in *Electricity Deregulation: Choices and Challenges, Griffin,* M. James and S. L. Puller (editors), Univ. Chicago Press.

Oren, S. 2005b. "Generation Adequacy via Call Option Obligations: Safe Passage to the Promised Land." *Electricity Journal,* November.

Pepall, et al. 2005. "Industrial Organization. Contemporary Theory and Practice." Thomson, SouthWestern.

Porrua, F.; Bezerra, B.; Barroso, L. A.; Lino, P.; Ralston, F.; Pereira, M. V. F. 2010. "Wind Power Integration Through Energy Auctions in Brazil." Proceedings of 2010 IEEE General Meeting, Minneapolis, MN.

Rodilla, P. & Batlle, C. 2010. "Security of electricity supply at the generation level: problem analysis." Working Paper IIT-10-027A. Available at: http://www.iit.upcomillas.es/batlle/ Publications.html.

Rodilla, P., Batlle, C., Salazar, J., Sánchez, J. J. 2011. "Modeling generation expansion in the context of a security of supply mechanism based on long-term auctions. Application to the Colombian Case." *Energy Policy* 39 (1): 176–186. January.

Roth, Alvin E. 2007. "Auctions create markets where they do not exist." Harvard Business Review 85 (10): 118–126.

Rudnick, H. and Mocarquer S. 2006. "Contract auctions to assure supply adequacy in an uncertain energy environment." Proceedings of the 2006 IEEE PES General Meeting, Montreal, Canada.

Schultz, C. 2005. "Virtual Capacity and Competition." CESifo Working Paper No. 1487, University of Copenhagen.

Schweppe, F. C; Caramanis, M. C.; Tabors, R. D. and Bohn, R. E. 1988. "Spot pricing of electricity." Kluwer Academic Publishers, Boston, MA.

Silveira, O. 2009. "A viabilidade da insercao da energia eolica na matriz energetic nacional." Dreen Re-energy. Presentation. Sao Paulo, Brazil. August 4.

Singh, J. et al. 2010. "Procuring Energy Services." The World Bank. Washington, DC.

Tezak, C. 2005. "Resource Adequacy—Alphabet Soup!" Stanford Washington Research Group Policy Research, Available at: http://www.ksg.harvard.edu/hepg/.

The Brattle Group. 2008. "Review of PJM's reliability pricing model (RPM)." Available at www.brattle.com.

Walker, M. 1989. "New Jersey's Competitive Bidding System—An Attempt at a Balanced Energy Supply Policy." *Public Utilities Fortnightly* 123 (4). February.

The World Bank. "*Implementation of Renewable Energy Market Development Policies in Brazil. Energy and Water Department*"—EWTEN. Washington DC. Forthcoming (2011).

Vergara, W. et al. 2001. "*Wind Energy in Colombia. A Framework for Market Entry.*" A World Bank Study. The World Bank, Washington DC.

Wang. X. "Legal and Policy Frameworks for Renewable Energy to Mitigate Climate Change." The World Bank, Washington DC. (Mimeo).

Whitfield, D. "Global Auction of Public Assets." Spokesman 2010.

ECO-AUDIT
Environmental Benefits Statement

green
press
INITIATIVE

www.ingramcontent.com/pod-product-compliance
Lightning Source LLC
Chambersburg PA
CBHW081505200326
41518CB00015B/2381